Ashanti Nyame, is the god the most important god.

The Religion,
Spirituality,
and Thought of
Traditional
Africa

Dominique
Zahan

Translated by
Kate Ezra Martin and
Lawrence M. Martin

The Religion, Spirituality, and Thought of Traditional Africa

The University of Chicago Press

Chicago and London

Originally published as *Religion, spiritualité, et pensée africaines,* ©1970, Payot, Paris.

The University of Chicago Press, Chicago 60637
The University of Chicago Press, Ltd., London

Library of Congress Cataloging in Publication Data

Zahan, Dominique.
  The religion, spirituality, and thought of traditional Africa.

  Translation of Religion, spiritualité, et pensée africaines.
  Bibliography: p.
  Includes index.
  1. Africa—Religion.   I. Title.
BL2400.Z2813   299'.6   78–23525
ISBN 0–226–97777–3

DOMINIQUE ZAHAN, professor of anthropology at the University of Paris V, the Sorbonne, is the author of a number of distinguished anthropological studies.

KATE EZRA MARTIN is a doctoral candidate in art history at Northwestern University. LAWRENCE M. MARTIN is a doctoral candidate in anthropology at the University of Chicago.

Contents

Introduction

We thus have no reason to assume for Maliki . . . something specifically different, in terms of logic, than what happens among us. It is enough to know that the beliefs and mystical experiences common to his group give reason to his words and acts. Given their ideas of sickness, abnormality, death, and the power and evil deeds of sorcerors, the rest follows.

Lucien Lévy-Bruhl
Les Carnets

To date numerous works in the field of African religious traditions have appeared. Of these many have been devoted to the description of particular religious phenomena, while others have attempted more or less broad syntheses of them. But in examining the efforts of the various investigators who have grappled with this task, one has the impression that they may have overlooked something. That "something," we think, is a very profound aspect of African spirituality, one which is certainly difficult to approach but not absolutely impossible to attain.

On one hand it can be said that spirituality is the very soul of African religion. It is found principally in the mystical emotion provided by an African's faith, and can also be seen in the meaning he gives to the dialogue between man and the Invisible. On the other hand, this same spirituality may be the feeling man has in realizing himself, not with the help of God (as we would be inclined to think), but by the exertion, sometimes conscious, often unconscious, of his humanity.

To attempt to penetrate this extremely complex domain, loaded with facts which by all appearances do not point to an advanced spirituality, would seem to be a thankless task. It is the very abundance of these elements which makes the job difficult, because if the existing material is an indispensable source of information it is just as much a screen blocking the way to the correct comprehension of things.

Certainly, when it concerns black Africa, the concept of "religion" appears to be among the most confused and treacherous. We automatically think of a corpus of doctrines and practices expressing the relationship between man and the Invisible, and by giving the word this meaning we immediately establish a fundamental distinction between man and the divine powers. But in actuality how do Africans themselves

1

conceive of this aspect of culture? Do they detach themselves sufficiently from the Other for spirituality to be felt in terms of an opposition, or do they merge themselves to a certain extent with the world, the universe, and God so as to see in religion, rather, a series of concerns for the harmony and placement of man within the whole formed by the visible and invisible world?

Despite the considerable number of ethnic groups in Africa and the apparent heterogeneity of their religious "customs," scholars sought for several decades to model the spiritual portrait of Africa with a single expression. This practice gave rise to the concepts of fetishism and animism, and was less a real attempt at understanding the phenomenon of religion than an intellectual satisfaction for Western rationalism.

In point of fact, black Africa has only recently revealed to us its secret thoughts on the subject taken up in the present work. Even if it is now possible to observe many peoples in the field, it is nonetheless true that we are often unable to penetrate the meaning of the rites, since for this type of investigation we are dependent in large part on the good will and ability of our informants. Unfortunately, many ethnic groups still refuse to participate in a collaboration of this type. I have therefore chosen to devote myself to finding the deeper meaning of those things which could be observed and understood in order to extract from them the overall spirit, the common denominator, and, as it were, the theology.

The diversity of African ethnic groups should not be an obstacle to such an undertaking since the variation in religion has less to do with the ideas themselves than with their expression by means of dissimilar elements linked to the occupations and the flora and fauna of the area. As anywhere else, here man partially expresses his ideas in terms of the geographical milieu in which he lives. It is impossible, for example, to prevent oneself from establishing a relationship between the "geometric" cosmogony of the Dogon and their environment overflowing with rocky masses of the most varied shapes. It is equally difficult, when learning of the belief among the Thonga people of the "issuance" of the first man from a reed, not to think of the swamps of the Natal coasts overgrown by these plants.[1] Among each African people man translates in his own way the constant thread of his conception of himself and his relationship to the Invisible. The permanent image of the human spirit is at times clothed in the richest of ornaments, at others left in its rough state. And yet it must be said, even in regard to the latter category, that not a single ethnic group exists in all of black Africa about which we can pride ourselves on knowing all the workings of its culture. Moreover, religion is like a language in which the complete understanding of each element would necessitate the knowledge not only of the many meanings which it encompasses but also of the entire spiritual heritage of the society which uses it.

These elements of religion can be likened to the features of certain islets off the coast of Africa, while the rest of this vast continent remains shrouded in mystery as dense as in the time of Herodotus. For, in spite of our progressively close contact with African culture over the past century, the West has chosen to see sorcery, savagery, and obscenity—in short a caricature of man—precisely in those moments in life when the African sets in motion his most genuine values. As strange as it may seem, no one in the West is astonished at the nuances and subtleties of Japanese or Chinese thought; but let an investigator document certain African ideas and he is considered a rash if not completely reckless "interpreter." It is almost as if the refinement of the mind were the heritage of one part of mankind and not another, unless one wants to assert by this strange value judgment that thought and reflection are necessarily expressed by a single category of signifiers.

Two approaches offer themselves for the analysis of African religious concepts. Either one may limit oneself to a very restricted number of ethnic groups or one may take into consideration, after a preliminary selection, the largest possible number of them. In no case can the inclusion of all African ethnic groups in the study give rise to a reasonable undertaking at the present time. Two of our predecessors, E. G. Parrinder and E. Dammann, to name only the latest, have each adopted one of these views.[2]

For E. G. Parrinder, the unity of African spiritual concepts can be perceived in the attitude which the individual may adopt towards the world and the Invisible. Paraphrasing a biblical verse, he says:

> Man beneath the sky lives on the land, not in a void but as a sovereign vital force. He has no doubt that he was made to have dominion "over every living thing that moveth upon the earth." It is his duty to "be fruitful, and multiply, and replenish the earth, and subdue it." On the other hand he knows that he is not able to do these things by himself, and he seeks the help of every available power, spirits and gods "that share this earth with man as with their friend."[3]

For this author, then, the common element in the spirituality of different African ethnic groups is found in the African's consciousness not so much of his power as of his lack of power. As for the substance of the religion, according to Parrinder, it is polarized in four directions: the earth below, the sky and the supreme being above, the ancestors on one side, and the deities and natural forces on the other.[4] In sum, with only a few differences, we find in this generalization the Christian conception of the relationship between man and God.

In contrast to this interpretation, E. Dammann marks a very definite retreat. For him it is of prime importance to find a definition of the word "religion" which can include all the phenomena of African religion. The formula presented by G. Van der Leeuw, "Relation with Transcendence," seems to him the most appropriate to this end. However, it is worth noting here the distinction which exists, according to him, between the "primitive" and the "civilized." The former has not yet learned to "distance" himself from his environment so that "transcendence and immanence, objectivity and subjectivity are not differentiated for him. . . . Thus primitive man is at an earlier stage of historical evolution. He is close to the origins."[5] In this way, if the African maintains relations with transcendence, it is felt by him above all as a magical power which acts involuntarily and which he can command and control "simply by knowing its laws and using them."[6] One finds in this conception of "primitive" man and of African religion the perspective of Lévy-Bruhl prior to the *Carnets,* as well as traces of an evolutionism which has today fallen into disuse.

These remarks are not, properly speaking, criticisms of these scholars of world renown. They are intended to indicate the present state of scholarship in the area of synthesis of African religious studies. For the reasons cited above, it is easy to see that such an endeavor is difficult and full of obstacles.

A great improvement has already been made in this effort by the recognition on the part of scholars of the vacuousness of such concepts as "fetishism" and "animism." But there remain still others which will have to be clarified before they can take their proper place in scientific anthropological vocabulary. This is notably the case for terms such as "magic" and "sorcery." Because even if today we have partially abandoned the thinking of Sir James G. Frazer on this subject, it nonetheless remains that through a lack of knowledge of the true nature of a multitude of African practices and a misunderstanding of the role attributed to numerous objects and ingredients used in these rites, we group all of these elements into the categories of "magic" and "sorceror." These terms thus become a catchall for our ignorance.

To speak of the multiplicity of "religions" in black Africa is likewise to demonstrate our ignorance of African spirituality. In this regard Africans are no more divided than are Muslims or Christians. Still, it is important to fully apprehend the unity of traditional African religion, not so much through some of its elements as through man's attitude towards the Invisible, through the position which he feels he occupies in creation, and through his feeling of belonging to the universe. In my view, in short, the essence of African spirituality lies in the feeling man has of being at once image, model, and integral part of the world in whose cyclical life he senses himself deeply and necessarily engaged.

All of African spiritual life is based on this vision of man's situation and role. The idea of a finality outside of man is foreign to it. Man was not made for God or for the universe; he exists for himself and carries within himself the justification of his existence and of his religious and moral perfection. It is not to "please" God or out of love for God that the African "prays," implores, or makes sacrifices, but rather to become himself and to realize the order in which he finds himself implicated.

The sky and the divinity are only thought of insofar as they represent something about man, who constitutes, so to speak, the keystone of the African religious structure. This does not in the least mean that the African is not profoundly religious. He is all the more so in that his fundamental concern is for the protection of the spiritual interests of the individual which, in the manner of a ball hurled into the orbit of time, rolls and rebounds periodically, thereby making short appearances on earth.

One sees definitively in these conditions that African religion is a kind of humanism, one which, moving away from man only to return to him, seizes in the course of its voyage all that is not of man himself and which surpasses him. This humanism is the basis for an individual and social ethic whose normal development culminates in mystical life.

Moral life and mystical life, these two aspects of African spirituality, give it its proper dimensions. They constitute, so to speak, the supreme goal of the African soul, the objective towards which the individual strives with all his energy because he feels his perfection can only be completed and consummated if he masters and surpasses himself through divinity, indeed through the mastery of divinity itself.

The aim of the present work is not to serve scholarship but to penetrate the African soul in depth in order to discover the animating principle of "life." This is to say how much it falls short of what a real synthesis of African spirituality should be, and how great the dissatisfaction of the author is in the face of the treasures which he guesses to be beneath the pile of documents—some perfect, others imperfect—which he has at his disposal.

Mankind, "Miracle-Workers," and the Divinity

The power to which the cult is addressed is not represented by him [the primitive] as soaring high above and overpowering him with its superiority; on the contrary, it is very close to him. . . .

E. Durkheim
The Elementary Forms of the Religious Life

1

Before beginning the study of African religion and spirituality, we must establish the position occupied by man in African thought and culture, since this is the foundation which will allow us to understand the relationship between God and man. From one end of the continent to the other the African affirms his conviction that the human being is superior to all else in existence. Man is the supreme and irreducible reality; the divinity itself enters his affairs in the same way as do other beings which he is close to and uses. This underlines the importance of the human being in the religious context and, consequently, the importance of the earth element in relation to the spiritual element.

This is not to say that in Africa man places himself in opposition to God or that he places the earth in opposition to the spirit; rather (and here western Europeans must adapt their own way of thinking) it must not be forgotten that the full cycle of human life includes reincarnation. In addition, when man venerates the divinity, it is not for the glory of God but for his own personal development. Religion is thus essentially a function of the human element and of its domain, the earth.

The primacy of man in relation to the rest of the world is due to his central position in the cosmos. Man is the microcosm in which converge the innumerable invisible threads spun by objects and beings between themselves, in consonance with the rules of correspondence given by categories and classifications. He is not the "king" of creation but rather the central element of a system on which he imposes a centripetal orientation. Thus the accounts transmitted by oral traditions always give a privileged position to man and, at least in part, to his destiny, both of which are never-ending sources of interest. At times he is "made" directly by the divinity,[1] at others he "emerges" from a reed[2] or a tree.[3]

At still other times he rises out of the earth,[4] or descends from the sky.[5] The "creation" of man is always accompanied by distinctive occurrences, such as the imprint of his feet on the soft earth[6] or some more detailed scenario.[7]

It is interesting to note that these "creation" myths often go hand in hand with a certain social organization in the ethnic groups from which they stem. Among the peoples of northern Yatenga, for example, society is divided into two categories: the Foulse and the Nioniosse. To the first group is assigned the chieftaincy and it is always from among its members that the kings of Loroum are chosen, whereas the second group is concerned with the cult of the earth itself as well as with all the customs pertaining to its nourishing soil. Furthermore, according to their myths of origin, the Foulse "came down" from the sky while the Nioniosse rose up from the bowels of the earth. Far from merely expressing the actual pattern of social relations between groups, as one might naively think, these correspondences (which one encounters elsewhere in Africa) are rooted in the human subconscious. There they arrange themselves around the concepts of order and harmony which are reflected by the social organization of all African peoples.[8] Understood in this sense, the "creation" of man constitutes the supreme effort of the mind desirous of situating man in terms of certain coordinates—inorganic world, vegetable world, animal world, spiritual universe—and affirming thereby both his attachment to all of these domains and his transcendent position relative to them.

As we saw previously, the special domain of man is, of course, the earth. It is the earth which predominates in the myths, stories, and legends collected by various specialists. Thus Paul Radin writes in connection with a series of oral traditions concerning "the universe and its beginnings":

> Rarely has man been depicted as more completely and inextricably anchored in this world, more obsessively earthbound. Contrary to the belief widespread elsewhere in the world, man in aboriginal Africa is never thought of as having once possessed a portion of divinity and having subsequently lost it. Even in the few myths that deal with the so-called high gods and the heavenly deities, one detects an almost obsessive geocentrism.[9]

This observation is eminently accurate provided it be recognized that the African never thinks of the earth as being sufficient in itself. He always conceptualizes it as a point of reference, and, as such, it is in opposition sometimes to the sky, sometimes to water.

The majority of African myths concerning creation note that, at the dawn of time, the sky and the earth were contiguous. We will see later how much this belief influences and orients African spiritual life. Moreover, it is almost unnecessary to insist upon the relation between earth and water in African thought. Water often dictates the orientation of habitations, and it always conditions human existence wherever the scarcity or lateness of rains endangers the means of subsistence. We can thus understand the immense role played by the personage commonly called the "rainmaker," who is in contact above all with the earth, and who is no less than a shrewd master of the elements.

Earth, sky, and water are, in fact, the notions which presided over the creation of a philosophy and a religion of matter in Africa. Nowhere else, perhaps, has the material world been investigated, observed, probed, and pondered as much as in Africa. Accustomed to considering others superficially or according to unfounded prejudices, many of us have tried to minimize, even ridicule, the African "healers" and "miracle-workers." But they, with a gravity touching upon drama, devote themselves to a veritable alchemy of the concrete, because they have the feeling of commanding matter and of being the masters of nature. Were their ancestors not among those who, when gnawed by hunger, cut off slices of clouds to feed themselves?[10]

Surely such practices of manipulating nature require very unusual "technicians." In particular they require that the human person not be a single, indissoluble entity, and further that he enjoy a certain plasticity which defines him more in terms of becoming than of being. The mobility of matter invites the variability of the manipulator. Thus the idea of the malleable concrete is as universal in Africa as are the notions of the duality of spiritual principles and the process of evolution of the human being.[11]

If we were to apply ourselves to the serious study of African psychology, focusing in particular on the analysis of the self and the personality, we would be driven to restrict the limits of the abnormality of perceiving one's body as alienated from oneself [*héautoscopie*]. According to African thought, the human being does not possess the unity which we attribute to him; the individual psyche is not felt to be an undivided whole. Among its component principles there exists an element which allows man to "double" himself at certain moments in his life. This conception is very widespread in Africa, if it is not universal.[12] Be it the *chitjhouti* of the Thonga or the *dya* of the Bambara, the fundamental idea is the same. The self normally and naturally possesses a point of fission, probably situated at the border of the conscious and the unconscious, and this characteristic "assures" man of a wide gamut of para-human possibilities, for example, the ability to be in two places at once, clairvoyance, and metamorphosis. But there is still more.

African psychology attributes to the self a broader and richer content than our classic treatises on the study of the soul. To define the self, we separate it from the other, whereas in Africa the opposite is the rule; nowhere is the African psyche ever limited to "that which is not the other and does not come from him." On the contrary, the African carries within himself, physiologically and psychically, his own genitors and their respective ascendents. His self is thus more "social" than "individual"; he defines himself precisely by that which he receives from others at any moment. This explains in part the real feeling of inadequacy often manifested by the ethnographer's informants since they deem themselves capable of furnishing testimony only when they feel supported by other members of their lineage.

The unity and identity of the personality doubtless affects man's vision of his own position in the center of the universe. From this point of view the individual does not constitute a closed system in opposition to the outside world in order to better secure his own substance and limitations. On the contrary, he enters into the surrounding environment, which in turn penetrates him. Between the two realities there exists a constant communication, a sort of osmotic exchange, owing to which man finds himself permanently listening, so to speak, to the pulse of the world.

This fluidity of the person is augmented by a plasticity which is not at all evident to the uninformed observer. Bringing to Africa our own conceptions, we have always assumed that the African possesses the same status as any man, undifferentiated and for as long as he lives (*ab utero usque ad mortem*). Such beliefs served to justify the punishments inflicted on child-murderers by our colonial administrative courts; they also formed the basis for the repression of human sacrifice and, in the name of morality and religion, for the battle against polygyny. However, in acting in this way we were proceeding contrary to the African conception of man, whereby man is only definable in terms of becoming. First of all, he *does not exist* as a human being prior to certain physical transformations or before the performance of rites designed to admit him into adult society as a new member. Among the Venda, the newborn child has no social significance until his teeth appear; he is "water" and not "person." Consequently, it should not be considered a crime to eliminate children with traits incompatible with the religious ideas of that people (e.g., those who are twins, who have birth defects, who cut the upper teeth before the lower).[13] Similar if not identical ideas are encountered among the Thonga,[14] all the Bantu peoples of southeastern Africa[15] and the matrilineal societies of Malawi.[16] These ideas occur in more or less attenuated form throughout the entire African continent, since for almost all the peoples conception and birth alone are not sufficient to assure the individual of his status as a human being. This status is acquired progressively and is not fully achieved until old age, during the final phase of existence.

Parallel to this notion, which is based largely on space, there exists another view, one related instead to time, which reveals man in continuity. We have already noted that Africans think of their existence as a cycle; for them the concept of existence-cycle includes the concept of prolongation.

It is notable that in Africa celibacy is not viewed with any favor and that, except for those who live alone for ritual purposes or who have been deserted by their spouses, men and women view marriage as the ideal human state in this world. This is so true and so deeply rooted in the minds of Africans that single persons (other than those special cases mentioned above) find no excuse in their eyes. They are treated with contempt, and may even be ostracized from their families and from society. Celibacy constitutes an incomprehensible upsetting of the social and religious order.

From this point of view sterile people are no less despised. They are compared to unproductive earth, having no value for anyone expecting from it an increase in power and a prolongation of life. Almost everywhere in Africa sterility constitutes a cause for "divorce" because a household without children signifies the extinction of the family line.

Polygyny becomes a means of defense for men against these two debasing possibilities. Polygyny is the opposite of celibacy and constitutes the preventive "cure" for widowhood; likewise it is insurance against the infertility of women. As such, polygyny is compared to the man who wants a drink and who digs several wells at different places to be sure of satisfying his thirst.

Celibacy, sterility, and polygyny maintain a certain relation with the notion of time, according to which man is viewed existentially. African thought assigns man different modes of time depending on his marital status. The bachelor is placed in a false human perspective; he registers his life in linear time and follows a straight path with no possibility of "returning." In this he resembles the infant whose eventual disappearance leaves his parents and society with only the regret of his lack of human achievement. The married man, by contrast, follows a curved line because he inscribes his life in cyclical time, and thereby finds himself in the true human perspective. Indeed, through marriage, and especially through fatherhood, man enters into the cycle of generations. He abandons the straight route in order to follow the gyrating movement of creativity and great undertakings; he becomes fully a man.

This double vision of human destiny projected into infinity explains the African attitude toward solitude as opposed to a union promising successive regenerations. It also unveils every man's immense desire to have a numerous progeny and reveals the underlying motivations of polygyny. Polygyny must be understood as a variable exponent (in relation to the integration of the individual in the cycle of generations) compared to the constant of monogamous marriage.

For certain West African peoples the union of man and woman is doubly symbolic and as such offers man another occasion for transcending himself. Above all it represents the union of the sun and the earth.[17] It also reproduces the "initial" human condition, androgyny, of which many African peoples seem to have retained "recollections" in their religions (if we may judge from the ritual "residues" which we encounter).[18] The idea of androgyny, the ideal form of the human being, reflects the concern for perfect equilibrium between male and female and for their total reciprocity in equality.

This ideal state only serves to bring out more clearly the second condition of mankind; in this condition, according to the Bambara and Dogon, mankind, having lost its androgynous nature through circumcision and excision, adopts marriage and thereby satisfies social requirements. Marriage is really only a poor substitute for the initial androgyny. Nevertheless, like androgyny, it is fundamentally characterized by the idea of complementarity, the leitmotif of African thinking in all domains.

This idea of complementarity is not completely the same in androgyny as in marriage. Androgyny makes few distinctions in this regard; it does not distinguish the oppositions that we will encounter in marriage. What counts in androgyny, fundamentally, is the being's dual nature as both male and female. When attributed to marriage, the idea of complementarity becomes a source of oppositions, although it still respects a rigid symmetry. If man is associated with the right because of the strength and action which he incarnates in the manner of the right side of the body, then woman belongs to the left because of the notions of obscurity and secrecy which she shares with that side.[19] Considered in spatial terms, on the horizontal level, if man is "in front," woman is "behind," while on the vertical axis man adopts an upright position and woman a horizontal one. The same concern for symmetry can be seen in the realm of activity. Man is linked to the "exterior," woman to the "interior"; the masculine world develops outside of the house, the feminine one inside it, as if the home, the hearth, and domestic life contrasted conspicuously with the rest of human activity.

All of these characteristics, which seem to overburden the seemingly simple concepts of male and female, show the extent to which the African is concerned with defining the human being according to all his attributes. Still we have not discussed all the fundamental problems concerning man; of particular interest are the ideas concerning the offspring produced by the couple.

It is well known that the African is not only desirous of having children but that he also shows them incomparable kindness and tenderness. The treatment accorded to twins is surprising in this context. In many societies twins are fervently desired and their arrival is greeted as an extraordinary event: the twins are practically worshiped, as are their parents. Many other peoples, however, are afraid of twins and their birth provokes a veritable catastrophe. Often both children are killed, sometimes only one of them. At times the mother is also sacrificed, or at least forced to leave the village. At best she remains "impure" for a certain period of time and then, following purification, is reintegrated into the conjugal household.

No one has yet undertaken a thorough elucidation of this feature peculiar to African culture. The question certainly deserves study since it appears to result from an evaluation of man made by himself; nowhere is human nature more directly at issue than in cases such as this one.

At first sight it would seem that there is a close relationship between the conception of the person held by various African peoples and the reception which they reserve for twins. In other words, one might think that the cultures in which man's original androgyny is considered an ideal state of equilibrium would have a reverential attitude towards twins because, by their ambivalent unity, they represent one of the social manifestations of the original equilibrium of man.[20] But the problem is certainly more complex than it seems at first.

It can be said that in general the feeling towards twins is universal. Two ideas seem to be confronted in relation to twin births: the fertility of the woman and the inferiority of the children she brings into the world. And since the former is transferred onto the latter, the twins enjoy a unique kind of ambivalence in society: they are at the same time positive and negative, good and bad. Their social polarity is accordingly defined in each culture in terms of criteria which no longer directly concern the children. And although black Africa does not present an exception in this regard, it remains for us to specify for each society the factors which give twinning its special meaning.

One fact which immediately occurs to any Africanist is the importance of social hierarchy in Africa. Here all men have their determined place in society; each has a function to perform or a role to play, and they arrange themselves in strata according to the order of their coming into the world.[21] Many African societies are extremely "sensitive" to this order. In addition, all take note of the interval between births, sometimes to the point of religious respect. They strongly prohibit any new conception before the last child has properly entered the family, this occurring sometimes two or three years after birth.[22]

In fact, what is valorized in these societies is above all the role and rank of the child. More often than not the preferential form of marriage is between cross-cousins, and a birth immediately poses the question of the choice of the future spouse as well as of the "price" of the wife. If this hypothesis is valid, it helps to explain how disturbing the birth of twins is to the social order. Under these circumstances the killing of one of the twins (at least) does not carry the criminal aspect which we attribute to it.

Other African ethnic groups turn to the second member of the mother-child dyad, the woman, and valorize the idea of fecundity. This attitude obviously leads to the appreciation of twin births and the veneration of twins, while the respect for the interval between births is blurred and the regulation of sexual relations between husband and wife after childbirth decreases. Certain peoples, such as the Dogon for example, even extend the notion of twinning in that they consider the child born before the recurrence of menstruation as the twin of the child which preceded him into the world.

Can we go further in these investigations of the relationship between cultural elements and say, as some have, that the cult of twins in Africa is characteristic of sedentary agricultural peoples?[23] No, for this would oversimplify things beyond measure and would ignore the profoundly human aspect of the problem. What we are concerned with here, essentially, is not eugenics, or economics, but a certain vision of the human being.

From the beginning of this synthesis we have seen that man appeared as the center of the world, and also as a being conscious of his strength. It was necessary to define him in relation to himself and to all creation in order to then place him in relation to the divinity.

The "God" of African culture appears to Westerners as the "great unknown." Anything and everything has been said about the Divine Being in this part of the world, but we are hardly more advanced today than yesterday. No doubt we grant ourselves the illusion of having progressed in the knowledge of African theology by having banished the notions of animism and fetishism from scientific religious vocabulary. But can one call this illusion an advancement in knowledge? Certainly not. What then do Africans think on the subject of the divinity? Is it a single being, or are there several "divinities" populating magnificent pantheons? What is the relationship between God and all the intermediary powers which we call "spirits" or "secondary deities"? What is the role of the ancestors in African theology? The number of these questions could easily be increased. Some people state that originally Africans must have been monotheistic, but that they lost that belief over the course of time in order to devote themselves to the adoration of several gods. Others criticize these assertions and uphold the belief in Africa's inveterate polytheism. "About no subject in social anthropology," said an eminent British researcher in 1936, "is there more conflict of opinion than about primitive theology."[24] And, after summarizing the various opinions of different scholars on one given people (the Zande), the same author concludes, "This diversity of opinion cannot be wholly due to religious convictions, or the lack of them, but must also be attributed to the amorphous, indefinite, character of the facts themselves which allows emotional and intellectual selection on the part of observers."[25]

African religious phenomena certainly are "amorphous" and "undifferentiated" when they are approached directly. In that sense they resemble all things which seem abstract to us but which are concrete to others: they are located, in one or the other culture, on different levels. On this subject we may well wonder what theology a stranger to our culture would make of our religion if he did not know the fundamental principles of Christianity and if he did not use the same conceptual language as we do.

In reality, African theology, which has barely passed out of the embryonic stage, must be approached both through the detailed analysis of its rites and through the narrations of oral traditions. Certainly this is an indirect way of revealing the relationship between man and his god, but, we think, it is the only method which allows us to avoid the impression of insubstantiality, fluidity, and vagueness which an overly direct approach will always produce.

In practical terms, all African peoples are profoundly religious. But the number and nature of their beliefs are extremely varied. In some cases we are confronted with cult objects and practices which seem disconcertingly insignificant at first sight. Hunting and nomadic peoples serve as examples here. Furthermore, it is very difficult to penetrate their religious life; one has the sensation of being in a world from which God retired long ago and to which he now turns his back. At other times, spirituality is expressed with exuberance, rites are found in profusion, and at almost every step one trips over sacred objects. In such areas one has the impression that the divinity still lives among the children of men and that a great intimacy exists between them. Almost all sedentary peoples fall into this category.

Whether we study one or the other of these two categories of peoples, or peoples intermediary between them (since our classification is not at all exhaustive), one conclusion becomes evident. As soon as we are able to penetrate beyond the superficial beliefs, and from the moment we pierce the "shell" of the superfluous elements of the religion of a given people, man appears with absolute faith in the efficacy of his approach to spirituality. It is certain that nowhere in Africa does man feel any philosophical or religious doubt. His "faith" and his thought show absolute certainty in the success of their undertakings.

Is this to say that the African is naive and credulous? Far from it, although all evidence might lead us to believe this. He simply feels assured that in acting in a certain way he is conforming to the order of things in the universe, that he is respecting the hierarchy of beings, the categories and classifications which correspond to those defined by his culture, that he is obeying "the rules," and that he is not guilty of violating its "prohibitions." For him this attitude places him close to God, like the Christian careful to fulfill his religious duties who with a good conscience can call himself "child of the Father."

From this point of view it is surprising that in approaching the study of the divinity in Africa, Western scholars have always begun by looking at the "African" supreme being through the prism of Christian soteriology. They have not for a moment thought that in cultures other than our own the God of Abraham, the God of Moses, and the God of the Christian era could easily blend into a single being who, abolishing the temporal perspective, manifests himself according to several modalities. In fact, we find in African religion ideas about God which conform to all the stages of the great adventure from the creation to communion with God through the eating of his flesh. The remarkable aspect of this religion is found in the absence of abstract theological speculations and in the feeling of quietude which it offers man.

The African does not possess theological *"summae"*; his ideas concerning God emerge during the course of rites, often the most soothing ones, and it is here that we must look if we want to learn his wisdom on this subject. The hunter is apt to symbolize the divinity in terms of a "gatherer" of human lives;[26] the elephant becomes the symbol of his immensity; the lion designates his royal character and his justice. Rites which are "obscene" to our eyes may represent man's joy in his contact with God. The African may use all of the "materials" which his environment puts at his disposal in order to express his ideas about God. For him everything which surrounds him exhibits a sort of transparence which allows him to communicate, so to speak, directly with heaven. Things and beings are not an obstacle to the knowledge of God, rather they constitute signifiers and indices which reveal the divine being. Thus a sort of communication is established between the "high" and the "low" by means of intermediary elements.

It is striking that in almost all African creation myths we encounter the theme of the sky pressed flat against the earth at the beginning of time. The contiguity of these two worlds was so bothersome that it often disturbed humans in their growth or in their daily activities.[27] In particular, women could not pound their grain without knocking against the sky, and so close relations finally ended when the sky's anger at the annoying blows of the women's pestles caused it to withdraw from the earth.

A similar theme is encountered with the same frequency in the relations between God and men. According to this theme God was once living among men (or men were living in the sky, close to God).[28] Then, following incidents between the two parties, God resolved to recede from men.

Some eminent researchers and scholars feel these themes are equivalent to the idea of the "fall" in Christian religion.[29] But this is not at all the case. The separation of the sky and earth, of God and man, simply constitutes the middle course enabling the mind to conceive of communication between these two realities. If a dialogue is to be established between them, "distance" becomes indispensable. Indeed, the mind can only justify the existence of intermediaries when a gap separates the communicators.

All African ritual practices concerning rainbows, clouds, and rain are based on the "distance" which separates the sky and the earth. Similarly, all relations between the divinity and men can exist logically only if the space between the creator and the created is acknowledged.[30] Thus, far from representing an action which unfolds in two eras, paradisiac life and the fall, these themes contain the element which establishes the possibility of religion as communication: distance.[31] In other words, in order to understand the significance of these mythical accounts it is necessary to reverse what they seem to suggest at first glance. The period of man's "religiousness" is not at all the "paradisiac" era when God lived in the "village" of men, but the period following, when God had lost his earthly and human qualities in order to live separately from mankind.

Furthermore, the withdrawal of God is not simply a mythical theme; it still constitutes one of the major characteristics of African religion to this day. Many Africanists have in fact noted that the worship of God was really addressed to a being so distant that it seemed completely ineffective. They have not even hesitated to speak of the Supreme Being as a *deus otiosus*.

It should be said that the "withdrawal" of the divine being is not in any way a negative aspect of African religion. It is very much the opposite. The African feels deeply that the more inaccessible God seems to be, the greater is his need of Him. This is, moreover, one of the unique features of African mysticism: it could be said that the intensity of religious emotion is directly proportional to the human soul's feeling of separation from God.

This God, made "smaller" by perspective, is not, as a result, a "weakness" of African religion. On the contrary, He is the dynamic element around which all the other elements of religion revolve; He procures for man true detachment. For this to happen, however, one must remember that God's correspondent, man himself, is in a unique situation. He is in some sense divine since his death will never affect him definitively. He disappears only to return and, in numerous cases, will do so indefinitely. In a sense it can be said that the "withdrawal" of God constitutes the only divine position in accordance with the doctrine of human reincarnation. The human adventure thus enjoys a freedom of movement which it could never have if the creator "clasped" his creation too tightly. But in another sense the distance separating man and God multiplies the need for intermediaries. In practical terms, in a system such as this one, anything can become a "means" of access to the divinity. In the same way the divinity can "disintegrate" into the form of metaphoric analogies and give the impression of being either a well-populated pantheon, or what has been called astrolatry, zoolatry, phytolatry, and so on.

All this indicates just how complex the relationship between man and God is in Africa and demonstrates as well the necessity of not approaching African theology through our own mentality.

The African attitude toward the supreme being is infinitely humble. True, man aspires to become God; certain rites even lead him there. However, he never leaves his human condition; he does not rise to the sky in order to peacefully bask in the beatific vision. Rather, he obliges God to come to earth, to renew his closeness to man, to descend to him in order to divinize him. Thus the favored place for the African beatific vision remains the earth. This is shown in all the African practices concerning trances and dances of possession, as well as in all the customs involving the ingestion of hallucinogenic substances towards a highly sacred end.

The Elementary "Cathedrals," Worship, and Sacrifice

What is quite certain is that material reveries change the dimensions of our powers; they give us demiurgic feelings; they give us illusions of omnipotence.

G. Bachelard
La terre et les rêveries de la volonté

2

In comparing the piety of the African with the religious sentiments of the Western European, one gets the impression that there is no common denominator between them, no more than there is between the spiritual needs of "believers." The entire apparatus which serves as a framework or support for these different forms of religion—places of worship, liturgy, celebrants, offerings, and so on—testifies to structures so different that it is impossible for the careful observer to penetrate the profound value of African religion without totally ignoring the fundamental ideas we call "civilized."

In our culture communal and public demonstrations of piety quickly took precedence over individual and domestic worship; churches and cathedrals were soon built to shelter such rites. Contrary to this, traditional African religion is characterized by an almost complete absence of temples erected for the express purpose of providing shelter for the officiants and faithful. Instead, both forms of religion, domestic and public, coexist on equal terms in black Africa.

There are many reasons for this scarcity or absence of cult buildings in Africa. First of all, African building materials and techniques are not easily adaptable to the construction of vast monuments. Certainly, Africa is not devoid of important archaeological remains of architecture: the continent has produced audacious builders who have left to posterity the vestiges of imposing edifices, such as those of eastern and southern Africa and the ancient kingdoms of the Sudan. These monuments, however, were not actually intended as places of worship, but rather as fortified enclosures or royal residences. As for the temples, they seem always to have had the smaller proportions still seen today in

Dahomey, Ghana, Gabon, and elsewhere, while their simplicity tended to hide rather than reveal religious mysteries.

In addition to material difficulties, the climate certainly contributed to the lack of emphasis on congregational religious structures. In intensely hot areas it is much more difficult than in temperate regions to tolerate gatherings in enclosed spaces. Furthermore, concern for preserving the secret and mysterious character of the religious act prohibits any public participation in religious "services." These services are thus performed by a very restricted number of officiants in the presence of only those who have been initiated into the beliefs.

To these material considerations can be added others which are even more important because they are inherent in the very structure of African society and psychology. From what we know of African societies since their contact with the West, it is quite clear that the nature of a people's religious edifices is linked in some way to its social organization. The more a society departs from the simplest forms of social organization—lineages and clans—in the direction of state structure, the more the places of worship tend to take on importance. In other words, political and administrative centralization itself requires a certain concentration of religion into well-defined buildings, while the division of society into lineages and clans favors the scattering of places of worship and diminishes their distinctiveness to the point that certain of them blend into the environment.

No less important is the natural tendency of African religion to maintain a close contact with the cosmos. The African "believer" does not willingly isolate himself from nature; nature must act without intermediaries or obstacles on the officiants and those who participate in the mysteries. As regulators of liturgical cycles, the sun, moon, stars, earth, animals, and plants directly influence people in "prayer." That is why the idea of a temple as a place of worship is foreign to the African "believer."

This can and must be followed by a further comment. The very nature of the liturgical life in traditional religion is incompatible with the temple. In Africa the sacred calendar of this religion, like the hieratic cycle of spiritual life, is not based on a succession of events related to the development of a human or divine being. Instead, it is founded on the processional rhythm of the stars and the seasons, on the movement and cycle of the year, and on the succession and metamorphosis of natural events, independent of the life and will of humans. However, all of these phenomena are difficult to summarize and register in human constructions. The most natural path to follow in this situation, and the one adopted by African civilization, consists not in reducing the phenomena and their cycles to the level of human existence, but in being guided by them. This explains the existence of natural landmarks scattered throughout the African continent in order to follow the "path" of the sun and the heavenly bodies. It also justifies the use of the biological cycles of animals and in particular of plants to determine divisions of time. The human being thus lives in close contact with the universe; he lives in symbiosis with it and does not artificially separate himself from it at any moment of his existence.

Since it is essentially in opposition to this self-generating notion of religion, the idea of a public religious edifice specifically intended as a place where people can come into contact with the Invisible can be of little interest to the African. He is resolutely turned toward the cosmos, where nature offers the human soul a vast range of supports on which to "seat" its prayers. This is again to say that the specific characteristic of places of worship is in large part determined by the geographical milieu. Thus it is not so much the being to whom the cult is addressed that varies from one people to another, or one region to another, but rather the various "means" of communicating with God and their expression, the latter being necessarily related to the former. So the African, being in almost constant communion with nature, will seek in nature to achieve harmony with the divine; it is there that he will establish his place of worship.

If we wish to attempt a systematic classification of these natural "temples," the four classic elements of water, earth, air, and fire will furnish the clearest outline. Besides, such a classification is not at all artificial. To be convinced of this we need merely look at the allusions, sometimes explicit, sometimes implicit, in rituals throughout Africa.

Let us begin with places of worship associated with water. It is curious to note that while in geographical terms the hydrography of Africa makes it a land of contrasts (humidity and dryness being found there to extremes), Africa can also reveal an astonishing uniformity if we consider the purely religious value of water. During periods of drought or in arid areas, man strives to erect a sanctuary on any small spot where water appears or can appear; when water abounds to the point of dominating the rest of the landscape, man still considers it with respect and veneration. All this arises from the fact that man always considers water as a source of life and that as such it is as indissolubly tied to human existence as are the very means of subsistence.

Springs, streams, rivers, lakes, and ponds constitute the great aquatic "temples" of African religion. Each one possesses its own meaning. According to the description of the *maziga* rite given by Evans-Pritchard,[1] the Zande attribute to springs the ideas of rebirth and resurrection. Of course Evans-Pritchard saw in these ceremonies only a simple technique for obtaining rain, yet it seems obvious that we must go beyond his interpretation and see in water surging up from the depths the return of the souls of the dead to this world. This symbolism becomes even more evident when we consider that the accounts concerning the vocation of the women diviners who perform this rite have death and resurrection as their themes.

Bodies of water are sometimes considered to be the residence of "ancestral deities." The Chopis, for example, say that these spirits live in rivers. Also, "when the chiefs make a national offering, they mix the meat with water when they present it to their gods, and the one officiating turns his eyes towards the river when he prays." Similarly, "he places the part of the victim which has been cut out for the gods on the bank of the river," expecting them to come and take the offering.[2]

Sometimes rivers and streams are also considered "residences of water Genies," and as such they also have significance in connection with fecundity. Many African peoples perform rites on riverbanks so as best to assure the fertility of people as well as material wealth and abundance. Junod rightly remarks that the word which designates water among the Thonga, as well as many of the names of streams among the Bantu of southeastern Africa, possess the feminine suffix *ti* (or for certain groups, the feminine prefix *mi*), "which seems to show that long ago . . . water was considered a feminine principle."[3] The connection between femininity and flowing water is also found elsewhere in Africa. For example, the section of the Niger River flowing through Bambara territory is given the same meaning. This part of the river is regarded as the body of *Faro*, who is associated with the multiplication and proliferation of beings.[4]

Among the Bozo a small ritual fishing party precedes the large fishing party into the entrance to Lake Debo at the end of the dry season. The small party is charged with furnishing the necessary victims and commodities for the large sacrifice performed on the banks of the river in order to obtain abundant fish and harvests. On this occasion a goat is slaughtered and "given" to the river, as are fresh milk and bits of certain grains and plants.[5]

Worship on the banks of rivers and streams is not only public. Often it is individual and personal, particularly when it involves prayers for the fecundity of women, as is seen in West Africa.

The still water of ponds and lakes carries a symbolism somewhat different from that of the preceding account. It is associated instead with the origin and creation of man and the world. For this reason the banks of these bodies of water are well suited to receiving "prayers" concerning the "return" to origins. Among the Venda, Lake Fundudzi represents the very place of creation, the primordial womb. It shelters the annual rites for obtaining grain, during which a young girl was supposed to be ritually offered to its waters in order to open the gates of heaven and drive out the drought. The same lake is compared to the courtyard of the royal palace, where the final initiation ceremonies (*domba*) of the Venda take place. Moreover, these rites specifically allude to the death and resurrection of the initiates who on that occasion experience "all ideas relating to the origins...."[6] Similar ideas undoubtedly exist among the Bantu of southwest Africa, particularly among the Kuanyama for whom the water of Lake Osamba plays an important role during the *efundula* initiation rites.[7] A rigorous inventory of beliefs attached to lakes and ponds in Africa would facilitate a better understanding of the meaning of these bodies of water which hold so much fascination for men. Their often "miraculous" origin prefigures their religious destiny among riverine peoples. For example, was not the creation of Lakes Kivu and Tanganyika due to the intervention of the God Imana?[8]

It is important to note that all of the examples mentioned up to now were concerned with fresh water, as if fresh water monopolized most if not almost all of the symbols of African religion. Still, it is quite surprising that a continent almost entirely surrounded by the sea would not give to salt water more symbolic value in its religion. Undoubtedly there are good reasons for this. As we have said before, Africans are earth-dwellers deeply attached to the soil. The solid ground is for them the best guarantee of existence; it is the element most exploited both materially and spiritually. Conjointly, fresh water, the nourishing principle of both the earth and man, is indissolubly associated with worship and prayer. Fresh water is human water, while sea water, as Bachelard points out, is inhuman water because it does not serve men directly.[9]

In another connection Junod has already remarked upon the African's fascination with the ocean's grandeur. He writes,

> The *sea*, with its immensity and its wonderful power, deeply impresses the Thongas dwelling near it. They do not, however, tell many stories about it, nor did I hear of any explanation regarding its confines and the shore on the other side. Some magicians claim to have gone and stayed for some time down in the depths: to have "crossed the sea" is for them a kind of diploma, which gives them the right of exercising their art.[10]

This behavior with regard to the sea can be clarified in a surprising way when we compare Junod's observation with Bachelard's remark:

> The hero of the seas always returns from afar; he comes back from the Beyond; he never speaks of the shore. The sea is fabulous because it is first expressed by the lips of the traveler of the farthest voyage. It

makes something imaginary out of the distance while natural dreams confabulate what one sees, touches, and eats.[11]

This does not mean that the sea plays no part in worship in Africa. There are marine "temples," places where people sacrifice and pray while facing the sea, just as there are marine fishermen along the coasts of Africa, particularly along the Atlantic seaboard from the mouth of the Senegal River to that of the Congo. Examples of this are furnished by the Lebou, Ga, Fante, and the Benga of the Cape Esterias peninsula, to cite only a few. However, when we study the traditions of many of these peoples we find that their relationship with the sea is "late" and, in a manner of speaking, accidental. These ethnic groups first experimented with the sea and made it a part of their worship as an extension of their earlier experience with fresh water. For example, the Lebou, prior to becoming ocean fishermen, seem to have learned and practiced fishing on the banks of the Senegal.[12] The Fante and the Ga possess analogous traditions.[13] On this subject we should note that down through the centuries authors have passed silently over marine fishing off the coasts of Africa as if it did not exist or was of such secondary interest that it did not merit their attention.[14] In truth, Africans seem never to have been intrepid "argonauts"; neither do they seem to have ever practiced sea fishing with as much competence or on as great a scale as they did freshwater fishing. From this latter point derives the important role played by fresh water in their liturgy.

"Temples" associated with the earth are likewise extremely varied. The ground itself, rocks, named places, crossroads, hollows, grottos, and mountains furnish a broad range of them.

Almost all African traditions consider the earth to be the symmetrical equivalent of the sky. As such, whatever the spot chosen, it is a perfect locus of "prayers." Its sacred nature undoubtedly results from its dual valorization by man: it is the nourishing force and the place of burial; it makes things grow and consumes them; it unites within itself the two opposite poles of existence, life and death. Among many African peoples the earth is thought to have given birth to the first human beings. Those places where man first emerged may then become favored spots for farming. Generally, inhabited and cultivated land possesses a much greater religious meaning and importance than does the barren or uncultivated bush (although for certain "prayers," particularly hunting rites, the bush is preferred). The conceptualizations which certain peoples have created concerning the earth prohibit us from thinking that Africans consider this element an undifferentiated cosmic unit. Among the Dogon, the earth is a "building" with fourteen stories, seven above and seven below, of which only the highest of the lower worlds is inhabited by humans. For the Fali there are two distinct primordial worlds which, by coming closer together and twirling around each other, finally unite and give birth to the present world divided into two zones, the known world to the east and the unknown to the west.[15] The earth is thus a focus for speculations that are often quite far-reaching, and its choice as a "temple" undoubtedly results from what man "knows" of it rather than from a sort of confused primitive experience.

Sometimes, characteristic signs seem to predestine certain spots. For example, among the Kabre of Togo it is said that a certain rock bears the traces of human steps. It is thought that the first pair of men created by Esso lived on this spot. Not only has this rock become a "sanctuary," but in the eyes of the indigenous people it incarnates the unity of the Kabre and even the identity of the human species. Sacrifices are made there, particularly to ask for rain. Such sacred rocks and stones are found throughout Africa. Their valorization seems to correspond first of all to the ideas of strength, stability, and everlastingness, and accordingly these places of worship are often in close relation with the chieftaincy. For example, among the Mossi of Upper Volta the new king must, at the time of his coronation, be seated several times on stones located between the capital and the city in which the enthronement takes place. But their semantic content is not limited to these ideas. Rocks and stones are also placed in relation to the sky, the sun, and fire. Thus any spot from which ore is extracted and then placed in a furnace for the fabrication of iron receives "prayers" and sacrifices beforehand.[16] Through the intermediary of iron, the celestial metal, the stone too is endowed with a heavenly character. "What is the thing," asks a Mossi riddle, "which is found in the sky and is transformed into stone when it descends to earth? The correct answer: a star."[17]

Of course these are not the only meanings given to stones and rocks. Many groups attach meaning to them and endow them with a "sacred" character for very different reasons. For example, it is thought that two rocks in the form of a skull located near the city of Astrida in Rwanda are the remains of two mythical serpents who play an important role in the beliefs of the Rwandans.[18]

Hills, mountains, and peaks constitute another category of places of worship involving the earth. They express the solid and unshakable character, and the power, of things and beings. "A mountain," say the Bambara, "will never collapse." Again, there is a close correlation between these places of worship and royalty. Very often in Africa the enthronement ceremony of a king includes a "visit" to a specific high place held in great esteem by the inhabitants, who make offerings and sacrifices there. During the year of their nomination, the sultans of

Kapka and Kobe in Zaghawa territory go to the sacred mountain of their clan and perform a sacrifice, which is renewed every three years thereafter.[19] Among the Mossi of Yatenga the coronation of the king takes place on a hill close to Gourcy.

In addition, elevations in the terrain are often considered to be related to the "sky," and are consequently chosen to be "temples" "in" which pleas for rain are likely to be taken into consideration by the divinity. That is why, among the Zaghawa, people climb the mountain not only for the enthronement of the chief but also to solicit rain.[20] Similar "prayers" are performed by the Mossi king of Ouagadougou and the earth chief of Sabatenga, on a hill located near the latter village.

Opposed yet intimately related to elevations are hollows, grottos, and caves, which are also predestined to be places of worship. Sometimes the entrance to a grotto or cave is located not at the foot or side of the mountain but at its summit, making its sacred character even more pronounced. In general, the symbolism of hollows, grottos, and caves reveals the profoundly female nature of the earth. These places offer man the possibility for deeper and more intimate contact with the nourishing ground. Because of them, man and his offerings can return to the womb of the earth in order to be renewed and reborn.

Two ideas seem to cut across the multitude of rites connected with hollows, caves, and grottos. It is through them that one gains access to the interior of the earth, conceived as a womb in which man descends in a spiral motion, to reappear, like a newborn child, remodeled, renewed, and remade at the beginning of his spiritual and mystical life. As material bases of this idea, hollows, grottos, and caves serve as places of initiation whose fundamental theme is almost always the same: the death and resurrection of man. It is often in this role that they are encountered in Africa. Among certain groups the grotto or cave is "replaced" by an artificial excavation in the ground when the symbolic death of initiates is to be performed.[21] At times, again through the intermediary of these temples, man enters the "digestive" stomach of the earth, whose role is then to "mash" the initiate, to "pulverize" his old personality in order to fashion a new one. In the past, initiation into the *Komo* society of the Bambara, which was intended to transform the individual by means of such a "crushing" of his personality, often took place in a grotto.[22] But the "rebirth" of the initiate can also be compared to the "rebirth" of vegetation when the rains return to make the earth fertile. This is why certain ethnic groups perform sacrifices in a grotto in order to solicit the return of the rains and the growth of useful plants.

Finally, caves and grottos may at times serve as tombs, as is the case among the Dogon. In this context their meaning is basically the same as when they are used for initiation. They emphasize man's wish to avoid putrefaction and his desire to be "reborn" through his return to the "womb" of the earth.

These complex and varied ideas are not always expressed clearly in the rites. Among certain groups, however, they are often easily perceived. Such is the case of the Zaghawa, who in the course of ritual sacrifice of a pregnant animal remove the fetus and deposit it in a pit at the top of the mountain.[23] This "prayer" can be interpreted as an offering by which men ask for the return of fecundating water at the end of the dry season, and also for the return of the vegetation indispensable to life.[24]

To all these places of worship related to the earth must be added crossroads and named places. It would not be an exaggeration to state that in black Africa every human settlement possesses one or more sacred crossroads, predestined for the performance of numerous rites. Normally the most important intersection is formed by the crossing of two paths, but forks with two and three branches are also generally called "crossroads." However, the semantic value of these places is different.

Among the Bambara the intersection with four branches represents the original "crossroad." It signifies the "God-point or God-'ball', *kuru*, the phase of creation in which the divinity itself was still no more than a dimensionless being in a universe without coordinates."[25] Thus, for the Bambara this place constitutes a "temple" in relation to the being in its concentrated form, its totality. This explains the names, strange-sounding at first, which this Sudanese people gives to this type of crossroad: "giant head of the limit" (*dāgū* or *dākū*), that is to say, the "initial point of departure," or the "old man," implying the being who existed before all other beings. The *dāgū*, as a temple, is frequented particularly during the important events in the life of the village: epiphanies of initiation societies, sacrifices commemorating the life led by men before the invention of agriculture, and "prayers" and sacrifices recalling the memory of the founding of the village. In the past, some of these "temples" were decorated with various symbolic designs.[26]

Among the Bambara the crossroad in the form of a two-pronged fork always signifies doubt, while among the Pygmies of the equatorial forest it is the "temple" meant to receive the umbilical cords of twins. "For twins," writes Father Trilles, "the cords must be buried at the fork of two paths, one at the beginning of each of the paths. All of the participants deposit a small branch, preferably forked, a twig, and some leaves. Several days later the father returns to spread out the piles . . . and ordinarily the two paths are then diverted for a few feet. Often a tiny hut is built at that spot in honor of the spirits."[27] A path splitting into three branches, called "chicken-foot crossroad" by the Bambara, is likened by them to the anisodactyle foot of the chicken. And as this bird is the symbol of the (apparent) movement of the sun around the earth, the image of the chicken becomes the basis for relating this kind of crossroad to the rotational movement of the world. The "prayers" and sacrifices reserved for the "chicken-foot crossroad" are those particularly concerned with the rites for the renewal of the year.

Named places mark those parts of space which the local population endows with special significance. Their religious valorization is most often due to a mythical event which is believed to have taken place there. The course of the Niger River from its source to Lake Debo is staked out by named places called *faro tyn*, where important rites are performed by the riverine peoples. All of these places were the scenes of mythical events.[28] In addition, named places often acquire their value as "sanctuaries" either because of their form or because of their peculiar vegetation. In short, any part of nature can become a place of worship. As soon as it does so, however, the idea of its use is confronted with the two structures of the named place turned place of worship: first, the structure in which the named place is naturally a part; and, second, that of the religious universe to which this spot is assigned. This change is usually imperceptible to the eyes of the uninitiated, who continue to "see" only the first "function" of the spot (first structure), while for the "faithful" the place is both *profane* and *sacred*. This explains African religion's apparent lack of conspicuousness, at least insofar as cult "edifices" are concerned.

Of all the "temples" of African religion, those associated with the air seem to be not only the most numerous but also the closest to the affections of the faithful. We speak here of "sacred" trees and groves.

Generally trees and plants offer Africans complete material bases for conceptualizations, since all of nature seems to bond together to accomplish those syntheses which, in their eyes, vegetable species represent. This is the reason for the immense prestige of these species, both medicinally and in strictly religious terms.

A tree is also directly involved with time since it develops according to the rhythm of the seasons or, at least, is linked to periods of time by its cycle of growth. This link is sufficiently precise for the tree to serve as an indicator of the periodic progress and retreat of the different phases of time.

If the tree is to be regarded as an entity related to the air, it is so related through the intermediary of time, although not in its abstract sense. The tree is rather concerned with concrete time as indicated by atmospheric changes, by the "air" of rain and by the "air" of sun, by the "air" of the wet season and by the "air" of the dry season. Trees follow the movement of the "air," say the Bambara, without directly alluding to the swaying of the branches in the wind.

For all of these reasons, through which we catch a glimpse of the close parallel between the kinetics of the cosmos and that of plant life, the tree, of all African "sanctuaries," is the one most directly and universally in touch with the divinity. Without exaggeration we can state that all African peoples have or have had their "fetish tree," to use a still popular term. Throughout the continent, including the forest regions, the forest species were, and still are, highly respected. Trees are not cut down, and are often not planted, until specific precautions have first been taken. In many areas man establishes a close bond between trees and human beings, as if the latter were an emanation of the plant world. Certain authors have even spoken of vegetable totemism, though they should have looked more closely beforehand at the poetic reveries of our own culture. Certain passages of Rainer Maria Rilke[29] or of August Strindberg[30] would have furnished them with the opportunity for finding as much "totemism" and "animism" in Europe as among the Ova Hereros, for example, whose ancestor is said to have been born from the tree *omumborombonga*.

Because of the diversity of their qualities and properties, trees are appropriate for representing attributes of the divinity towards which they lift their branches. Thus, in making these vegetable species his favorite "places" for worship, man is not addressing himself to the tree but to that which the tree represents: the power, wealth, uprightness, and everlastingness of the Invisible. Speaking of the role of the tree in Thonga religion, Henri A. Junod states:

> When travelling through the country, you may come across a tree round which a rag has been tied, evidently for some religious purpose. One's first idea would be that this tree is worshiped, but this is by no means the case.... In fact I never met with any worship offered to a plant as such.[31]

And Junod is not one to be suspected of partiality.

Placed on the path of relations between man and the spiritual powers, the tree acquires an even greater value when it forms a part of the thickets and groves in which man holds religious meetings, and by which he isolates himself from the view of the uninitiated. In fact, groves are the most preferred places of worship in African religion. In our judgment they are never man-made. Man can occasionally improve a bit on nature's work, but the location of the vegetation and its variety of species depends on chance.

Generally the "sacred" wood is formed by a ring of thorn trees of the acacia genus with branches crossed in all directions in an inextricable tangle. In its center is a more or less large, clear space which can be reached by one or more paths worked into the living wall. The "sacred" trees may be located in the interior "courtyard" of the thicket. Sometimes ponds are found there containing crocodiles and fish which no one ever tries to catch. Permanent altars may also exist inside the clearings.

Although quite common in Africa, these sanctuaries have been generally ignored by investigators. In their defense it should be stated that access to these places is difficult for anyone not integrated into the community to which these "temples" belong; the *kãgo* of the Mossi, the *tũ* of the Bambara, the *sinzang* of the Senufo are highly sacred and inviolable. The reason they are forbidden to the uninitiated is undoubtedly to preserve the mystery of the numerous symbolic meanings given to them by the initiated. To judge from a well-studied example, the sacred wood of a Bambara initiation society, these "temples" are symbolic of mystery, of that which is, first and foremost, impenetrable, thus entered with only the greatest difficulty. The thickets are usually used for initiations. They are the symbol of knowledge. The thorns of the living fence represent the harshness, the difficulty, and the shadows which the intelligence of the neophyte must overcome before advancing further into knowledge. The thorns, their sharp points bothersome and cutting, connote difficulty, pain, and tension. In addition, each species of thorny plant possesses its own symbolism which is grafted on to that of the type.

But if the grove, sacred in its entirety, constitutes the image of knowledge, then the interior clearing represents the end of the path toward learning: the sky, the abode of pure souls, the "holy" space par excellence. This is why it is generally prohibited for anyone to enter with his shoes on; would it be proper to soil the sky with all the impurities collected by shoes on earth?

These summary remarks suggest the scale of the desolation which strikes the hearts of Africans when, in the name of town planning, the administration cuts down these sacred woods in order to construct whitewashed buildings in their place.

With the element of fire we touch on that which is among the most profound and hidden of all the treasures of African culture. No African rite is as surrounded with secrecy as those concerned with fire. According to numerous myths, fire was originally stolen, and even in the context of the cult it still retains something of the illicit character of an object which must always be concealed. The jealousy it inspires is equalled only by the jealousy of a man on account of his wife. "Temples" related to fire are more numerous than one might think, since any hearth where an African woman prepares food can be properly considered a sacred place of worship. This is not so much because of the holiness of the food but because of the "sanctity" of fire. But hearths form only one of several types of fiery "sanctuaries"; there are the blacksmith's forge and active volcanoes besides.

Little systematic research has been undertaken concerning African religious conceptualizations of the hearth, despite the fact that it is one of the richest and most vital parts of the household in all the regions of Africa. The fire which burns there constitutes the most visible image of the unity of the living and the dead. Among the Pygmies of the equatorial forest the importance of the hearth is underscored by the fact that the spirits of the dead "live" there. In addition, it represents an "altar" where numerous rites are performed, particularly by hunters, who offer there a bit of fat taken from the side of the right ear of any elephant killed in the hunt. Similarly, a domestic fire should consume as firstfruits those parts of the game reserved for the divinity.[32] Among the Bantu peoples of southeast and southwest Africa the individual hearth and the village hearth both play an important role in religion. As the "soul" of the household, the hearth turns the house itself into a humble "sanctuary" of prayer, of silent invocation addressed by man to the divinity or to the family's ancestral souls. When an offering is made of food cooked in the fireplace before it is taken into the body to be transformed into blood and life, this is not only a way of "nourishing" the ancestors but also a way of thanking the Invisible for the gift of fire, the symbol of life.

After the hearth, the most important "temple" of fire is the forge. Here the blacksmith, who usually belongs to a special caste in black Africa, devotes himself to the difficult task of working iron to furnish the tools for farming or the weapons for hunting and warfare. But the forge is often a place of worship, too. Its ground is sacred, and one enters barefoot in order not to communicate to the "temple" the impurity of the shoe. It is also a place of peace. No dispute is tolerated there, not because of the "spirits" which live there but because it represents a celestial space. There are still other characteristics of the forge which can be added. It is often attributed with the ability to overcome stubborn cases of sterility in women, who seek the intervention of the blacksmith when plagued by such a disgrace. The artisan-priest's mediation with the invisible powers takes place in the enclosure of this workshop-temple. In addition, the forge offers a place of refuge for unfortunates seeking asylum. Connected to the notions of fecundity, life, and liberty, it is the most typical sanctuary in African religion, the one which, after the hearth, possesses the widest extension. It is intimately tied to the soil and, relative to the cult of family ancestors, it stresses the importance of the community. If the comparison were not so extreme, we could almost say that the forge is the church of the African village.

But the most impressive manifestations of fire to human eyes belong to the phenomena of nature: these are volcanoes. Such "temples" of fire have a very limited geographical distribution in Africa and are still not well known. In Rwanda, the cult of Ryaangoombe focuses on the volcano Muhabura on whose peak the hero established his residence and still continues, it is said, to cultivate such useful plants as bananas, sorghum, and tobacco (the latter in the form of giant lobelia).[33] Elsewhere certain women become the "wives" of the volcano and maintain a permanent cult near these fiery "sanctuaries."[34]

The great variety of places of worship which we have just discussed does not exhaust the list, because in Africa—as elsewhere in the so-called archaic world—any location may become a "place of worship." This derives in part from the fact that any portion of space can offer man, in a more or less durable fashion, a material base for his religious conceptualizations. In other words, in this religion man does not visualize space as a homogeneous concept but as a multitude of meaningful elements which he can utilize as he pleases to express his "faith." On the other hand, the function of the various parts of space in the cult results from the very nature of the rite in African religion. It would not be an exaggeration to say that in Africa the rite encompasses all human actions because, at least in its origins, any such action is always religiously meaningful and requires the "sacredness" of the space in which it is accomplished.

Still, this should not lead us to conclude that in Africa every man is a "minister" of a cult. There too public prayer requires specific officiants, persons destined for that role either by vocation or because their society chose or named them according to definite rules.

In general, any human group forming a self-sufficient social "system" (especially for "controlling" the "entrances" and "exits" of women for purposes of marriage) possesses a "priesthood." Thus it seems that there is a certain relation between any religious unit and its power to direct the movement of its most precious human resource, women. This should not come as a surprise to anyone who is aware of the fundamental role played by women (often unbeknownst to them) in African society. In fact, even though religion in Africa is principally a man's affair, its reason for being is woman, guardian of life and link between the living and the dead, between the past and the future. The ability of the group to dispose of its own "life" goes hand in hand with the autonomy of religious life.

The religious life is almost always placed under the aegis of the chief of the group—the eldest or the patriarch of the family. This personage is not seen, as we might think, as a precursor, opening the way for the family line. Instead, the African mentality places him at the other end of the human chain: he belongs to the past. He is the final element, living at the border of this world and that of the departed, and because of this he is destined to be the liaison between the living and the dead. His role on the religious plane mirrors that of woman on the biological plane: both act as intermediaries between two worlds. But while woman in this context is a movable element, placed under the authority of the chief of the group, the latter is sovereign. He gives and receives women to seal unions between men, as he grants "prayers" and receives the benefits of the Invisible to maintain the homogeneity between man and God. He is above the incessant circulation which operates between the two groups ("takers" and "givers" of women) in terms of both human and spiritual goods because he is the one who rules it; he is permanent. Often his subordinates see this characteristic in him in such a realistic way that he is·said to be exempt from death. Thus in numerous African societies, these patriarchs are believed to transform themselves at the end of their earthly lives into quiet animals, preferably snakes, so they can go off unperceived to join the world of the ancestors.

The religious powers of the chief of the group are often numerous and complex. Theoretically and schematically, he alone is responsible for addressing "prayers," offerings, and sacrifices to the divinity. In reality, however, African societies have often opted for specialists in the "priesthood": "prayers" and offerings are frequently the responsibility of an old man, while the performance of sacrifices is entrusted to an appointed sacrificer. At times we even find specialization within the "oratory" function of African "ministers" of worship. In a single society, some members are in charge of general spiritual relations between the divinity and the ancestors, while others insure the performance of "prayers" for rain and·harvests, and still others preside at rites concerning the harvesting and threshing of the crops. Thus in the *moaga* society of the Republic of Upper Volta these three functions are performed respectively by the *kim soba,* the chief of the earth, and the *bugo.*

In truth, African religion has a tendency to multiply these functions and the agents responsible for the spiritual life of the group. Religious "despotism," the concentration of spiritual authority in the hands of a single person, is a cultural trait not at all suitable to black Africa. This does not mean, however, that the idea of unity is absent from this religion; quite the contrary, it has a conception of unity which is most often diffuse and radiating outwards.

The oral element in African "liturgy" is of prime importance. Speech, in the form of sacred formulas, is present in all religious acts but, by their nature, is most evident in "prayers." It also accompanies, indeed brings life to, offerings and sacrifices. Speech possesses the characteristics of both water and heat and so is a fecundating power.

In their "devotions" Africans are particularly responsive to offerings and sacrifices. Offerings generally precede sacrifices and are intended to favor and facilitate contact with the Invisible. Through them, man tries

to provoke contact with spiritual powers, either by making them re-
laxed, calm, and tranquil or by making them animated, excited, and
moved. Cool water, milk, honey, and light cereal porridges are examples of soothing offerings. Palm wine, various beers, mead, and all
fermented drinks constitute the "erethistic" offerings. These are the two
major categories of offerings which are universal in Africa. Others,
apparently more limited in their geographical distribution and more
adapted to the specific circumstances of life, include saliva mixed with
various products (kola nuts, diverse fruits, and parts of certain plants)
previously chewed by the officiant, or the contents of the stomach of
certain even-toed mammals (in practice among Bantu pastoralists). The
"dosage" of these offerings, as well as the priority observed in their use,
give evidence of a veritable "choelogy" of which Africans are the incontestable masters. The fundamental principles of this science depend on
the profound knowledge of the semantic value of the materials utilized
and their adaptation to the different situations in which man finds
himself.[35] Of course nowhere in Africa does this "science" of offerings
exist in the form of a corpus of doctrines. Rather, it consists in the
application of rules of a mode of thought which constantly strives to
grasp the relationships between beings and things, and between beings
and the conditions which determine them. It constitutes one part of
man's spiritual and relational universe, the other part involving
sacrifices.

African spiritual life is so impregnated with the idea of immolation
that it is practically impossible to find a people on that continent whose
religious practices do not include the slaughter of the most diverse
victims. It can even be said that sacrifice is the keystone of this religion.
It constitutes the supreme "prayer," that which could not be renounced
without seriously compromising the relationship between man and the
Invisible. By sacrifice we mean the flowing blood of slaughtered animals. And it is from the actual blood of animals and human beings who
have fallen on innumerable altars that its entire value in Africa derives.

What are the possible reasons for the African's fascination with this
life-sustaining liquid? Also, by what mechanism is man able to unite the
sky and the earth by means of blood?

One important fact attracts our attention: victims of religious practices
are almost always chosen from among domestic animals.[36] It is almost as
if through these sacrifices man was trying to offer the invisible powers
something of himself. For, if we can believe the different myths and
legends about the domestication of animals, tamed animals did not only
belong to the "supernatural" world prior to their capture but were also
an "extension" of man. Domestic animals receive their subsistance from
the hands of men; their life depends on contact with their masters and

some among them even eat the same food as he. Thus, in regard to sacrifice we may speak of a kind of preferential order which classifies victims in relation to man, who is the supreme "host."

These reflections are of course very general and do not prejudge the different kinds of sacrifices and the specific victims which they require.

A second fact should now be noted, that is, the dominant place of the chicken in African liturgy. It could be said that this bird is a universal sacrificial animal, for it is used as much by nomadic as by sedentary peoples, by farmers as by pastoralists, in the savanna as in the forest.[37] Several reasons seem to have contributed to its religious valorization. First, the chicken is not costly, so even a poor person can obtain one easily enough. Raising chickens poses no problems because these domestic fowl are usually raised freely and without concern for their food, laying, or reproduction. Furthermore, as a sacrificial victim, no other animal offers as many individual variations as the chicken. Bodily peculiarities, coloration, voice, laying, and disposition vary so greatly from one to another that there are hardly two that resemble each other. All this is important from the point of view of religious symbolism, which, when applied to the sacrifice, can be given free rein to find the appropriate victim for each occasion. Thus in a single African ethnic group we were able to distinguish more than seventy kinds of chickens representing the appropriate victims for as many different kinds of sacrifices.

There are still other, no less important, reasons for the high valuation of chickens. These concern the ease with which the body of the victim can be divided after the sacrifice. The anatomy of the chicken is relatively simple; its body is naturally divided into a specific and unequivocal number of parts. Because of its size this bird is suitable for small religious groups. It is adaptable to the communal level of African religious groups but can also be consumed by the "priest" or sacrificer alone. Finally, the principal factor in making the chicken the supreme sacrificial victim seems to reside in the relationships established between this animal and time.

The rooster is the first in the household to announce the arrival of the day, and this is of particular importance since dawn in the tropics is very short, night being more sharply separated from day than in our regions. This fowl is accordingly credited with being in possession of the "science" of time. His song marks the rhythm of time, which for many African peoples allows him to be considered as equivalent to the succession of days and nights. Thus the rooster and chicken are generally likened to cosmic values, bearers of a destiny on which man feels himself dependent. This explains their high estimation as sacrificial victims. To offer them in sacrifice means at once to present oneself before the Invisible and to demonstrate the desire to match one's "time" with the rhythms of the cosmos. For the African the sacrifice thus becomes the act by which man penetrates the very heart of the universe.

This brings us back to our earlier suggestions that Africans are fascinated by blood, a fascination better understood now because blood conveys life. It contains the active force of the beings which carry it and constitutes a dangerous vital element which if carelessly wasted has serious consequences. But blood, like the sacrificial offerings about which we have just spoken, is above all intimately tied to rhythm. Blood is the sustainer of the body's life-movement and reflects the allotment of time to each being, a little like drum music which in a series of intervals sends naked time to the ear enriched by this new dimension, rhythm.

What could be more natural than this intimate and almost necessary relationship between sacrifice and the spilling of victims' blood? Man could not find a more proper element to inscribe his "prayer" upon the life of the world.

To attain such a goal there is no need for imposing temples or for ceremonies which attract attention. Little piles of sand or earth, mud cones which can often barely be distinguished from the other elements of a disorderly environment, stones, bushes, trees: for generations these have been the altars on which thousands of victims have lost their lives, imparting to their blood, in a final leap of life, the rhythm which opens to the faithful the door of the Invisible.

Life, Death, and Time

> To be born, to live, and to die,
> that is to change form.
>
> Diderot
> *Le rêve de d'Alembert*

3

In Africa the problem of life and death constitutes the basis for religious feeling and is the unconscious foundation of philosophical reflection. Life and death are both "given" to man by the creator; they are the fundamental terms of existence and are so closely linked that one cannot be conceived without the other. Death, however, enjoys the incontestable advantage over life in that it is necessary, for it was not inevitable that life be given, but as soon as it appeared death had to follow. It is fair to say that death seems to be the unavoidable consequence of life.

Almost all African myths of the origin of death (long analyzed and classified by Western scholarship) deal with this dialectic. Their themes reveal the great variety of motifs called upon by their users to "justify" the appearance of death in the world of men. However, this diversity allows certain main strands to be detected as soon as we look through the meshes of the narrative. Some of these myths are simple, repetitious signifiers of the human condition. Others are presented as superficially plausible lines of argument linking man's immortality to a certain requirement which he cannot satisfy because it implies the negation of one of the essential aspects of that same human condition.

A considerable number of these accounts relate to what certain authors have called the "message that failed."[1] According to this theme, the divinity decides to send man two messages, one of mortality, the other of immortality. The first to reach its destination will determine man's destiny once and for all. In most cases God entrusts the message of immortality to a slow animal, while a fast animal is delegated to carry the message of mortality. A Thonga myth on this subject can be considered typical.

When the first human beings emerged from the marsh of reeds, the chief of this marsh sent the Chameleon (Lumpfana) to them, with this message: "Men will die, but they will rise again." The Chameleon started walking slowly, according to his habit. Then the big lizard with the blue head, the Galagala, was sent to tell men: "You will die and you will rot." Galagala started with his swift gait and soon passed Lumpfana. He delivered his message, and when Lumpfana arrived with his errand, men said to him: "You are too late. We have already accepted another message." This is why men are subject to death.[2]

Myths of this type have a wide distribution throughout Africa and even elsewhere. Among the Bantu peoples, where they are most in evidence, one of the two messengers is generally the chameleon, either in the role of the herald of immortality or as the one charged with informing man of his mortality. He is set against a wide range of animals carrying the opposite message. Sometimes the chameleon and his antagonists are replaced by other animals, or the message leaves the world of men in the form of a request addressed to God, or it happens that we find only a single message instead of two.

The diversity in the forms of these accounts need not conceal their meaning, which is easily revealed by applying the methods of communications theory. These myths possess three fundamental postulates, the first two of which are discernible at the narrative level, while the third must be inferred from those preceding. These postulates are: (1) the distinction between the world of men and the world of God; (2) the existence, between these two worlds, of a "space" which alters the message, a sort of "black box" which "explains" the difference between the message when it "enters" and "leaves"; and (3) the inversion of the relationship between "speed" and "slowness" on one hand, and between life and death on the other, in passing from the world of God into the world of men.

It is important to note first that the myths of the "failed message" do not confuse the celestial world with the terrestrial one. In accounts of this type there is never cohabitation between God and men; the raison d'être of the message is opposed to this. Certain of the myths are so definite on this subject that they take care to clearly specify this postulate. An Ashanti story recounts that long ago men had familiar dealings with God, who gave them everything they needed. One day, the women, annoyed by the divine presence, compelled God to withdraw, which he did, leaving the world to the power of the spirits. Some time later the Invisible sent men a goat with this message: "There is something which is called death (*owu*). One day it will kill some of you. But, even if you

die, you will not be completely lost; you will come to join me in the sky."
The goat dawdled along the way in order to eat. Seeing this, God sent a
second messenger, a sheep, to carry the same message. This animal,
however, altered the contents of the message to mean mortality and,
arriving first among men, communicated it to them. Afterwards, when
the goat presented himself and transmitted the words of God, no one
believed him. Men had already accepted the sheep's message.[3]

We must also consider the "black box," the space between the two
worlds which relays the message. It "contains" the factors which alter
the message and the information it carries. These include: the bush
(which in the preceding myth offers food to the goat and slows him
down), the grass (which in a Kratchi account "captures" the medicine of
immortality intended for men and benefits from it in their place),[4] and
the termites (which according to a Tikar legend become the food for the
frog who carries the message of life, thus delaying him in his mission).[5]
The "black box" essentially accounts for the lead taken by the message
of mortality over that of life. Indeed, as we will see later, it furnishes on
the narrative level the justification for the semantic change in the ideas
of speed and slowness.

These two concepts do not possess the same significance in the world
of God as in the world of men. In the former, speed connotes death,
while slowness is tied to life. When the dead are "agitated" they constitute the Invisible's greatest menace towards men; in this sense their
"activity" is synonomous with irritation and wrath. Similarly, when the
sky kills it does so by means of a thunderbolt, and with the celerity of
lightning. The dead must exist in slow time, for them "life" is equivalent
to calm, rest, and peace. The living, by contrast, only merit their status
by virtue of activity. Movement, speed, exertion, and zeal are the surest
indices of their vitality. Inactivity, sleep, and torpor bring them closer to
death and the inertia of the corpse.

We can now see that having left the "sky," each of the two heralds
sees himself entrusted with the message which conforms to his behavior: the fast animal brings the message of death, the slow animal
"conveys" life. According to human "logic," however, to receive
"speed" is to have life, while to welcome "slowness" is to accept death.
In addition, the swift messenger arrives in the terrestrial world first not
only because he is more diligent but because, according to men, he
signifies life. In sum, death introduces itself among the living under
cover of the idea of speed, which signifies "life" from the human point
of view and death according to the "logic" of the sky.

The "black box" and the messengers play the role of mediator between the celestial and terrestrial worlds. They allow the changeover

from one signification to the other in the ideas signified by life and death (see fig. 1).

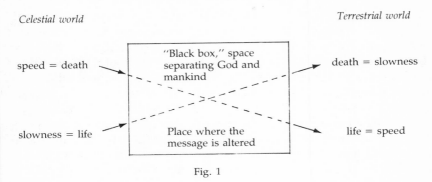

Fig. 1

The "black box" in particular assures the proper functioning of each of the worlds according to its specific modality. Without this mediating space human beings would pass without transition from their own "life-speed" to the "death-speed" of the sky, and the notion of speed would overlay the confusion of life and death.

This eventuality is not at all theoretical, since sometimes the sky sends death to men without the consideration shown in the myths which concern us here. Thus those struck by lightning, who enjoy a unique status throughout Africa precisely because they constitute points of immediate impact between the sky and the earth, pass from life to death without, so to speak, changing their "manner" of existing: they remain in a rapid time and yet belong totally to the sky.[6] The practices concerning lightning follow the same idea: the spot touched by this unmediated irruption of the sky becomes "sky" and must be withdrawn from ownership by men.[7]

It is interesting to note the way in which the peoples who have "failed-message" myths treat the two messengers. Aversion to both is practically universal. The chameleon in particular is held in disfavor by almost all the Bantu peoples and by others as well. This dislike for the slow animal is doubly justified, first because on the mythical level he let himself be overtaken by his teammate, the messenger of death, and second because in the human world slowness is associated with death.[8] The way in which the chameleon is "punished" for its slowness by those who "hate" it is also significant. The Thonga, Zulu, Venda, Xhosa, Lamba, Acholi, Nyanja, Ngoni, and Mushikongo tribes force its mouth open and then throw in a pinch of tobacco, which causes the animal to die while its color changes first from green to orange and then from orange to black. This practice undoubtedly has the aim of showing the relation between the chameleon and lightning in terms of death: one kills by its slowness, the other by its speed; one is "slowness-death," the other is "speed-death." Even better, the chameleon may be considered a being permanently struck by lightning, like the albinos of the Baronga, who are called "lightning-ember" because they are thought to have been "burnt (hisa) by lightning in their mother's womb before their birth."[9] The bringing together of lightning, the person struck by lightning, and the chameleon is further justified when one realizes that this animal is used by "magicians" as if it were a piece of a tree struck by lightning in order to discover thieves. "It is used by certain magicians to discover thieves. They smear a chameleon with a drug which makes it turn white and then let it go: 'Then the thief, wherever he may be, also turns white, and if he does not confess his theft, he dies.' "[10]

Thus, insofar as it mediates between the sky and the earth regarding the "origin" of death, the chameleon is in an exceptional position. It is both "slowness," like "life" in the world above, and the celestial "cause" of human death, like lightning. In other words, the chameleon is the "incarnation" of the two contradictory ideas, life and death, united in one and the same being.

It is now easy to establish that the "failed-message" accounts of the origin of death are devoid of etiological intentionality concerning their apparent theme. Instead it can be said that they emphatically affirm the distinction between the world of God and that of men, the existence of a "no-man's-land" (the "black box") between these two worlds, and the mortal nature of men and the immortality of God. This manner of "speaking" about death is not without interest. It indicates the concern for locating the problem of human existence according to coordinates which are certainly open to question, but which conform to the culture and philosophy of men who cannot conceive of life and death without reference to the intervention of the "sky."

This same concern is reflected in another group of myths which fully accentuate the human condition. The stories of this category can be validly grouped into various referential sectors corresponding to essential life processes.

The ability to reproduce which man shares with the animal and vegetable world and which, at the same time, distinguishes him from the inorganic world, is most appropriate for allowing us to understand the origin of death. There is nothing more striking than the succession of beings endowed with life issuing from a single founder in which the offspring replace one another over the course of time. In a certain way isn't death linked to this very ability to reproduce? If life regenerates in order to preserve itself, it is fair to think that death is hidden within the act of life like a "portion" of the living person. Furthermore, to suppress the reproduction of the living would be equivalent to confusing the organic world with the inorganic world.

A Nupe myth on this subject recounts that in the beginning God created tortoises, men, and stones, and, with the exception of the stones, he made them both male and female and provided them with life. However, none of the species reproduced. One day the tortoise wanted to have descendants and asked this of God, whose response was that he had granted life to the tortoise and to men but had not given them permission to have children. At this time, the story adds, men did not die; when they became old they were automatically rejuvenated. The tortoise renewed his appeal and God warned him against the danger of death, which would result from a positive response on his part. But the tortoise took no notice and pressed his request. He was joined by men, who had decided to have children even at the risk of death, while the stones refused to join in with them. Thus God granted tortoises and men the ability to have a posterity, and death entered the world, but the stones remained unaffected.[11]

No less essential to life is sleep, which periodically plunges the living person into a state of unconsciousness which men in all times and places have likened to death. If the similarities between the two phenomena recall their "necessary" connection, then the absence of one will provoke the disappearance of the other and give rise to the idea of immortality. From this isn't it perfectly logical for mythical thought to establish just as "necessary" a connection between immortality and the state of wakefulness?

At the beginning of creation, states a Bassa myth, men were immortal. At this time there were no animosities or disputes, and animals were respected as brothers by men, who in return were done no harm by the animals. *Lolomb,* the divinity who never slept, enjoined men to stay awake at all times or else death would make its appearance in the world. But men could not resist sleeping and for this reason death began its work.[12]

Other accounts emphasize the need for food and relate death to the consumption of the nourishment essential for life. In the Congo basin, where bananas constitute man's basic source of food, it is natural that this fruit be chosen as the significant element in the narrative. Among the BaSonge, the creator Fidi Mukullu made all things including man. He also planted banana trees. When the bananas were ripe he sent the sun to harvest them. The sun brought back a full basket to Fidi Mukullu, who asked him if he had eaten any. The sun answered no, and the creator decided to put his response to a test. He made the sun go down into a hole dug in the earth, then asked him when he wanted to get out.

The sun answered "Tomorrow morning, early." "If you did not lie," the creator told him, "you will get out early tomorrow morning." The next day the sun appeared at the desired moment, confirming his honesty. Next the moon was ordered to gather God's bananas and was put to the same test. She also got out successfully. Then came man's turn to perform the same task. However, on his way to the creator he ate a portion of the bananas and denied doing so. Put to the same test as the heavenly bodies, man said he wanted to leave the hole at the end of five days. But he never got out. Fidi Mukullu said "Man lied. That is why man will die and will never reappear."[13]

Aversion to the dead body and decay constitutes another of life's distinctive traits. Contact with organic matter in the state of decomposition, especially when it is the mortal remains of a fellow man, is a serious menace to the living being. Even in those societies which practice "desiccation" of the corpse, man eventually separates himself from anyone, no matter how beloved. Myths in the category of "premature burial" seem to ignore this requirement and associate the immortality of man with the nonburial of the corpse.

Among the Kongo, Nzambi created man and woman. The woman gave birth to a child. The creator forbade the parents from burying it in the event that it died; they were told to simply put the child in a corner of the hut and cover it up with wood, because after three days the child would come back to life. The parents did not believe the words of God and when the child died they placed it in the earth. Then Nzambi declared: "I told you not to bury the child and you have buried it. For this reason all your descendants will be subject to the same malady; they will die because you violated my prohibition."[14]

This second category of myths about the origin of death is noticeably different from that of the "failed message." In the latter case we witnessed a complex "discourse" based, it could be said, on a veritable "theory" of information. But here the story is simpler and more direct. It takes the form of a line of argument whose conclusion consists of an option which conforms to the present human condition concerning one of the essential characteristics of life. Indeed, each of the myths in this category forces man to choose between mortality and immortality. But while the first alternative (mortality) expresses the present condition of man, the second (immortality) leads to its negation.

It is evident that the keystone of this line of argument, the human condition, is characterized among other things by reproduction, sleep, nourishment, and aversion to decay.[15] If mythical thought establishes a connection between death and each of these characteristics taken separately, it is because such a link exists beforehand between them and man's nature. Moreover, immortality is opposed to man's nature in the same way that the negative aspect of the essential characteristics of the human condition is opposed to their positive aspect. The result is that man "opts" for mortality because it conforms to his condition. In no way can he "opt" for immortality without automatically rejecting his very nature (see fig. 2).

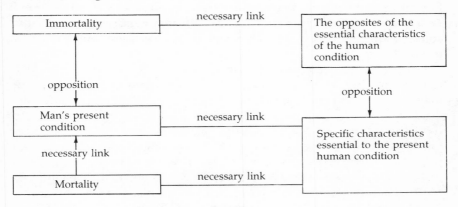

Fig. 2

Beyond this, what is interesting in the myths of this category, other than the type of reasoning for which they have a predilection, are the specific aspects according to which the human condition is grasped. These most often relate to the functions judged to be vital: sexuality, strength-regenerating rest, food, hygiene, and so on. But there are others which are concerned with, for example, knowledge or the emotional state which death causes among the living. Serer and Korongo myths deal with the first of these elements. In the beginning, say the Serer, men did not die. The first being to experience death was a dog. He was buried in a termite hill at the foot of a baobab tree, and, as no one had ever before seen a dead creature, this was a great event. While the women danced, the dog was wrapped in a cloth and gunshots were fired. When God (Koh) saw all that men were doing for the corpse of a dog he became angry, and from that moment on death became the lot of men as well.[16] The Korongo story chooses a tree trunk as the object to be buried. In the beginning of things, it is said, men did not die and their number seemed to be increasing indefinitely. In their happiness men began to perform mock burials and carried in procession tree trunks which they later buried with great ceremony. When God saw this he was irritated and sent sickness and death into the world to punish men for their mockery.[17]

It is easy to establish the structure of these two narratives in terms of what was said earlier. The present human condition is linked to the distinction between men and animals (Serer myth) and between men and trees (Korongo myth) in that men are buried but animals and trees are not. Thus death is found to be associated with an element which confirms this distinction, while immortality ("impossible" to realize) goes together with the confusion of men with animals or men with trees. Both of these stories emphasize the aspects of intelligence and the mind which are given the highest value by the two cultures involved: the ability to distinguish and classify, oppose and associate things in order to avoid confusion.

The emotional state resulting from death is the object of a Bena Kanioka myth. A hunter named Kassongo was visiting the village of Mauesse without permission during the dry season, a period marked by death and the desiccation of the celestial beings. One day Mauesse reprimanded the hunter and at the same time gave him a package. Shortly thereafter Kassongo's son died. Kassongo, not understanding what had happened (since at this time men enjoyed eternal life), returned to Mauesse's village to find out. He was given to understand that the package received by him contained the punishment for his transgression and he was advised to return to his home, place his dead son on a mat, and cry. Kassongo did what Mauesse prescribed. All the people assembled around the corpse and began to dance while they lamented. Meanwhile, Mauesse sent his dog to see if the humans were eating and laughing instead of crying. The dog returned to his master and said, "First, I saw men lamenting. Then I saw them eating, then I saw them lamenting. After that I saw men playing and laughing." Mauesse then pronounced his sentence: "Since men cannot even be sad, they must all learn to die."[18]

The structure of this myth is similar to that of the preceding stories. The present human condition involves complex funerary rites whose execution does not exclude, and in fact requires, feasting, drinking, exaltation, and even a certain gaiety. Thus, in order to avoid death, the men of the myth would have had to confine themselves to tears and lamentation. This requirement for immortality contradicts man's nature and thus becomes "unacceptable."

As can be seen, all these myths—like the "failed-message" stories—are not intended, despite their appearances, to inform us of the origin of death. Rather, by means of the problem which they set out to resolve, they make known their possessor's conception of the human condition. Life (the original "immortality") constitutes the fundamental principle of man's nature, from which all others derive. It can only be grasped by endowing it with all the attributes opposite to those which characterize mortality. This goes without saying since, on the one hand, death is the opposite of life, while on the other death furnishes men with an experience far more realistic and convincing than life.

Life also has priority in terms of time, since it precedes death. As a result of this intellectual requirement (which is so evident in the myths), these stories constitute the human being's first attempt to apprehend himself diachronically. They are man's attempts to find the elements of his own history, or even rough outlines for the first history of human destiny. This means that death and the myths of its origin lead the mind directly toward the problem of social time, of time lived and of duration.

For the African, time is inconceivable without generations as its framework. The succession of human beings issuing one from another offers to African thought the ideal basis for establishing the three fundamental correlative stages of duration: past, present, and future. However, contrary to what we might expect, a succession of individuals linked by ties of birth appears on the ideal axis of time facing not the future but the past. The human being goes backward in time: he is oriented toward the world of the ancestors, toward those who no longer belong to the world of the living, while he turns his back on what is to come, the future. Future and past are thus determined in relation to the two major sides of the human body, the back and the front. Between them, the flanks, containing the ribs, are analogous to the present, connecting the two extremes.

From the point of view of the generations, the woman is equivalent to the rib because in bringing children into the world she assures the link between successive generations, between ascendants and descendants, between the past and the future. For this reason the woman remains the most engaging image of the present.

Within the lineage the past and the future are represented by the head of the family and his son. Between the two of them, the mother, carrying their descendants on her back, is extra-generational. As the present she belongs to both at once. She is above all a mediator, since the child perched on her hips is none other than an ancestor returned to the world of men through her. Thus everything occurs as if woman were the crossroad where future and past, death and life intersect. She results from ambiguity, from that which is at once tomb and resurrection, decay and vitality. But she incarnates the junction, the beginning and the end of the cycle of human existence. It is within the entrails of woman that we should locate the *ouroboros* as a symbol of rebirth. The mythical theme of the woman giving birth to a snake thus acquires its full meaning.[19]

Within this context the limits between life and death do not really exist. Life is born from death and death, in turn, is the prolongation of life.

Many so-called barbaric and savage customs may be explained in the light of these brief remarks. Take, for example, the alleged indifference if not cruelty towards the elderly, who are often abandoned to their fate. Certain Bushman tribes do not burden themselves on their difficult travels through the desert with old people who are helpless or hard to transport. Instead they build them a small enclosure of brush wood and abandon them there with, if possible, a small provision of wood, food, and water. If the rest of the community finds game and water quickly they send someone back with new provisions for the old people left behind. If not, they avoid even returning to visit those they deserted, knowing that the old ones would not be able to prolong their existence for very long and that soon the hyenas would not allow them to survive.[20] The Hottentots treat the elderly of their communities in a similar way. According to Kolb, when an aged Hottentot reaches extremely bad physical condition, his oldest son, or a close relative, asks the residents of the kraal for authorization to unburden himself of such a load and to deliver the old person from his misery. Since this permission is never refused, a bull or several sheep are killed for a feast and then, on the appointed day, the old person is placed on a carrier bull and escorted to a small hut constructed for this purpose at some distance from the kraal. He is abandoned there with only a small amount of food. The old person soon dies of starvation or is devoured by wild animals.[21]

These and other such customs encountered in Africa have often provoked the indignation of researchers, who have denounced them as cruel and inhuman. But these denunciations have constituted a rather quick judgment without accomplishing beforehand the necessary unraveling of the intricacies which order these practices.

We must add that it is essentially the indifference to death and the contempt for life which cause astonishment. Bowdich reports that during his voyage to Kumasi he found himself one day in a village where the chief, accused of committing a serious offense, was awaiting execution. "He conversed cheerfully with us," recounts the explorer, "congratulated himself on seeing white men before he died, and spread his cloth over his leg with an emotion of dignity rather than shame; his head arrived in Coomassie the day after we had."[22] Winwood-Reade relates the story of an Akropon woman who had been stripped before the sacrifice, then clubbed unconscious but not killed. He writes,

> She recovered her senses and found herself lying upon the ground surrounded by dead bodies. She rose, went into town, where the elders were seated in council, and told them that she had been to the land of the Dead and had been sent back because she was naked. The elders must dress her finely and kill her over again. This was accordingly done.[23]

Almost everywhere in Africa the royal burial ceremonies of the past were accompanied by numerous human sacrifices, of which many were voluntary. "It is said," reports le Hérissé, "that for the kings of Dahomey those wives [of the deceased chief] not designated to be sacrificed would ask for it as a favor."[24] And R. S. Rattray adds, concerning the Ashanti,

> Among the scores killed at royal funerals were some of the highest of the land—high court officials, relatives and wives of the dead monarch, who, no longer having any desire to live once "the great tree had fallen," compelled their relatives to slay them by swearing the great oath that they must do so, thus not leaving them any option except to carry out their wishes.[25]

Innumerable cases like these could be cited, and others from different areas could be added. Think, for example, of the impressive custom of ritually putting kings to death, and of the ease with which in the past human beings were sacrificed (particularly certain types such as albinos). Africa was undoubtedly a land stained red with human blood. All these deeds denote a religious "confusion" on the part of Africans between life and death, or rather an astonishing sense of life which in their eyes could only be fully realized if interrupted by momentary stopping points. Instead of diminishing and weakening life, these moments of rest give it a new vigor each time, to the extent that life continues reinforced and renewed after each ordeal.

This conception of life and death, and implicitly of time, has extensions in other areas. Being oriented towards the past, the African finds the justification and meaning of his actions not in the future but in time already elapsed. His reasoning is thus "regressive": "I do this because my forefathers did it. And they did it because our ancestor did it." The profound and necessary connection between present activity and the past thus appears. The aim is to trace the present from the past and thereby justify it. This line of thought reveals on one hand the role played by tradition in African culture and, on the other, the meaning which is given to action.

This single word "tradition," when applied to African "customs" and beliefs, too often makes us think of some simplistic system of habits and routines according to which, turning against progress, Africans content themselves with the inability to grasp the new. However nothing of the kind is included in the notion of tradition as it should be understood to explain African religious behavior.

For Africans, tradition is above all the collective experience of the community. It constitutes the totality of all that successive generations have accumulated since the dawn of time, both in spiritual and practical life. It is the sum total of the wisdom held by a society at a given moment of its existence. If we admit that the ancestors do not constitute a closed community, but that they are seen as an assembly which is perpetually increasing and incessantly evolving, then we must recognize that tradition too is not at all static. In the same way that the past augments the "group" of those whom it keeps in its den, the living enrich their spiritual holdings owing to the experiences of the dead. Thus tradition is like the continual reappearance of buds from the protective scales at the tip of the supporting branch.

Tradition for Africans is, then, a means of communication between the dead and the living, as it represents the "word" of the ancestors. It belongs to a vast network of communications between the two worlds which embodies "prayer," offerings, sacrifices, and myths. In this relationship tradition possesses a real originality. At times it is direct, that is, it precludes any intermediary between man and the beyond. The living "feel" the wills and prescriptions of the ancestors; they divine them by a kind of intuition which does not seem to be based on any consciously perceived sign. In this sense tradition is a sort of tacit agreement between the past and the present. This is why in all good faith many Africans justify their religious behavior by invoking the similar comportment of their ancestors. At other times tradition is indirect, and in this case the human being perceives more or less clearly the reasons for his religious actions. By means of perception he seizes upon one or more indices (accidents, disasters, and so on) which justify both his conduct and the religious act which he performs. To an observer located outside the "system" this is particularly striking in medicine and the treatment of diseases according to traditional methods and remedies.

Whether in the form of one or the other of these two types of communication, tradition as the "word" of the dead remains the most vital means of assuring the link between the dead and the living. Owing to this "speech," which is transmitted through the ages, the presence of the ancestors among men is assured at each instant. By conforming to the legacy of the dead, the living in turn recognize their authority and avoid "dangerous" undertakings. Presence on the one hand and submission on the other, this is the very object of the exchanges between two worlds whose reciprocal permeability is never contested by any African. On the contrary, the African lives with the idea of a perpetual osmosis between the two interfacing realities. Yet one can see that it is the world of the living which occupies the unfavorable position in this exchange. It exists at the expense of the other, which is proof enough of its imperfection. From this fact spring the sad laments of the living, who wish to abandon the earth and "rise" to the sky. Take for example a funeral chant of the BaSotho, as reported by E. Casalis:

> We stayed outside,
> We stayed for the sorrow,
> We stayed for the tears.

Oh, if there were a place in heaven for me!
That I would have wings to fly there!
If a strong cord came down from the sky,
I would tie myself to it, I would climb up above,
I would go to live there.[26]

H. Callaway[27] and H. A. Junod,[28] respectively, cite almost identical threnodies from the Zulu and the Thonga which demonstrate that this theme is quite widespread among the Bantu peoples of southeast Africa.

But it is not simply because the world of the ancestors is automatically associated with ideas of repose, tranquility, and peace that it appears as the quintessence of perfection. It is "magnificent" above all because of the prestigious character of its inhabitants. Not just anyone can become an ancestor. The society of the living "directs" towards this "paradise" only those dead who satisfy certain well-defined conditions.

Proceeding to the analysis of the notion of ancestor in African societies, we notice that it constitutes the crossroads of many ideas concerning the individual, society, time, and the divinity. In each society the notion of ancestor is formulated in relation to certain key ideas and according to a dialectic of thought which puts into play the law of oppositions and contrasts.

The ancestor is, first of all, a man who has reached a great age and who has acquired along with longevity a profound experience of people and things. He is thus distinguished from people less advanced in age and whose credulity and inexperience in life classify them with children or youths; the latter are usually not given elaborate funerals and are never the focus of a "cult." Second, an individual who dies from a "dishonorable" disease is definitively struck from the list of ancestors. Thus it is impossible for a man dying from, say, leprosy to become an ancestor. There exist in Africa several specific illnesses which are incompatible with the esteem, radiance, and glory of the dead.[29] It seems that the dead can only be honored by the living if they have ended their lives in conformity with the rules of society. An accidental death also constitutes a humiliation and a stigma, and its consequences in the hereafter are inauspicious for gaining a "halo." A mortal accident breaks in some way the natural and regular progression of things; it constitutes a distressing event which is striking because of the suddenness with which it shatters order by brutally destroying the continuum of time. In addition, physical and psychic integrity represents a fundamental condition for aspiring to the rank of ancestor. All those who are abnormal, all those who deviate from the usual type of person in a society, are automatically excluded from the category of "illustrious" dead. Thus the deformed and mentally ill can never figure among the "chosen." The same ostracism applies to perjurers and any individual who does not enjoy moral integrity. It should be said here that, for the African, moral integrity is of prime importance; he places it before all else in the mastery of the self and, in particular, in the mastery of one's speech. Finally, the ancestor in Africa is always and everywhere an "organic" member of the community of the living; he is one of the links in the chain. Thus the stranger, even if he is adopted and integrated into a given society, cannot pretend to the title of ancestor there, since he is forever a juxtaposed component. The stranger lacks participation and communion with the life of the group in its spatial and temporal continuity.

Considered closely, the body of norms which govern the elaboration and preservation of the notion of ancestor seems to rest on two key ideas: (1) the purity of a type of man, conceived by the group as a social and religious model to which individuals must conform in order to avoid their destruction; and (2) the concern for the continuity and identity of the group over time and despite the vicissitudes of existence. In this regard it is interesting to note that the characteristics of the ancestor—wisdom, physical and moral integrity, passage through life without deviating from its normal course, and communal identification with the society to which one belongs—all constitute attributes involving the idea of completion. And ideally, if they are extended to their highest degree, we arrive at the supreme ideal, superhuman perfection, the divinity. We can thus understand that according to African thought God is often located at the farthest extension of the idea of ancestor, the latter sometimes envisioned as the eponymous hero of the group, sometimes as the intermediary between the divinity and men.

Whatever the circumstances, the ancestor can only fully play his role in the spiritual life of the society of the living if he withdraws from it to a certain extent. This separation is sometimes more symbolic than real. Among the Bantu of southeast Africa solitary old people are assimilated in anticipation with those from their age-set who have disappeared, that is, the ancestors.[30] Normally, however, wise men do not enjoy this status until after their death, and particularly not until after their clear separation from the society of the living has been marked by second burial ceremonies (the lifting of mourning) or by alterations to their tombs.

Even if in principle all dead people who have satisfied the social and religious requirements discussed above can be considered as ancestors, in reality few of them are invoked as such by their descendants. From the total number of the "chosen" each society seems to distinguish a "useful" portion, arranged at various points in the series of generations, who alone are advantageously put to the service of the living. The remainder become blurred in the memory of the living and constitute the refuse of the hereafter, whose memory is recalled without precise reference particularly during new-year rites. Thus, in the same way that some people join the lot of the useless dead at the time of their departure for the hereafter, so the ancestors themselves become partially unusable through the weakness of the living.

We see from this brief analysis of the notion of ancestor that men are doubly indebted to their "glorious" dead. On one hand they owe them their knowledge and wisdom as well as the guarantee of authenticity with respect to tradition, while on the other they are indebted to them for their intervention and mediation on the level of spiritual life strictly speaking. This explains the considerable hold which so-called "ancestor-worship" has on the African soul.

But the relation between the past, present, and future also generates the meaning which the African attributes to his own action. As we have seen before, this action is rooted not in the future but in the past. Action is also synonymous with realization, which is why it is opposed to speech, which has neither form nor measure and which, once spoken, takes off and dissolves in the air. By contrast, action is what man does, what supports him when he undertakes a new effort. And yet one cannot be understood without the other. Speech and action are like two aspects of the same reality, which, in the eyes of Africans, constitutes the full realization of man himself. The balanced dosage of word and act expresses the perfection and completion of the human being.

Still, it is the past which gives measure and volume to this completion, on the condition that man relies on the experience and wisdom of the generations which preceded him, that he agrees to be subject to the authority of the ancestors and tradition, and that he accepts their example as the stimulus and norm of his behavior.

In this aspect of African thinking we are witness to a total reversal of our usual conceptions of the ideal and of progress. For the African the ideal takes the form of an exemplary past which is realized in the present. The supreme ideal for him is the indefinite repetition of the normative past, enriched at each realization by the acquisitions furnished by the present. The ideal does not constitute a model or standard tied to the future but rather an ensemble of values ascribed to the past.

It is easy to see that under these conditions the African, living according to tradition, sees progress above all as the realization by a given generation of stages which others have reached before it. It is always the present generation which is at the point of progress, but this generation is in some way unconscious of the acquisitions which it makes and which will form the first step for the next generation in its own climb to the past. Any religious or social innovation is thus less profitable to its authors than to those who come after them. Like the ideal, progress too is intimately linked to the past.

But the reference to the past is a human reference, because, of all the moments of time, only the past carries traces of human action. It is the only truly humanized period. This explains the profound relation which exists in the eyes of Africans between the idea of progress and the moral achievement of man.

Initiation and Knowledge

> The body is the first and most
> natural tool of man.
> Marcel Mauss

4

The religious behavior of the "believer" has given rise to misapprehensions on the part of Westerners and has often led them to erroneous conclusions as to the nature of African spirituality.

It is known that despite his exuberance the African hardly reveals his inner thoughts. He often allows uncertainty to cloud the essence of his thought or, even worse, he is content to leave his interlocutor in error when the latter has not succeeded in penetrating the workings or meaning of an act or institution. As a general rule an African rarely anticipates the curiosity or the research of an investigator by suggesting clarifications concerning problems he would like to resolve. He prefers above all to be examined on his own cultural values and, when he agrees to answer, he surrenders only that which strictly pertains to the question posed. In so doing he observes time-honored pedagogical principles and, perhaps, the rules dictated by the conservation of knowledge. These spare the master by saving his energies and thus encourage the pupil's research by stimulating his desire for knowledge.

The religious domain is more affected by this attitude than any other because in it, by definition, things are hidden and by their nature more subtle. Further, the sense of "modesty" which surrounds sacred things causes *homo religiosus* to retire in the presence of mere man. That which is "profane" thus appears with greater importance; it forces the "sacred" back into the obscurity of the interior. One should also not forget that the absence of exterior signs confers on it a disconcerting diminution of apparent value.

But in Africa that which is hidden is truer and more profound than that which is visible. The inner man is esteemed more highly than the outer man; thought has a greater value than act; intention prevails over action. To be convinced of this we need simply consider the current and universal African practice of substituting sacrificial victims. This practice justifies a seemingly childish game with the divine: an important sacrifice requires a victim of high rank, but if this victim is lacking, another of lesser importance may be substituted. If this one in turn proves impossible to find, another, even more "insignificant" one may replace it. It is thus possible, by a series of descending stages, to replace a sacrificial bull with a pinch of ashes taken from a domestic hearth which has been passed over successively by a goat and a chicken. However, in the minds of the officiants, the ashes effectively "are" the bull and the value of the sacrifice is not in the least diminished by the use of such an unusual "victim." Here then is one of many possible demonstrations of the importance which Africans give to the interior domain, to that which remains hidden and escapes the notice of others.

It is then this aspect of religion which constitutes an achievement for man. It is through the valorization of the interior man that the human being raises himself beyond his natural limits and accedes to the dimensions of the gods. He becomes something other than himself by refusing to valorize appearances, by instead deeply mining his secret being. This does not happen without the acquisition of a veritable "sense of what is within," of a science of the soul. Neither does it happen without a total transformation of the personality, one which is accomplished during the course of initiations chiefly marked by the death of the "old man" and the resurrection of a new being. This is what constitutes, strictly speaking, man's passage to knowledge. Thus, the human being goes beyond himself insofar as he acquires a new vision of himself.

It is difficult to define initiation in Africa solely in terms of certain social criteria, such as the integration of the individual into one or several initiation societies, submission to puberty rites marked by circumcision or excision, or the extraction of certain teeth. This is because in reality all of these criteria constitute only the visible aspect of initiation; they serve as the bases for hidden meanings, but they are not at all the essential elements. Initiation in Africa must rather be viewed as a slow transformation of the individual, as a progressive passage from exteriority to interiority. It allows the human being to gain consciousness of his humanity. This ascent may be marked by solemn events invested with such social importance that at times the society in some way finds its justification in them, or it may pass practically unnoticed, developing quietly throughout the entire life of the individual, like a long period of meditation.

Certain peoples, such as the Bambara, admit all males without restriction into their initiation societies, while others, like the Dogon, are selective. Still others have no initiatory systems, while women, it should not be forgotten, are generally considered as naturally carrying knowledge within them and are thus eliminated from systems of initiation (except among the few groups which practice a distinct initiation for them). The absence of initiatory practices does not imply the absence of spiritual life. Whether or not he participates in initiation societies, the individual feels himself drawn toward the interior life, toward the search for the Invisible and a dialogue with the divinity. Spiritual life is developed, perfected, and completed by constant meditation. Thus defined, initiation becomes a long process, a confrontation between man and himself which ends only with death. It becomes an experience which is enriched with every passing day, being in principle more complete in an elderly person than in an adult, and more in an adult than in a child. This explains why many informants take refuge behind their "inexperience" and "ignorance" and refer their interlocutor to their older "brother," who alone is capable of responding to the questions posed.

We can thus understand that while it is possible to chart the distribution of certain cultural elements which accompany initiation and its social signifiers, it is impossible to concretely locate initiation itself. It exists everywhere, asserting its authority as the spiritual base of the African soul, as the background on which all religious revelations—from the most insignificant to the most imposing—are registered.

In a synthesis such as the one we attempt here it is not possible to treat all the forms taken by this passage to knowledge in Africa, for to do so would involve running into insurmountable obstacles. Indeed, many of the social aspects of initiation have not yet revealed their deep significance. That which has already been accomplished in this domain is modified as more advanced investigations are undertaken. Yesterday's studies give way to the more pertinent analyses of today, which are conducted according to more rigorous and complete methods often based on the researcher's direct participation in the religious rites. For example, as a result of the investigations of Audrey I. Richards[1] and J. Roumeguère-Eberhardt[2] we now know the profound meaning and implications of the puberty rites of Bemba and Venda girls,[3] whereas not long ago we possessed only commonplace generalities concerning these rites. However, since such studies are not numerous, it would not be an exaggeration to say that we are still far from possessing a true spiritual picture of African puberty rites. In general we have only a limited knowledge of the hidden side of the entire imposing group of practices which physical anthropologists call "mutilations," yet these affect almost all visible parts of the human body (notably the skin, nose, ears, teeth, lips, neck, and limbs). Other, less traumatizing practices involve the hair, nails, epidermis, and body hair. What an enormous chapter could be written on African spirituality as revealed through its immediate foundation, the human body!

While such a study cannot be undertaken here, we can at least try to approach it by uncovering certain of these "techniques," specifically those which deal with the passage of individuals into initiation societies. Still we must impose limits, and focus on the common elements of the institutions rather than on the multiplicity and diversity of acts.

One thing becomes remarkably clear as soon as we begin to look at initiation. This is that, first and foremost, initiation constitutes a progressive course of instruction designed to familiarize the person with the significations of his own body and with the meaning he gives to the environment. Moreover, each of these is in a sense a function of the other: the human body and the world constitute two inseparable entities conceived in relation to each other.

J. Roumeguère-Eberhardt reports that among the Bantu of southeast Africa (the Venda, Lovedu, Pedi, Karanga, BaSotho, Swazi, Thonga, Zulu, and Xhosa) religious, intellectual, and moral training occurs in three stages, the relationships between which define a gradual development of the knowledge dispensed to the neophytes.[4] Corresponding to this knowledge there is also an increased mastery of the environment. In the course of the first initiation, the *khomba,* young girls learn at the level of their family villages the laws of the body (the seat of social and reproductive functions), the laws of fire (related to the categories of persons distinguished for the Bantu by the symbolism of the three colors— white for man, red for woman, and black for old woman), the laws of the hearth (representing the union of man and woman), and the laws of cooking (evoking the conception and birth of the human being). At the time of the second initiation, the *tshikanda,* young men and women are assembled on a regional basis for a period of a month. Here the novices are familiarized with the laws of the house in order to explain the symbolism of each part of the family residence and its relation to the individual and to procreation. At the same time they learn the logic of "the things which go together," that is, the science of the categories of the Bantu universe. Finally, the third phase of initiation, the *domba,* which is conducted on the national level, is intended to instruct young men and women in the laws of the court. And since the court is in fact the counterpart of the mythical space of creation, the instruction given to the candidates at this initiation, as well as the rites which they perform, refers to their accession to the status of completed persons. As such they are ready to fulfill their role in society by marrying and giving birth to other human beings. The teachings of *domba,* focusing on the procreative role of men and women, are associated with apprenticeship to the laws of the drum, which are inculcated in the novices at the same time. This is because the drum, in Bantu symbolism, is nothing else than the "creative voice of God."

Thus it is clear that

> the conquest of space, of the Kingdom, is [among the Bantu] above all a taking possession of the Person, and that the laws of the body, as taught during the first *khomba* initiation, are presented as a microcosm. . . . The house is then introduced [during the second initiation, *tshikanda*] as a macrocosm of the body, as a new matrix, the place of procreation. And this corresponds to an enlarging of the horizon of physical space, since for this instruction the family-village level is replaced by a regional one. . . . Finally, the third school, *domba*, which is national, teaches that the court in turn is a microcosm, the epitome of the entire mythical space of creation. Thus, as the person gains knowledge, through participation in ritual and initiation, of the three territorial zones—village, region, and capital—he also enlarges his ontological, mythical, and social knowledge, which permits him to assume his role in society and be integrated in it.[5]

Seen in the form of an evolution in three stages, Bantu initiation appears to be similar to the observations made by Edwin M. Loeb among the Bantu of southwest Africa (the Kuanyama, Nyaneka, Hembe, Ondonga, and Ukuambi).[6] Here again we find three initiatory stages. The first corresponds for girls to the onset of menstruation. Then, for both boys and girls there is a one-month period of living together (called *oijuuo* in Kuanyama). Finally, for both sexes there is an imposing ritual called *efundula*, which continues for four days and ends with the seclusion of the girls and their preparation for impending marriage. Even though Loeb does not give as many details about these rites as we have about those just cited, it seems clear that the peoples which he describes have the same schema of initiation as the southeast Bantu. Indeed, we find again among the Bantu of southwest Africa that the mastery of the self goes together with the conquest of space. During the *oijuuo* rites boys and girls are brought together and "play" at being married couples. They sleep together at night, and during the day perform tasks according to their sex, in imitation of the chores of married people. Boys pretend to be taking care of the cattle and go out to hunt small animals while their "wives" busy themselves in the kitchen preparing meals for their "husbands." But in no case may cohabitation entail sexual relations between the initiates; rather it constitutes a school of endurance as part of the individual's apprenticeship in the mastery of the body. Parallel to this discipline, the person also takes possession of physical space. The rites of the first menstrual period are individual in character and take place within the family village, while those of the *oijuuo* occur in front of

the entrance to the royal palace. Finally, the *efundula* rites are so intimately tied to the life of the kingdom that

> in former times the welfare of the king and the state did depend on
> the proper observance of the *efundula*, for the birth of a child to a girl
> who had not as yet undergone the ceremony was considered an evil
> omen foretelling the death of the monarch. Even today such a birth is
> considered an ill omen for the Kuanyama as a whole and is very much
> dreaded.[7]

This same schema of initiations is found among African peoples seemingly quite distant in culture from the Bantu of southern Africa. Among
the Fulani of West Africa the candidate for initiation begins by practicing
patience, perserverance, and, later, discretion. Finally, at the end of his
initiation he develops obedience to his master, modesty, and the understanding of discipline. These virtues form, as it were, the physical and
moral basis for the instruction he receives. The instruction is progressive, as is the slow acquisition of the qualities just mentioned. This is
because prior to his gaining knowledge of cattle and the bush (which
constitutes the most important knowledge in terms of religious meaning), the postulant is required to learn such techniques as farming,
leather- and wood-working. Once the neophyte has been admitted to
the pastorate he will no longer practice these techniques. They must
then be considered, rightly, as a small, minor "space" in comparison to
the immensity of the bush, whose most adequate equivalents are the
universe and the divinity.

> Once he has decided to be initiated and to seek a master, the young
> Fulani is under a certain number of obligations for several years. From
> the age of fourteen until he is twenty-one he must beg, cut grass for a
> wage, or sell dead wood in order to buy with his earnings and the
> gifts he receives a handful of cereals and the seeds of three types of
> calabash-plant. He must then clear land in the bush to make a field
> where he will plant the grains and the calabash seeds. This work must
> be done in secret; the boy must hoe, harvest, and thresh his grain
> alone. He then transports his harvest to sell in a market which is
> regularly held on Saturday and on no other day of the week. The
> earnings obtained by the sale are assigned to the purchase of a
> he-goat and clothing, in particular a tunic, pants, a bonnet made from
> indigenous cotton woven by hand, and shoes. It is usually necessary
> to begin anew several years in a row and to make several harvests in
> order for the profits to enable him to make these purchases.
> When he reaches this last stage he must kill a he-goat and remove
> its skin without emptying it. Then he tans the hide to make a
> container for water all the while alone and in his field. At the same
> time he makes a gourd, a bowl, and a spoon with the fruit of his

calabash plants. When the skin has dried, he must fill it with pure water and again go to a Saturday market, dressed in the garments which he procured for himself and equipped with his utensils. There, the first person who asks him for a drink must become his instructor or lead him to a master. If the person is an old man, the initiate begs him to be his teacher; if he is young, he asks him to take him to an elder of his family who will become his master.

From the moment the postulant is accepted by his master he becomes his servant, and this lasts until the end of the initiation. . . .[8]

With age and practice and in relation to the extent of his knowledge, the initiate pastor . . . progressively gains the title of *silatigi*, a term . . . which can be interpreted as follows: "he who has been initiated into the knowledge of pastoral things and the mysteries of the bush."[9]

From "beggar" or "grass-cutter" to the state of *"silatigi"* is a considerable distance, not only because the *silatigi* is the priest of the community, but because he is also the supreme expert on everything that concerns the life of the flock. Furthermore, he is the "master of the plants," having the knowledge of their classification and therapeutic virtues, and he is a diviner, experienced in the interpretation of the "signs" with which the universe is endowed.

In fact, knowledge concerning the structure of the world represents the final goal of the Fulani pastor's initiation just as, on the personal level, the conquest of the self marks the end of the struggle waged against himself for the attainment of spiritual perfection. Thus the path to knowledge among the Fulani is seen

as a progressive instruction in the structure of the elements of space and time, whose essence must penetrate the postulant. At the same time it is presented as a succession of tests symbolizing the struggle which he must undertake against himself with the help of God in order to progress. The postulant must successively enter twelve "clearings," which symbolize on one level the year and its twelve months and, on another level, his movement over an area where, in passing from one clearing to another, he encounters the mythical personages who must instruct him. In addition, he is put in contact with wild animals, which symbolize the forces with or against which he must battle, and with the principal plants which are encountered in the pastoral life. For the postulant, crossing the entrance to the first clearing signifies passing from the disordered world of men, the "troubled city" (*ngenti d'ibuya*), where he resides, to the bush, "the city of God" (*ngendi geno*), and the organized world of the pastorate. . . .

After the twelfth clearing, the initiate receives from the wife of Koumen (who personifies initiatory instruction) a small cord with twenty-eight knots. [These knots] correspond to the days of the lunar month, which must be "untied," that is whose succession must be consciously understood.[10]

This moment marks the high point of Fulani initiation: that knowledge which only divine knowledge can surpass.

After this brief analysis of these few types of passage to knowledge, it is evident that, when considered as a means of introducing man to the mysteries of the universe and of his own being, the schema of initiation appears with remarkable similarity among the most diverse peoples. This can be seen as clearly among the people of southern Africa as among the nomads cast across the steppes, although culturally speaking the two groups appear to be quite distant.

Neither are these examples isolated cases separated by the immensity of central and eastern Africa. To be convinced of this, one need only carefully study, for example, the initiation ceremonies of certain Gabonese peoples[11] and those of the peoples found between the Congo River, its tributary the Kwilu, and the Angolan border.[12] Also instructive would be a careful review of the rites of admission to the cult of Ryangombe-Kiranga (practiced among the Banyaruanda and Barundi)[13] and an analysis of the complex ceremonies of the Chagga,[14] Masai, and Nandi.[15] Among all these peoples, as man advances on the path to knowledge the conquest of the self goes even further, and the taking possession of space and time leads the individual to mystically overflow into his creator. The initiate in Africa thus reveals himself to be like a gentle wave which, starting at the point of contact between the surface of the water and an object touching it, spreads out in wider and wider circles before dying near the banks.

But initiation in Africa entails another aspect, which is no less interesting than the one just discussed. Initiation is meant to be a sort of sacrament with the ability to grant the initiate resurrection and a new life after he has been symbolically put to death. This aspect of the passage to knowledge is by nature even more prominent and obvious than the first. This is why it is also the most easily perceptible during the initiation rites. We must be careful, however, not to limit the extent of its significance within initiation.

It is generally held that the death and resurrection of the neophyte corresponds to the idea of the renewal of the human being who, owing to this symbolic trauma, sheds the "old man" that he was in order to be transformed into the "new man" of his new spiritual state. This is accurate if we look at the initiation rites "close up." As soon as we step back from these ceremonies and consider their most minute details, we notice that in reality they involve the idea of a fetal stage situated between the "death" and "resurrection" of the neophyte. These stages

then become, respectively, "return" to the "maternal" womb and rebirth. The period separating the two critical phases of initiation is thus
not "dead" but "active" time. Its length varies according to the fullness
of the rites among the various ethnic groups; in some cases it is spaced
out over several years, while in others it is marked by a short rite of only
momentary import. In any case, the true formation of the postulant
occurs during his "fetal" state. This phase marks that other passage to
knowledge, one characterized by the "passivity" of the candidate, the
resigned acceptance of the test to which he is submitted, and his profound spiritual transformation.

Among the Senufo peoples of West Africa, initiation into the *poro*
society is divided (according to B. Holas and G. Bochet) into three
phases, each lasting seven years.[16] The final period, called *tyologo,* is that
of the maturation and completion of the initiates; it involves the major
ceremonies intended for adults. During the course of this phase the rites
and tests concerning the postulants' "return" to the womb of the divinity *Kâtiéléo,* and their subsequent rebirth, take place. Among the Dieli,
from the beginning of this phase of initiation, when the neophyte is
preparing to enter the sacred wood, he is confronted

> with a device composed of two vertical cords tied on top to the branch
> of a tree and on bottom to a stake. The young man hesitates and
> usually goes around this obstacle, which is an error punishable by a
> *fine* or a *beating....* The young men are then shown the proper way of
> passing through this barrier. They must back into it, face turned
> towards the entrance to the wood, and spreading the two cords with
> their hands behind their backs they should pass backwards through
> the space made. There is an element of "riddle" in this test which is
> shared by many of the poro tests, but there is also a symbolic element.
> It seems in fact that this moment corresponds (although in more suc-
> cinct form) to the entrance into the *kâtioul* among the Tiembara. The
> *kâtioul* is an enclosure made of logs located inside the sacred space [of
> the wood] into which the neophytes enter by a sort of damp tunnel. The
> Tiembara, whose *poro* is very explicit, point out that the young men
> return to *Kâtiéléo's* womb by passing through her vagina. Among the
> Fodombélé the *tiologo* phase begins with a similar ceremony: the
> young men crawl through a damp trench to the center of a small
> subsidiary sacred wood which acts as *kâtioul.* Even though no clear
> explanation is furnished [by the Diéli] , it is likely that they too are
> concerned with the same process of return.[17]

For the postulant this regressive process marks the beginning of a
series of "trials" whose complex plot can only be imperfectly discerned
at present because of the lack of detailed information and serious research. Nevertheless, Holas, while taking into consideration the inclu-
sive nature of *poro,* notes: "The final goal of this instruction is to lead

man from his primitive state of animality to that of a perfect social unity, or in other words to create, *to realize man. . . .* In fact, we are witness here to a laborious and lengthy metamorphosis at whose end is a sort of divinization of the mortal, who achieves a central place in the phenomenological system."[18] Let us take as an example the "ring" trial. This trial consists of three stages: the neophyte must first untie a ring held by a "cow knot" on a small cord without detaching the cord from the rods which hold up its ends; once the ring is freed and is hidden in a pile of dust, he must search for it with his nose and grasp it with his teeth; finally, the same ring is thrown into a jar filled with water seasoned with red pepper, and the postulant must retrieve it with his teeth. Bochet has an interesting remark to make concerning this test: "*The first search for the ring* evokes, according to the elders, the difficult 'quest' of *Kâtiéléo*, which is the *goal of initiation.*"[19] In reality, as is seen in the similar institution of *Korè* among the Bambara (a group culturally related to the Senufo), the "fetal" period reflects the concern of the spiritual community that the initiate be assured of a divine gestation in keeping with his birth into the life of God. The trials to which he is subjected during this period are intended to make him a being of a particular "nature," superior to the common run of mortals, in other words another God.

The "rebirth" of the initiate takes place at the end of the fetal period. He is not, however, "born" fragile; having become a participant in the life of God, he incorporates the power and majesty of that life. This is a new state for the neophyte who, for the Senufo, is symbolized by the wildcat, whose agility and suppleness reflect well the ease and talent of the man who has become God. On this subject Bochet writes:

> The young men are finally presented with a device made of *two arches* of supple wood and of unequal size which they must crawl through one at a time. This operation is called *Kâtiéléo dwo*, which can be translated as *Kâtiéléo's feline,* because, according to the elders, "the young man who crawls under the arches has the bearing of a cat, and his character, formed by the tests, is as supple as the spine of that animal."
>
> As is often the case, this name alludes to the material aspect of the symbolic behavior, to the correspondences which it evokes, and to its formative role in the area of social relations, but it does not shed any light on its *esoteric significance.* In this particular case, for example, it is evident that the *passage under the arches* (taking into account that in every poro at one time or another there is a *trial involving crawling*) corresponds to the trial of the vertical cords which opened the cycle. The young men *returned to the womb of Kâtiéléo,* where they were transformed; they are now *redelivered,* but this time with a very discrete symbol, which does not seek physiological realism but instead tends towards abstraction.[20]

Among the Bambara of the Republic of Mali the rites concerning the "destruction" of the "old man" and those marking the reappearance of the same being in divinized state are even more eloquent.[21] The "superimposed" image of involution-death and of rebirth-resurrection is stated here with a remarkable clarity.

The candidates for the *korè* secret society are "killed" on the first day of their initiatory life by means of a symbolic gesture: their throats are touched with two knives, one of iron and the other of wood. But prior to this the neophytes had been "introduced" into the "womb" of the divinity, that is, they were covered by an immense hide symbolizing the sky. This operation is intended, on the physiological level, to produce a numbing of their intellectual faculties in order to accentuate more strongly their "return" to the vegetative existence characteristic of the fetal state. To promote this numbness the senior initiates were careful to sprinkle the "skin-sky" beforehand with various irritants whose suffocating substances affect the postulants' throats and plunge them into a veritable state of lethargy.

Beginning with this ritual and for two weeks afterwards, the neophytes may not go back to their homes. They sleep in the sacred wood with a bed of green leaves between them and the ground. With the exception of the senior initiates, no one has the right to see them during this period. Their meals are regularly brought to them by their families but are handed over to the senior initiates, who act as intermediaries. This seclusion symbolizes the "existence" of the corpse in the tomb and also the wait of the fetus in the maternal womb.

This life is a period of formation and transformation during which the postulants must acquire the taste for knowledge and wisdom which will allow them to detach themselves from earthly things and orient themselves towards the life of God. Of the tests which they undergo at this stage of their existence some are intended to purify them of the pollution contracted during their previous, terrestrial life. Others are meant to remind them of their weakness and lack of power in the face of divine knowledge. In addition, some of these "exams" represent the definitive completion of the man, who lets himself be fashioned by the initiatory practices and who thereby becomes worthy and savory nourishment for the "mouth" of the divinity. The latter "consumes" the postulants in his own way. Through the appropriate rites the divinity is believed to grind their spirit, giving it special qualities, such as receptivity, vivacity, docility, and stability.

In sum, the spiritual gestation period of the neophytes and their life "in the tomb" corresponds to a transformation: they withdraw from humanity by acquiring a kind of divine nature. Endowed with such an "asset" they are "reborn" or resuscitated at the end of their spiritual seclusion.

The ceremony of "return" is modeled after the one which occurs at an ordinary birth and whose principal stages are the following: placing the infant on the ground, washing it with water, having the newborn taste that water, insufflations, making ablutions with millet beer, moving its limbs, and dressing it. In the center of the sacred grove the postulants are seated on the ground in a circle, legs spread apart. The chief of the *korè* society fills his mouth with water drawn from one of the brotherhood's altars and sprays it like rain over the initiates. He then takes some mud from the same altar and, placing himself between the legs of each initiate, uses his right index finger to mark them with it in the following places: between the first two toes of the right foot, on the solar plexus, on the forehead, and between the last cervical and the first dorsal vertebra.

After this ritual the neophytes are bathed by an older initiate of the *korè dugaw* grade[22] with water drawn from the village's sacred pond. The officiant also blows into their ears and onto their faces. When they have all been washed and insufflated, the chief of *korè* sprinkles them again as he did previously. This second aspersion corresponds to the ablution with millet beer in the birth rites. Then the same officiant calls the candidates up to him in pairs and, while the elders place a segment of *sambe*[23] branch on their heads, two other postulants, armed with lashes, take their places behind them. With sharp blows the neophytes strike their comrades on the torso, then change places with their victims and are beaten by them. All the candidates are called up in pairs to undergo the same treatment. This rite evokes the movements impressed upon the limbs of newborn infants and the taps which matrons administer to their backs.

Finally the neophytes all go to the sacred well of the village where they are washed. They then assemble in the vestibule of the *korè* chief's residence, where they remove their old loincloths and put on new fringed ones. This corresponds to the "dressing" of the infant when it comes into the world.

As can be seen, the rebirth-resurrection of the Bambara initiates is replete with allusions to the rites performed at an ordinary birth. This is because, for the Bambara, the acquisition of spiritual knowledge is fundamentally linked to the complex notion of the acquisition of personality. This ethnic group grants a great deal of importance to the individual and to each man's consciousness of his own temporal individuality.

A common element characterizes all these ceremonies, whether Bambara or Senufo, that is, man's attempt to go beyond himself. That a certain asceticism is required in this movement of spiritual conquest is not at all surprising. On the contrary, what is striking to our Western mind, accustomed as it is to a monopoly on knowledge, is the realization that to achieve this transcendance man takes the same path in Africa as he does in the West. The African, too, is aware that knowledge alone can free the human being from the limitations of matter and allow him to raise himself above the ordinary conditions of existence. And what is still more surprising is the discovery of the extent to which these ideas are found on the African continent: there are virtually no exceptions there to the passage to knowledge, a passage that constitutes the African's true mark of nobility.

Man on the Scale of the World

This world which seemed to exist without me, to surround and surpass me, it is I who made it exist.

M. Merleau-Ponty
Sense and Non-Sense

5

We have already seen that for the African the passage to knowledge cannot be achieved without a certain conquest of space, and that this in some way constitutes a spiritual transformation of the African soul parallel to the mastery of the self. Thus, according to the African way of thinking, there is a close correspondence between man and the world. These two entities are like two mirrors placed face to face, reflecting reciprocal images: man is a microcosm which reflects the larger world, the world the macrocosm which in turn reflects man.

Given the present state of our knowledge of African thought, it is difficult to state precisely the extent and limits of these correspondences either within the cultures of specific ethnic groups or in the framework of the vast culture areas of Africa. It is also difficult to determine their exact religious and cultural value for those who employ them. Still, those aspects of the problem which we do understand are significant and worthy of attention even though it is impossible to review them all here. We will only discuss those aspects which seem most characteristic.

Through initiation, man in some way becomes a living temple of the Invisible. By means of the space he inhabits, and in particular the dwelling in which he is born and dies, the human being expands his own religious dimensions to the scale of the cosmos. What follows will provide a demonstration of this new dimension of the African's religiosity.

Two key ideas seem to stand out from the apparent jumble of notions concerning the relationship between man and the world: (1) in his approach to the cosmos, the African behaves as an organizer of space; and (2) he tries to act on the universe, periodically remaking it, and thereby, he believes, bringing about its constant "rejuvenation."

In man's environment certain elements emerge as targets for his most audacious speculations, family residence and the village being among them. Beyond the settlement—enclosing a society complex from all points of view—the region as a geographical and social unit attracts man's attention. But further still, space becomes blurred by its being merged with the "world." The African passes without a break from the territory possessing certain specific characteristics to the universe. His vision of the world thus remains very "egocentric"; he only conceives of the environment around him to the extent that he can conceive of himself within that environment.

In terms of its total meaning, space is most often valorized and organized according to its East-West axis. Among the Bantu of Kavirondo in Nyanza province, Gunter Wagner reports that North and South are regarded with indifference while the two other major cardinal directions are involved in an ensemble of emotional, ritual, and social correspondences.[1] The East is identified with life, health, well-being, and prosperity, the West with sickness, evil, bad luck, and death. Each morning the Abuluya turn towards the East to solicit the help of the divinity throughout the coming day. The Logoli do much the same at the time of the first sacrifice offered in honor of a newborn child. Among the Lamba of northern Rhodesia the path of the mythical hero Luchyele followed the same East-West axis when he organized the area by endowing it with streams, mountains and ant-hills, trees and meadows. This orientation is still visible during the performance of important rites, funerary ceremonies in particular.[2] The lagoon peoples of the Ivory Coast hold these two cardinal directions in similar esteem. The Abure, Aladian, and Abidji attribute that which is beneficial to the East, while they associate the West with sickness, disorder, and evil.[3]

This formula for organizing space is sometimes replaced by another based on two other cardinal directions: High and Low and, concomitantly, North and South. The most distinctive example of this is found among the Shilluk. For this people, the sky and the earth constitute the principal divisions of the world. Between them is located the stream.[4] These three elements possess numerous references in the religion, cosmogony, and even the economy of this Nilotic group, and similarly the North and South are valorized on the level of their social organization. Water does not only separate High from Low but also the Boreal from the Austral and, consequently, the northern from the southern tribes.

We can well wonder whether these arrangements of the cosmos are conditioned solely by the geographical environment or whether other elements must be taken into consideration. For example, it has been noticed that the Shilluk division of space actually corresponds to well-defined categories in the geography of the region. The area inhabited by this people is a savanna region devoid of elevations, depressions, and forests; there are no natural elements providing variations to attract the attention or imagination, or to overcome the homogeneity of the relief. The only elements which can be opposed in such an area are the clouds and the ground, that is, the sky and the earth, with the stream as the distinguishing feature at once separating and reflecting them.[5] Similar observations have been made concerning the spatial organization of the Bantu of Kavirondo. While East and West constitute the principal axis for ordering the world, it should not be forgotten that in this region East is also the direction from which the rains generally come and from which the principal bodies of water flow.[6]

Among the lagoon peoples of the Ivory Coast the East-West orientation of space, also polarizing a vast body of cultural features, is complemented by the North-South direction, whose valorization seems to be a direct consequence of the contrasting appearance of the relief. The part of the Ivory Coast in which the lagoon peoples live consists of a vast plateau inclined in a North-South direction, and this generates the ideas of High and Low which determine the location of peoples in relation to each other, as well as the position of the dead in their tombs.[7]

But it is possible to go even further in the analysis of the motivations which permit the ordered apprehension of space by stating that in Africa it is the very position of that part of the continent south of the Sahara, in relation to its sidereal coordinates, which may have influenced man in the ordering of its geography. Indeed, we should keep in mind that the majority of the continent is located between the two tropics, and in this region the human being is in the presence of a natural element capable of dictating the organization of space. By its incessant repetition as well as by the amplitude which it possesses in these latitudes, the (apparent) diurnal movement of the sun across the celestial vault imparts a fundamental significance to the space oriented in the same direction. What we call East and West become parts of space perceived by Africans in terms of opposition and are placed in the same conceptual categories as all things which can be conceived according to the same oppositional model.

Conversely, the variability of the sun's declination, with its extreme limits at the two tropics, furnishes man living in the area between the tropics with the two other categories, pertaining to high and low, which are also brought to consciousness in terms of opposition. But while the first two directions connote the plane of being and daily existence, the high-low axis is concerned with seasonal activity and cyclical existence. It is significant that many African peoples celebrate the periodic festivals of chieftaincy at the solstices, while rites involving epiphanies are performed facing the East.

But often the two spatial axes are not conceived independently of each other. High and low are in fact categories common to both planes. Thus the Bambara and the Dogon, for example, assimilate high (North) with East and low (South) with West.

Of course this conceptualization of spatial organization seen as a whole is intentionally schematic. Its only aim is to give a rough idea of the conceptualization of geography. In point of fact each African people introduces other factors into its way of orienting space in order to situate itself in the world. Such sidereal elements as the Pleiades are retained virtually all over the continent, undoubtedly because, being close to the line of the solstices and in immediate proximity to the ecliptic, they mark the qualitative change of nature in the two hemispheres in the manner of the sun when it reaches the limit of its declination. Other constellations enjoy the same attention, such as Orion, Ursa Major, the Milky Way and, for the southern hemisphere, the Southern Cross and Canopus. With the help of these elements the African combines the characterization of space and time and validly locates himself within area and duration. Still, it is the sun with its two movements which can constitute to African eyes an absolute system of reference registering itself as the sole generator of pertinent spatial determinations.

In the universe thus defined the house constitutes the smallest portion of the cosmos but also the most noble, as it is entirely subject to the uninterrupted organization and control of man. The house is that part of space in which man most thoroughly imparts his conception of the world. Thus, it is not surprising that everything concerning the house is determined by cosmic references.

As a general rule in Africa, the home is conceived in terms of the couple: only the family can lay claim to use a house because it alone realizes the plenitude of the human being. Like the couple, the house is a complete and self-sufficient "being."

Among the Fali of northern Cameroon the residence is conceived of and realized on the basis of symbolism which is at once cosmic, anthropomorphic, zoomorphic, and dendromorphic. The system of thought which presides over its erection is dualistic and static. Because of this the choice and organization of the materials of construction refer to binary oppositions of which the most fundamental can be reduced to the distinction established between male and female substances. The right side of the house, associated with the East, corresponds to the earth and man, to the known world and the tortoise (the animal symbolic of a subgroup of the Fali). The left side of the house, associated with the sunset, corresponds to water and woman, to the unknown world and the toad (the animal symbolic of the other subgroup of the Fali). The arrangement of the Fali home actually reproduces the successive phases of the myth of origin in terms of the establishment, preparation, and possession by the human being of a "universe" cut to his scale.

> The single room of the first house represents the primordial egg from whence issued man's earth, whose square form is reflected in the rectangular courtyard. The roundness of the room itself suggests the equilibrium of the nascent but already organized world, which contains its own future, and whose completion will be marked by the large oval family enclosure divided into four sections connected two by two. This is the image of a "finished" world. The cycle will be completed by the circular shelter away from the family residence where the patriarch settles, detached from human activities and marking a return to the starting point.[8]

We see that the references to the primordial myth involve the intervention of a dynamic principle correlative to the dualism to which the construction of the house is related. The Fali house is likened to the living being, who is born, develops, and dies;

> the buildings are constructed in an order such that the right side of the house goes up at the same time as the left, and the construction of an edifice on the right is necessarily followed by that of another on the left. This back and forth movement is carried out in relation to the central post.[9]

Once completed and inhabited, the house, like humanity, is suited to procreation; it is also similar to the finished world. "Being the place of existence of the family, of which it constitutes the points of beginning and completion between which human existence unfolds, the house constitutes a total conceptualization of the life of the universe."[10] When in ruins it is comparable to the extinction of mankind and of the world.

The Mossi of northern Upper Volta are no less rich in conceputalizations concerning the residence. It is the core of a complex symbolism in which the divinity, the world, and the individual play parallel and concomitant roles. With its door and lock, the Mossi hut represents the divinity conceived as a four-faceted being, that is, doubly male and female.[11] But it also symbolizes the world and, more precisely, the "stomach" of the world. What happens in the house is similar to that which occurs in the world, that is, fundamentally, according to the rhythm which results from the alternation of work and rest. Domestic rhythm is engendered by the man and the woman, who are themselves represented by the posts of the house's framework; the cosmic rhythm is created by the male and female principles, and these are evoked by the system of closing the house. Finally, the Mossi house recalls the human stomach in that it resembles a person. Entering and leaving the hut evoke the introduction of food into the body and its ejection in the form of waste.

As can be seen, the basis for the conceptualizations concerning the Mossi residence is, again, the human being considered as a paradigm for that which transcends him. Still, man is not seen as a single being but as a being conceptualized in terms of both masculinity and femininity. Thus the Mossi house, too, is organized in terms of the dual sexuality of its underlying principles.

The Dogon give evidence of analogous ideas with regard to the great family house, *ginna,* where the patriarch of the family resides.[12] The *ginna* consists of a central room around which are arranged the kitchen, the storerooms, the goat stable, the "great chamber" supported by the entrance, and a second stable. At the corners of one of the rooms as well as on each side of the entrance rise four towers capped by a dome.

The plan of the *ginna* is the image of the Monitor of the world, the *Nommo,* in his animal avatar. The four towers represent his limbs.

Conversely, the kitchen and the stable form the celestial placenta and its terrestrial homologue, the whole representing the head and legs of a man lying on his right side. His every part has its architectural counterpart: the rectangular kitchen recalls the oblong head whose eyes are the two stones of the hearth,[13] the torso is symbolized by the great chamber, the stomach by the workroom, the arms by the two broken lines of the storerooms, and the breasts by the two jars of water placed at the entrance to the central room. Finally, the genitals are represented by the vestibule which, by a narrow passageway, leads to the workroom where the jars of water and the grinding stones are placed. On these stones the ears of grain still fresh from the first harvest are crushed; they yield a liquid paste likened to semen, which is brought to the left side of the vestibule, the symbol of the genitals, in order to be poured over the ancestral altar.[14]

This arrangement of the house thus represents a human being stretched out on his right, his procreative side, a position which is equally that of the man on the conjugal bed and of the corpse in the tomb.

These few examples are not exceptional in Africa, although the quantity of structural elements revealed here does not attain the same dimensions everywhere. As in other cultural domains, here we should consider certain fundamental principles which might be found in all cultures. It seems to us that these basic principles can be reduced to masculinity and femininity, which ultimately form the basis of the ideas more or less elaborated in the total organization of the house. Among the Kung Bushmen, for example, the hut is simply seen as divided by the hearth into two complementary parts assigned respectively to the man and the woman.[15] This initial dichotomy of the residence, associated with fire and the fireplace, seems to be more universally in evidence than any other.

Above the "arrangement" of the house in order of increasing conceptual complexity is the organization of the village. By its nature, however, this "social unit," which often unites different elements, is less easy to grasp from this point of view than is the family residence. Even so, among the Bantu peoples of southeast Africa the ordering of hamlets appears with remarkable clarity.

Among the Zulu, a pastoral and agricultural people for whom animal husbandry is valued higher than farming, the village is built around a central space consisting of the corral.[16] Diametrically opposite each other on a circle wider than the corral are located the principal entrance to the settlement and the hut of the family head's wife. This axis is important because it separates the village into two distinct parts: the right side, which is occupied by the first wife of the patriarch, and the left, which is occupied by his second wife. Each wife has responsibility for and authority over all the households located on the side in which she has her hut. Across from these buildings, and located symmetrically on either side of the village's principal entrance, are found the huts of the sons, of the persons connected to the patriarch, and of the strangers who have been adopted into the village. The right and the left side of the habitation each possess a private exit; similarly each group of inhabitants is provided with granaries and huts for the preparation of beer.

This organization of Zulu village space points in an obvious way to the dualism of this people's family structure. Indeed, among the Zulu, the legacy of the head of the family can only be transmitted to the group of persons stemming from the principal wife, whether the eldest or the first married, who occupies the right side of the village. Right and left thus become spatial elements associated respectively with the continuity and noncontinuity of the family. In other respects the central position of the cattle corral marks the place where the family's spiritual forces operate, since this spot represents the sky and constitutes a propitious place from which the ancestors can be invoked.

Analogous ideas are encountered among the Thonga, where one finds the same circular arrangement of the village with a cattle-pen as the center. Here, however, the fundamental opposition seems to be that established between inhabited space and the uninhabited bush. The village is seen as a basic concept established in relation to the bush, the latter being devoid of order and open to chaos and confusion. It is thus at the death of the family head or his principal wife that the village is abandoned, since it is considered to be like the "bush," that is, participating in the primordial chaos.

The arrangement of Tswana settlements demonstrates the same concern for ordering inhabited space. These Bantu villages are constructed in such a way that their entrance is oriented on the East-West axis.

When they are constructed, the family patriarch erects his hut at the eastern extremity of this axis and then, as the settlement expands, the sons and daughters (the latter prior to their marriage) of the first and other "uneven" marriages are placed in houses located to the left of the patriarch's hut, that is, toward the North, while the descendants of "even" marriages are assigned to the right side, towards the South. Tswana villages thus grow on both sides of the median East-West line but with a consciously formulated tendency to inscribe this development in a circle and not in a straight line. One day a native informant of J. Roumeguère-Eberhardt declared on this subject:

> the *kgotla* is solidly constructed in the form of a crescent, like the moon when it begins to wax. Similarly, the family must grow and a man's sons increase so that the village can become a circle like the full moon. When the circle is closed, it is time to create a new village. This is discussed by all the assembled members of the village, then the affair is brought before the *kgotla* (court) of the regional chief, who adopts one of two solutions: either the people split up to form two new villages, or the whole population moves and rebuilds the village in another place where there is more room.[17]

Among the Venda, whose principal occupation is agriculture, the cattle corral does not occupy the central place in the village as it does among the pastoral Bantu. Rather the central place is given to the mortars fixed in the earth in which women pound the grain for food. This place is called "the milky way" because, among the Venda, grain is put in direct relation to the stars. The settlement of the village develops around the "place" of the mortars, generally on a hill or on the side of a mountain. The patriarch's hut occupies the top of the elevation, while the other homes are arranged to the sides according to an order of precedence determined by kinship and rank.

> Frequently the only access to the Venda village is a small winding path on the side of the mountain ending at the entrance to the *khoro*, a large ceremonial courtyard surrounded by a stone wall or a post fence. Concealed in the bushes to the right of the *khoro*, a small, labyrinthine trail leads to the *Thondo*, the men's secret house where youths between the age of eight years and puberty undergo their tribal initiation.[18]

While this labyrinthine path seems to be a marginal element in the organization of the Venda village, it is central among the Bantu of southwest Africa, the Ovambo. Among them, the whole kraal is constructed according to a complicated network of interlaced lanes and alleys, whose point of convergence in the center of the village corresponds to the site of the sacred fire, to the hut of the first wife of the owner of the kraal, and to the spot where the owner usually sits.[19] For some if not all of these peoples the principal entrance of the circularly constructed village is oriented towards the East and the sacred fire is located on the extension of the East-West axis. This fire is believed to be the substitute for the sun. It is maintained night and day by the first wife of the head of the family or by his daughter, although no menstruating woman is permitted to approach it.

Certain authors have compared the organization of village space among the Ovambo with the settlements of the Bantu of southeast Africa described above. Even further, they have attempted to draw a parallel between these labyrinths and the stone ruins discovered at Zimbabwe, the plan of the temple of Marib in Yemen, and the habitations of the ancient Canary Islanders.[20] To these diverse comparisons they have added certain elements of worship (the cult of the moon, of the sky god, and of the bull), and have concluded that by diffusion Mediterranean influences spread as far as the pastoral-agricultural cultures of southern Africa. Certainly, when one is acquainted with the brewing techniques of African peoples, it is not impossible that such influences had occurred concurrently with the introduction of cattle, in particular among the Bantu pastoralists. But if the maze-like form of the Zimbabwe ruins is considered by specialists to be authentically African,[21] are we not justified in assigning an equal authenticity to the Bantu villages? Indeed it should not be forgotten that the labyrinth constitutes a conceptual model reflecting the sinuosities of thought itself and, as such, can very well be realized by man in his architectural constructions at any latitude. The thesis of convergence seems preferable here to that of diffusion.

Whatever the case, the settlements of the peoples just reviewed illustrate in a typical way man's concern for inscribing his social life in an ordered framework according to categories which, in the final analysis, stem from the innermost structure of humanity itself.

The settlement does not constitute a limit on the relations uniting man and the world but is rather an intermediate stopping-point. Geographically, the village unit always belongs to a wider unit which unites the conditions favorable to life and to the development of the people who compose it. To be sure, when men settle somewhere they are aware of a certain number of elements essential to their existence, such as proximity to water, the quality of farmland, the value of the pastures and security. But religious factors also arise in determining the choice of the region where the settlement is to be established. The existence of such and such a plant symbolically linked to the beliefs of the group, the presence of such and such an animal also related to the spiritual life of the people, or a remarkable occurrence can all influence men in their search for a place to live. Furthermore, these are only preliminary conditions in

the organization of a spatial infrastructure in which the human community is founded. The actual ordering of the area, considered on this
scale, appears based on the utilization of certain distinctive traits in the
environment, with respect to their meaningful function. It is thus that
Lake Osamba polarizes the "meridian" of Kuanyama space and Lake
Funduzi that of Venda space, while the structure of Zaghawa space is
fashioned on the mountains around which the clans are concentrated and
that of the Dogon region by the cliffs in which that people live.

It should be noted that at this level of environmental organization, the
limits between restricted space (such as the region or the country) and
cosmic space are not always very clear. Cosmic space easily subsumes
restricted space, and man merges into one his own country and the
world. Among the Mossi, the kingdom takes on cosmic proportions and
is arranged like the world; moreover, Mossi country is called "the
world" by its inhabitants. The same phenomenon can be observed in
Africa each time kingship is significant as a form of social organization.

The principles contributing to the structuring of the world are still
more complex, for they stem from celestial and terrestrial coordinates.

The first elements in the organization of the world seem to be the
notions of "high" and "low." Almost everywhere in Africa the universe
is fundamentally perceived according to the oppositional pair sky-earth,
with the sky stemming from the concept of high, the earth from that of
low. This correspondence is not universal, however, since among the
Efe we find a myth according to which in the beginning the earth was
above and the sky below. Nonetheless the story adds that the relative
position of these two elements was later inverted when men begged the
divinity Tore for food. The earth then came down and took its place
below while the sky ascended and settled up above.[22] It seems then that
at least for this pygmy group the vertical organization of the cosmos is
arranged according to oppositional pairs: high-low, sky-earth, hunger-
food. Other African peoples enrich this ensemble of relationships by
adding a fourth, light-heavy, which is integrated perfectly well. Among
the Abure, who in the past used the egg of the pagoda cock to determine
the time, it is said that "the egg of this bird, full around six or seven
o'clock, empties itself of its substance as the sun rises in the sky, and
becomes completely empty at noon. The egg becomes light. It is then
time to stop work in order to eat. In the afternoon the egg refills as the
sun goes down, until it is again completely full at about six o'clock. It is
then time to stop work in the field and return home."[23] Thus if the
separation of sky and earth, as related in numerous myths, locates itself
in terms of a way of thinking which divides and "separates" in order to
conceptualize (as was said above), then food and the work which is
required for its acquisition seem to be the criteria which have deter-

mined the apprehension of space as a function of the oppositional pairs
high and low, sky and earth. Furthermore, the myths which bear witness to the "confusion" of the two realities in general describe concurrently, and with incomparable logic, the "celestial" food of man. In
ancient times men used to eat slices of clouds which they cut from the
firmament and cooked in their pots, while the women were obliged to
adopt the uncomfortable position of kneeling in order to pound grain in
their mortars.

It should be noted that the sky-earth complex is also organized according to other criteria. The sky is not seen as a homogeneous concept.
It is divided according to the relationship which the various sectors of
the celestial vault are believed to maintain with the earth and the activities of human beings. Thus for many African peoples the Milky Way is
used to divide the sky in two halves, each endowed with its own
significations in terms of its turning movement. The Pleiades, the
Giraffe, Sirius, Canopus, the Southern Cross and the polestar offer,
according to various peoples, as many meaningful landmarks to which
other stars and constellations are related. The configuration of the sky
thus reveals the parallel organization which operates in the terrestrial
world.

But, perhaps more than all other celestial elements, the sun and the
moon have provided men with the opportunity to order the world in a
more precise fashion by bringing it back to proportions closer to the
human scale. With the combination of the two "apparent" movements
of the sun, its diurnal course and its annual "oscillation" between the
two tropics, the African is led to realize the circumscribed image of an
"intertropical" world which is his own universe. This space is sometimes "square" in form, sometimes "rectangular"; at times it is even
visualized as a corkscrew, which is said to have been the first form taken
by the earth during creation. Above and below this space the sun turns,
weaving a double spiral around the earth in its incessant rounds
throughout the year. The helix is often schematized by its projection on
a flat surface as a zigzag line which decorates utensils and various other
objects, as well as the facades of houses and sanctuaries. The space
delimited by the sun is supremely man's world.

In its own distinctive way, the moon contributes to the ordering of the
world thus defined. It seems to confer upon it its qualitative value: it is
tied to the life of the world. By its cyclical appearances and disappear-
ances it reflects life and death themselves, while by its waxing and
waning during its visible periods it illustrates the gradual process of
transformation of all that exists. While the sun is a symbol of permanence and stability, the moon constitutes the most brilliant sign of
change and transformation.

Under these circumstances it is not surprising that in almost all African cultures the organization of the cosmos is felt in terms of kinship, beginning with the sun-moon couple. The two celestial bodies sometimes appear as brother and sister, sometimes as husband and wife, and sometimes even as maternal uncle and uterine nephew[24] (although the distance separating them never seems to go beyond the sphere of the minimum social signifier).[25] The connections uniting the sun and the moon in such a context undoubtedly reveal the parental couple which, socially speaking, supports the weight of the structure of relations between the members of the "familial" group. In the same way it is possible to justify the sexuality attributed to the two heavenly bodies and the tie which unites sky and earth in close communion.

Space thus conceived does not constitute an unchanging concept for Africans. For various reasons the qualitative value of space seems to run down, a condition which leads men to "remake" it.

Death, and the contamination which is felt to follow it, are often the causes of a reordering of the residence and the village. This is the case among the Bantu of southeast Africa when the chief of the settlement dies. His successor founds his own settlement, leaving the old one in ruins. For the same people lightning striking the village's central square constitutes another reason for leaving their residences and relocating. But the most characteristic reconstruction is that observed among the Tswana, of whom we have previously spoken.[26] For this people, when the settlement has completed the circle according to which it develops, it has attained the limit of its realization. It is then thought to have come to the end of its existence and must be rebuilt elsewhere.

Similar practices are found among the lagoon peoples of the Ivory Coast (for example, the Ebrie, Mbato, Attie, and Abure). There the ceremony known as *Epwe atwe,* which occurs every seventy years, consists of the destruction of all the homes in a district whose oldest generation is in the process of dying out. The new generation then reconstructs a new district on the same land and gives to it its own name. The author who describes these practices adds the following justification:

> A village or a district, it is said, is born, lives, and dies like a human being; when dead, it rejoins the next world so that the members of its generation can live in it. In this order of ideas, there is a world identical to the one of the living where the souls of the dead pursue the same professions as during their time on earth. The villages and districts beyond the grave rebuild themselves as the districts and generations disappear on earth. The individual never dies, he simply rejoins the ancestors and his district.[27]

As can be seen in the case of either of these peoples, the criterion which presides over the transformations and the renewal of inhabited space is of a cosmo-biological order. The home as well as the settlement possess their own lives linked to the life of the world. The pulsations and the rhythms of the latter reverberate in the human world and affect those human works most intimately linked to the notions of increase, development, and advancement.

The remaking of space takes on a still more grandiose appearance when it is concerned with the renewal of the world. The world, too, is subjected to the restorative action of man, who intends thereby to give it a new brilliance, a rebirth of life, of which man in the end will be the first beneficiary. Undertakings of this type are not well known to Africanists because of their cyclical character lasting considerable periods of time. However, there is no doubt that all the ceremonies for the renewal of the year, as well as those consecrated to the renewal of the kingdom among African royalty, once included—and do to this day—rites concerning the restoration of the cosmos.

Among the Mossi, for example, the solemn rites of *basga* in the kingdom of Ouagadougou, and those of *filiga* in the kingdom of Ouahigouya, constitute rites devoted to the coming of the new year. But they take place around the time of the winter solstice, at a period when, having reached its maximum declination, the sun begins to regain the northern hemisphere. The lunar calendar also plays an important role in fixing the date of the ceremonies: the rite is performed on the new moon closest to the solstice. This moment is propitious for the "opening" of the "path" of the sun, which the Mossi think is made possible by the cleaning and opening of the trails leading to the royal palace, which at that time are actually cleared of the encroaching vegetation. At the same time, the king leaves his palace and returns the day the "paths" are "unlocked." Thus, in one and the same rite, this people bring about their entrance into a new period of time, the renewal of their kingdom, and the "reconstruction" of the world.

Similar rites take place among all the Bantu peoples of southeast Africa. The various writers who have described the *louma* of the Thonga and Ronga, the *dya ñwaka* of the Nkouna, the *thevula* of the Venda, or the *inkwala* of the Swazi have emphasized their "firstfruits" aspect, while the total significance of these ceremonies clearly goes beyond this meaning and is actually related to the reorganization of the world and of the kingdom. In fact, each so-called "firstfruits" ceremony among the Bantu is preceded by the renewal of the great "medicine" of the country, with which are mixed the first "fruits" of the earth prior to the harvest. Furthermore, this "medicine" constitutes a sort of "epitome" of the kingdom and the world.

Among the Swazi the collection of plants included in the composition of this "medicine" is carried out by emissaries spread throughout the kingdom, while the water used in its preparation is drawn from the rivers swollen by their tributaries. As the Swazi say, "The waters of the world are fetched to give strength and purity to the king."[28] Hilda Kuper also notes in regard to the *Incwala* among the Swazi that as this national holiday approaches the essential question entertained in the conversations of all those concerned is at which moment the sun and the moon will be in agreement. The royal advisors scrutinize the sky morning and night to determine the "agreement" of the two heavenly bodies in terms of their respective positions, taking into consideration certain terrestrial references for the sun and the proximity of the stars for the moon. This author continues:

> The importance of the sun and moon in relation to the *Incwala* ceremony hinges on their Swazi correlates. The sun is the more important, for the date of the ceremony is fixed by observation of the solstices. . . . [On December 21] the sun is considered to rest in its "hut" in the south, and then to leap out to start its journey anew, and the *Incwala* should begin the day after the sun has reached its hut and is "resting," i.e. on the longest day. The Swazi, however, correlate the lunar with the solar year, though inevitably there is confusion and "a moon is lost." The moon, as in nearly all mythology, is thought of as a woman who follows her male lord, the sun, and when she "dies" she is hidden by him and then reappears. The *Incwala* should begin when the moon is "dark," though the Swazi appreciate [by other ways] that the coincidence of the December solstice with the wane of the moon is rare. They therefore decide on the moon before December 22nd and have the ceremony end after the sun has reached its southernmost point. "The king races the sun."[29]

Among the Venda, the gathering of medicinal plants is carried out by all the men under the direction of the "doctor" of the country. They spread out all over the area

> following the course of the four rivers representing the four cardinal directions. They all assemble in the East, where the four bodies of water meet and there sacrifice a bull, which they eat while offering the ritual portions to the water. . . . They then return to the capital carrying the branches picked along the way, and it is after this that the *thevula* can take place.[30]

The same concern for associating the kingdom, and consequently the world, with the preparation of the country's "medicine" which "may be considered as belonging to the royal treasure, of which it is the most important part,"[31] is described among the Thonga.[32] Among this people, the dramatization of the solstitial period (equivalent to our month of December) and its relation to the reorganization of the cosmos seems to appear in the old ritual of *rongúe*, of which H. A. Junod has collected the last vestiges and the full meaning of which he undoubtedly did not suspect.[33]

The Dogon also possess an imposing rite of remaking the world, the *sigi*. Here, however, the point of reference is no longer the solstice but the equinox. In addition, astronomical factors concerning Sirius (of the Greater Dog constellation) are involved in it. The entire Dogon region is traversed by the "ambulatory rite," beginning at Yougo Dogorou (in northeast Dogon region) and descending towards Iréli (in the southwest). In Dogon thought, the top of the cliffs, the northeast, represents the God Amma, the sky; the foot of the cliffs, the southwest, symbolizes the Nommo genie, the earth. *Sigi* last for six years, three in the upper region and three in the lower, and the whole ceremony is felt to be the restoration of the cosmos and of its cardinal points. Informants explain it in the following way: "during the entire duration of *sigi* the sun does not rise; it is as if there were no East in the world."[34]

It is difficult at present to evaluate the place accorded to the reorganization of the world in the religious concerns of the various African peoples. Numerous traditions on this subject have been forever lost or forgotten, while many have been unintentionally omitted from the investigations of researchers. From what has survived and from what we know, it can be inferred that the idea of cosmic renewal was profoundly anchored in traditional African religion. It may have even constituted one of the dominant features. In sum, everything occurs as if through these imposing rites man were looking for himself, and, by outlining on his own scale a new genesis, he were announcing the renewal of his own humanity. The operation is only simple in appearance, since the individual and the society to which he belongs constitute an uninterrupted chain of orderings leading from the visible link to the very borders of the universe.

The Messengers
of the Unknown

On the other hand, this art [divi-
nation by astragals] is so perfect
that bone-throwers can find any
amount of satisfaction in practis-
ing it. . . . This system is so elaborate that I do not hesitate to say
that, together with their folklore,
it is the most intelligent product
of their psychic life.

H. A. Junod
The Life of a South African Tribe

6

In the eyes of the African, who valorizes it to the utmost degree, in fact
(as we already know) almost as much as he does himself, the cosmos
does not constitute a fixed, cold, and mute world. On the contrary, it is a
world charged with meanings and laden with messages, a world which
"speaks."

Thus man finds in his surroundings a partner with which he can enter
into communication, with which he must in fact maintain an almost
constant dialogue if he wants to be informed about himself. This is
because the macrocosm contains in itself all the potentialities of the
microcosm which is man. In this sense the world possesses an absolute
value. Consequently, to know oneself it is necessary for one to know the
messages which the universe continuously sends. It is through these
messages that one can interpret one's own destiny.

In this context it is the diviner who holds the code which allows the
decipherment of the various messages intended for man, the society in
which he lives, and all else related to his destiny, while it is the various
systems of divination which fulfill the role of decoding grid. Although in
a certain sense any man is a diviner to the degree to which he under-
stands and can transmit the messages of the cosmos, there is a basic
difference between this everyman-diviner and the professional vatici-
nator. For the latter is not content to possess great proficiency in the
science of interpreting common messages but also knows how to elicit
others. He possesses the skill of penetrating the universe of signs, which
mediates between the world and the human being, and, by ordering it
according to his own method, he is able to make it clarify the situations
at hand.

Like the healer and the priest, the diviner thus possesses a significant social personality and plays a considerable role in African culture. Often the same person takes on all three functions. His services could not be dispensed with either by the individual or the society: he is consulted on any outstanding occasion in life (or one judged as such). Does one want, for example, to undertake a voyage, the construction of a new residence, or the preliminary steps towards marriage? One will consult the diviner in order to know the outcome of one's plans. Similarly, determination of the sex of an unborn child, birth, naming, circumcision, marriage, sickness and death are all "questions" to which the diviner can be called upon to respond. It would not be an exaggeration to say that he is the man most informed concerning the individuals and the psychological and social tendencies of the group in which he lives. By virtue of this, we can understand why he is often considered by his fellow men as the representative of the divinity.

In essence, the nature of the diviner can be summarized by his great intellectual capacities, his intuition, and his facility for probing the universe and translating its messages. To these qualities can certainly be added his aptitude for entering into contact with others by his keen sense of human relations, by a kind of gift for penetrating the soul, and by a special "state of grace" consistent with his religion. The function of diviner does not tolerate improvization; on the contrary, to become a "seer" it is indispensable to follow a long and hard apprenticeship. It is often even necessary to undergo a veritable initiation, a transformation similar to those which lead man to the sources of religious life, to God.

Among the Bantu of southeast Africa,[1] when an individual feels he possesses the requisite qualities for becoming a diviner he sets off in search of the necessary astragals.[2] As soon as he has been able to collect ten of these small bones, he begins to practice divination for himself and his friends. This is a sort of preliminary step which allows him both to obtain the confirmation of his vocation and to amass a bit of "capital" which he can use for his future "studies."

These studies are conducted under the direction of an experienced master who begins by killing a fowl and putting in its body the small bones brought by the novice. After having cooked the fowl, the apprentice eats it and returns to his home with the small bones, which he buries on the path at the entrance to the village. Then he hides himself in such a way that he is able to observe the spot. Although Junod does not specify it, the rite up to this point seems to have as its goal, first, the bringing about of a conjunction between the divinatory objects and the spirit of the future diviner through the intermediary of the fowl,[3] and then the alienation of these same objects and their entanglement in a state of confusion. The latter is done in order to be able, in a second phase, to classify them according to another conjunctional axis, that of objective correspondences. Indeed, the novice observes from his hiding place the persons who pass on the path where the bones are buried. After a man passes he digs up a male astragal; after a woman passes he digs up a female one. If the passerby is a mature man, the uncovered bone must be that of a billy goat; if it is a young boy, it will be that of a kid. This classification constitutes at the same time a reacquisition of the divinatory objects by their owner because, as Junod remarks, "in this way all his bones are said to 'have returned to him'."[4] Finally, the rite completed, the novice returns to his master. The latter then lines up the bones in front of his pupil, whom he has just asked to close his eyes; then he has him touch and grasp each bone while calling it by its name. If the novice successfully passes this test of recognizing and identifying the objects, all that remains for him is to undergo a long ablution prepared with the leaves of the *nkouhlou* (*Trichilia emetica*), a tree which marks the profound transformations of beings and things.

By relying on Junod's statements alone, one sees that this initiatory rite seems more concerned with the intellectual and pedagogical aspect of the acquisition of the science of augury than with the strictly religious side of the process. But among other peoples the opposite is the case.

Among the Azande certain women-diviners become mediators between spirits and humans as a result of a sort of death and resurrection which they recount as if they had been witnesses to the phenomenon. E. E. Evans-Pritchard tells us:

> Nambua said that, "She died and they [her co-villagers] dug a grave for her and everyone wailed. Her soul went forth and appeared at the place of ghosts. She was just looking about when all her [deceased] relatives collected and made a circle around her. It was her mother who said to her, 'What have you come here for? Get up and go whence you came. Go away quickly.' She departed from amongst these people and her eyes at once opened. Everyone ceased wailing and she began immediately to wake from death and recovered completely."[5]

It is through this contact with the beyond that this woman acquired the ability to transmit to humans the spirits' wishes, particularly during rituals concerning rain.

According to J. A. Tiarko Fourche and H. Morligheni,[6] the diviner among the Lulua, BaSonge, and BaLuba in the Kasai, Republic of Zaire, is always an intermediary between the souls of the dead and his clients, the living. Among the various specialists in this art, those who practice *tshilumbu* (literally, "affair to settle") constitute the highest class. There are numerous women in this category of "magicians." In *tshilumbu* the diviner is more like a medium, with the revelation of the future taking for him the form of prophecy. He delivers his oracles in the course of a trance during which he is believed to visit the souls, who possess him, inhabit him, and make him speak.

Initiation into *tshilumbu*, which takes three days, is of great complexity and involves specifically the theme of the death and resurrection of the neophyte. When the candidate desires to have confirmed the powers which she attributes to herself on the strength of some unquestionable signs, she is isolated by the diviner-initiators in an enclosure behind her hut. Previously a pit had been dug there with two openings connected by a tunnel which is not cut through.

> They make the applicant enter it after she is supplied with sweet and starchy bananas, flour, and meat so that she will not be tempted to accept the food which the souls will offer her. . . . Placed next to her as well are manioc mortars and plants believed to repel evil influences, specifically the leaves of *tshikote, dikanga bakishi,* and basil.
>
> Having thus prepared her for her voyage, they close up the pit with mats. Outside, her husband assists her by his close presence. The mediums [initiators] blow into their horns and make incantations to the souls, with whom the neophyte immediately enters into contact. Meanwhile, her children sing accompanied by musicians:
> "Wa a lele–lele–lele–lelele–lelele–
> Mother we accompany you on the path of the secret;
> You have left us to follow the Milky Way;[7]
> Let us sing for our father, head of the family;
> Father, the day appears and we do not hear the cocks;
> Listen to what the *tam-tam* player says;
> Listen to what the medium says:
> When women are good, the market overflows;
> Why marry a woman who follows the taboos?
> Why marry a woman medium?
> I, a medium, I appeal to the children;
> The children appeal to her;
> A good marriage requires examination;
> A forced marriage will be broken;
> I, the Souls have delegated me to reveal the 'taboos';
> The 'taboos' will not come to an end on this earth;
> They will come to an end only in the land of the Souls."
>
> At the first crow of the cock the mediums, children, and musicians intone the song of the dead. The oldest medium calls the neophyte who, having finished digging the tunnel, leaves the pit by the second opening.
>
> As in any important initiation, she is believed to have been dead, to have traveled to the land of the Souls and to have then returned to life.[8]

On leaving this improvised "tomb," the candidate goes to sit on the exterior terrace of her house while her children in turn pass through the tunnel, symbolically retracing her voyage. They follow her when she enters her hut. She then settles herself on the overhead log supports where provisions are usually stored. Towards noon she cuts an opening in the roof and, still followed by her children, she slides through it to come down on the outside and squats on the same terrace as before.

At this time one of the initiators approaches and submits her to two trials. The first consists of catching an antelope horn used in the initiation which the initiator has thrown into the air. The second calls for saying precisely the name by which the Souls summoned her to the other world, that is, *Mutumina Mikiya*, the Harbinger of "Taboos."

The candidate's entire body is then smeared with kaolin and the master of ceremonies attaches a small bell to her belt. Then, after a crown of basil is made for her, the sap of certain "stimulating" plants is blown into her nostrils. One of her brothers hangs a chicken around her neck, because according to the authors: "It is by this lure that she will henceforth exercise the power to attract the Souls of deceased mediums in the bush in order to bring them back and fasten them close to the trees consecrated to them."[9]

Finally, the initiator proceeds to the sacrifice of a chicken and, at the end of the ritual, returns the attributes of divination to his pupil. It is the candidate herself who cooks the victim of the offering, preparing it with a porridge of manioc or corn. The sacrificer offers one portion of this to the Souls, puts another into the mouth of the postulant, while he himself consumes a third.

By studying the descriptions of the last two initiatory rites one can judge the distance which separates them from the initiation of the Thonga diviner, as described by H. A. Junod. For the Zande womandiviner, as well as for the BaLuba prophetess, apprenticeship in the craft is practically nonexistent since the diviner does not find herself confronted with having to analyze the relationship between a signifier and its signified (or signifieds). She is but a channel, the route taken by the Souls so they may appear and "speak"; she is a tool in the strict sense of the term. Back from her trance, revived from her symbolic death, the diviner in Kasaï reveals and exhibits what the Souls communicated to her; in reality it is they who took her place. In this she resembles the shaman of American and other cultures, even though the initiatory techniques are different in the two places.

The distinction which has just been established between the Thonga and the Zande or BaLuba diviner according to their initiatic substrata may deserve to be extended to other African peoples. A thorough study would allow two great modes of divination to be discerned on the African continent. One of these would be based on the apprehension of the relationship between things (intellectual process), while the other, lacking intellectual participation on the part of the diviner, would be based instead on his instrumental role in the divinatory operation (mediumistic process). The diviners who practice the first kind of divination are interpreters; they judge and appreciate the conjunction of the signifiers and the signifieds in a divinatory theme. Those devoted to the second augural mode are the "messengers"; practically speaking, they do not "touch" the content of the communication. The former establish the oracle, the latter reveal it. [10]

The interpreter-diviners employ divinatory equipment, objects which permit them to exercize their intuition and clairvoyance and with whose aid they establish the augural theme according to the needs of the clients. These tools are extremely varied and their enumeration alone would necessitate a separate chapter. Still, they obey several rules which allow a certain unifying strand to be discerned within this diversity. First of all, the divinatory equipment is intimately tied to the culture in which it is used. Thus, it is not possible to understand the use among the Dogon of the jackal and the matrices traced by the diviner in the sand without relating this to the role played by this animal on the mythic and social plane. [11] Similarly, the use of cowries, which is very common in Africa, becomes clear only when one grasps the relationship which exists in African thought between these "coins" on the one hand and man and the world on the other. Among the Bambara, for example, the postulant pays for his rights of entry into initiation societies with cowries, as if this currency had become the substitute for the initiate himself. [12] This is equally the case with kola nuts, diverse fruits and nuts, small bones and dice—in brief, with all kinds of materials—since, in practical terms, any sufficiently significant cultural element can become divinatory material. Secondly, this material is endowed by augural science with a specific and conventional meaning in relation to the signified elements. By its multiple possibilities for ordering, it must in principle exhaust all the situations in which these elements can be found. The divinatory material thus appears as the middle term or intermediary between the diviner and reality. It is a certain symbolic expression of reality and, as such, can only be utilized by specialists who are intimately acquainted with its exact nature.

The messenger-diviners use little or no divinatory material. Still, such material seems to be indispensable in the "minor" forms of the art of the "mediums," that is, where the diviner has not yet succeeded in serving, or been entitled to serve, as intermediary between the Souls and the world of humans. But, as soon as these conditions are achieved, the augural objects are replaced by the very person of the diviner. It is thus that in Kasaï, among the groups cited above, there exists a form of consultation with the Souls called *lubuku* which utilizes numerous different procedures. These include divination by hands, a statuette, a rubbing tool, a spatula, a squirrel on a liana, a winnowing basket, a water spider, a needle, a chick, rods, a teetotum, water, a mirror, a scout, a calabash, and hypnotism (*musangu*).[13] Nevertheless, this divinatory material does not play the role of signifier. It is intended only to transmit the response of the Souls—a response expressed by a yes or a no—to the questions which they are posed by the diviner. As soon as the other divinatory procedure, the *tshilumbu*, is tackled, the diviner substitutes himself for the augural material. He enters into a trance and personally makes the voyage to the Souls, from whence he reports the messages awaited by the clients.

The distinction drawn between the two types of diviners and, consequently, between the two great African divinatory modes, should not make us lose sight of the single psychological presupposition which underlies all these practices, that is, the conception of the constitution of the human person. The "fluidity" of this conception has been indicated above (pp. 8–10). According to Africans' ideas on this subject, there exists a plane of cleavage within the spiritual principles which constitute the human being. This permits the revelation there of the soul, properly speaking, and of an element, strange at first sight, which is the double. The double is a sort of mobile principle which can temporarily leave its owner in order to "walk" and roam in the world. (This it does regularly during sleep.) The person whose double is absent finds himself in a state of prostration and lethargy, as if his will and his intellectual faculties were failing. If the double definitively leaves its "abode," the person is considered to be dead. Divinatory practices are based on this psychological postulate, that of the existence of the double and of its mobility in comparison with the soul, which, only at death, leaves the body to which it is joined.

The case of the interpreter-diviners is not, strictly speaking, concerned with the double as a mobile element, but with it as a centralizer of psychic powers and energies. This is because, in contrast to the soul, the double represents the total set of intellectual functions and the faculties bearing on action. It sums up the individual in his capacity as a conscious, thinking, and active being. It can be acknowledged that, owing to a remarkable genetic endowment, or following repeated and sustained exercises, the interpreter-diviner is equipped with a particularly rich and active double. Owing to this, he is so sensitive to conjunctions that he acquires, as it were, the gift of double vision, the aptitude of the mind to move about with ease in the realm of meanings and a special sharpness in terms of discernment, insight, and the grasp of the relationships between things.

The diviner is not merely a being endowed with exceptional powers of clairvoyance, but, through his double, he is mobility itself. He penetrates things and beings; he is the world. He lives through his clients and through the society which shelters him, and they live in him. This copenetration is so far-reaching that one can not dispense with the other, as if this were a case of "consubstantiality." This is why the place occupied by the diviner in African society is so important, even though it is rarely mentioned in the works of ethnologists, sociologists, and specialists in religion.

The same role is played with no less distinction by the messenger-diviner, although the basis of his science is different. The "medium's" double is turned towards the world of the Souls; it detaches itself from the body of the diviner during his "voyages" so as to make contact with the true seers of men and things, the spirits. The science of this sort of diviner is more "celestial" than earthly and, in a sense, it is "second-hand." This, in the eyes of the clients, does not in the least diminish its quality, rather quite the contrary.

Owing to his relations with the beyond, the messenger-diviner is closer to religion and mystical life than his colleague, who acts through the intermediary of human intelligence. The "medium" dies and revives intermittently. While remaining a man he already belongs to the world of the Souls, which brings him closer to the divinity. This is why, in Kasaï,

> the *Tshanda* or meeting place of the magicians [of this category] is laid out according to the same plan as the World and the Sky. Its great dignitaries are grouped around their "invisible Master," following the same quadrangular and spiral order as the Genies around their celestial Master. The Magicians work in the image of God; hence the sacred character of their labors.[14]

Because of his special vocation and condition the African seer cannot exercise his art without taking rigorous precautions, the most striking of which are abstinence from certain foods and sexual continence. Yet these precautionary measures should not be confused with commonplace prohibitions. The negative practices which the diviner imposes upon himself in order to exercise his art derive instead from the incompatibility of the knowledge which he must exhibit at the time of vaticination and the acts tending to diminish his psychic and intellectual lucidity. Sexual abstinence, for example, can be interpreted as a guarantee of the integrity of the diviner's knowledge, since carnal relations, even with his own wife, are believed to create a void in the knowledge of the seer. Among certain peoples such acts also anticipate the joy of knowing, which diminishes the effect of the final act of knowing involved in divination.

Still, a fundamental question arises concerning divination in black Africa. The African is the being most careful to "read" his future in the composition of things and is one for whom this sort of prognostication has always been a habitual activity, but does he actually concern himself with the future as we ourselves understand it?

While there exist various terms for marking the different stages of the past, from "yesterday" to "long ago," it is quite striking to realize that in many African languages the future is only slightly differentiated. Usually it is in terms of a very close future, "tomorrow," that it is abstractly characterized. This is to say that, linguistically speaking, the future seems to be less conceptualized than the past. The reason for this lack of sensitivity in language for future time is undoubtedly the "non-humanized" character of the future. In opposition to the past, the future possesses nothing that can remind the African of man's nature and mark. And yet, as we have just seen, in his daily life man constantly calls on the knowledge of the diviner, who apparently broods over exactly what must or might happen in the emptiness of the future, in that time which to our mind is not yet "filled." Is this a contradiction? Certainly not. The African applies here again, and with implacable logic, his conception of life and time. He can only conceive of a future situation with reference to the past. "Tomorrow" is made up of elements of "yesterday" and "long ago"; it is the expression of the will of those who, though swallowed up by time, continue to testify to their presence in the multiple combinations of human destiny. In the light of this conception, can we not claim that for the African "what-will-be" blends into "what-already-was," that the future is in a certain sense the past, and that man is and will be only what he was? From this derives the diviner's profound belief in the ineluctable character of his "predictions" and, also, society's unlimited faith in the statements of its "seers."

All this can explain, at least in part, Africans' repulsion with regard to forms of divination in which human intervention is weak or nonexistent, such as astrology. Likewise, it explains their infatuation with any omen which is inscribed within a human framework, in relation with the earth, plants, and animals.

But this reversal of temporal perspective according to which the future becomes a tributary of the past seems, at first sight, to exclude the new and unusual. This is so only in appearance. The new and unprecedented in the destiny of a being or object results from the multiple possibilities for combining the "preexistent" elements. Nevertheless, these assemblages are not infinite in number, given that the elements which they call upon are themselves limited in number. Thus, for example, according to this point of view man is formed by the contribution of his paternal and maternal sides, by the geographical, biological, and social milieu in which he was born and in which he lives, by the history which he has experienced, by all that has contributed to make of him what he presently is.

In addition, even though the African is eager to know the "future," he is not terrified by it, as he knows that it cannot be "substantially" different from the past. This is the raison d'être for the feeling of resignation with which his soul is profoundly impregnated. To be convinced of this we need only observe the attitude of the African confronted with situations which change the initial composition of the elements of destiny by introducing new material.

The African's apprehension and anxiety concerning travel and hazardous and perilous undertakings is well known. These activities of course enrich the experience of the human being; but they also change the "capital" provided by his past, and he is no longer himself. Hence the multiple precautions taken by the African before deciding to leave on a risky "venture": consultation with a diviner in order to know the outcome, diverse baths and medications to safeguard the integrity of the traveler and assure his return, and choice of the time of departure and direction to take in order to reduce the risks of the trip to a minimum. Hence also the special rites performed for its members "abroad" by the community which remains behind. The return to the fold is celebrated as an event intimately tied to the life and "resurrection" of the traveler.

In sum, in the same way that the transformation of the personality of the BaLuba prophetess is symbolized by the "voyage," so does a voyage mark the change and renewal of the human being to the extent of making him a "resuscitated" person. The distance between someone who has traveled and someone who has never left his native soil is immeasurable. The latter always belongs to the structures in force in his cultural setting, and the elements constituting his destiny may always be revealed in spite of their multiple possibilities for ordering. The former destroys "the order of things" which existed at his birth and he also modifies the network of units which make up his destiny. Society and the diviner possess a firm hold over the one who remains at home—they know him or can at any moment know him—but this hold becomes ineffectual over the one who leaves, for he has become something other.

The religious and social repercussions of this concept of how man relates to his future are important. As a result of the innovation introduced into African societies by different cultural contacts, the role of the diviner diminishes more and more. His real function can only be under-stood in a society profoundly tied to its past and its traditions. Further-more, contact with foreign civilizations and the utilization of new techniques introduce new modes of thought. All this upsets the Afri-can's conception of the world and of the place he holds in it. The African diviner feels more than anyone the drama of this new state of things, because his intelligence and his spirit strike against the strange unknowns which escape his wisdom.

Nyctosophers and "Healers"

> ...sorcery [and] magic...try, by operating on matter and using mysterious processes of which neither the falseness or the efficacy can be proven, to capture a power forbidden to man.
>
> Baudelaire,
> "Le poème du hachisch," *Les paradis artificiels*

7

As much as if not more than the diviner, "sorcerers" and "magicians" occupy a place of the highest order in African culture. Like those who reveal the future, these personages, versed in the so-called occult science, polarize important social tendencies and attitudes around themselves and around the institutions of which they are the basis. Traditional African religion acquires its full meaning only when the existence of "sorcerers" and "magicians" is acknowledged as one of its constants.

To the uninformed mind the word "sorcerer" applies indiscriminately to the diviner, the blacksmith, the healer, the person in charge of a cult, the chief of a secret society, and finally to any individual who distinguishes himself from the common run of mortals by details of his dress or by duties whose meaning remains mysterious. The most regrettable misunderstanding however is the one which identifies "sorcerer" with "magician," as was the case during the era when the magician was considered to be someone who called up the dead or invoked the devil. It is possible that Anglo-Saxon ethnological literature has contributed somewhat to this mistake, given that the English word "sorcerer" designates equally the caster of spells and the doctor-healer.

In African societies, however, a great distinction is made between these two personages who, viewed linguistically, most often answer to different names. Thus the Kissi, for example, distinguish the *kuino,* an evil man given to killing and eating his victims, and the *wulumo,* who is dedicated to hunting down and neutralizing the *kuino.*[1] Similarly, the Ashanti possess both the term *suman* (or *dunseni*) to indicate the "medicine-man" and the term *bayifo* to designate the sorcerer (witch).[2] Among the Songhai the word *shantye* refers to the magician-diviner, while "sorcerer" is connoted by the word *tyarkaw.*[3]

In fact, the terminological distinction between "magician" and "sorcerer" corresponds to a differential gap between two social roles, between two incompatible offices, and between two diametrically opposed orders of phenomena. The "sorcerer" and the reality to which he belongs are classed on the side of evil, the night, destruction, and the antisocial, while the "magician" belongs to goodness, light and the day, construction, and the social. The world of the former is a universe of decay and shadows, decomposition and transformation, nonsatisfaction and incompletion; that of the latter, in contrast, displays a remarkable stability and a profound accomplishment, and seems always to be in a state of freshness, limpidity, and vigor appropriate to life in full bloom. When transposed to the plane of knowledge and wisdom, these two worlds oppose each other as knowledge which is tortuous, obscure, and sown with contradictions and antinomies is opposed to knowledge which is clear, based on evidence, and in conformity with the logic of the mode of thought which serves the community.

From whatever perspective the sorcerer and magician are viewed, one can always detect a certain antagonism which opposes one to the other. Still the rivalry is not absolute. As we will see later, sorcery and magic can overlap with each other so that in certain cases they present but a single domain, that of the magician-sorcerer, the ideal form of self-rivalry on the religious, ethical, and social planes.

On consulting the immense literature relating to sorcerers and sorcery in black Africa, one cannot help but notice that certain constants appear as leitmotifs over almost the entirety of the continent: the sorcerer usually reveals himself and acts at night; there is a close relationship between sorcery and femininity; the sorcerer generally destroys his own kin; and he often operates by means of an alteration in his personality. It is not possible here to analyze these themes for all of Africa. We will limit ourselves to a few ethnic groups, it being understood, however, that the conclusions drawn from this approach cannot lay claim to any rash generalizations.

Among the Bambara the sorcerer is called *suba*, a term which folk etymology semantically defines as equivalent to "great night" (*su*, night, and *ba*, great). This Sudanese people of the middle Niger say that the sorcerer is the "great night," or the most absolute darkness, because his actions are the result of a knowledge so profound that it escapes the ordinary methods of investigation. Some even consider the knowledge of sorcery to be the highest degree of all wisdom.

But the sorcerer is the "great night" in another sense as well. He never shows himself during the day. In conformity with the nature of the obscure and refined knowledge which he possesses, he acts at night. Darkness and shadows constitute his own domain because they form a favorable framework for transformation and secrets. Furthermore, there is a proverb which says: "Whatever the flight of the sorcerer, he will wait for the night to make it."

It seems that the relationship between sorcery and the night is based on the similarity between this period devoid of light and a certain form of mental activity whose development transcends the principles and laws of logic and ordinary knowledge. It would not be out of place to call such mental activity "nyctosophy" or "wisdom of the night," while its holders, the sorcerers, might merit the name of "nyctosophers."

Until now this aspect of the problem of sorcery has not, to our knowledge, been pursued by researchers. They generally considered it insignificant and were content to merely mention the nocturnal activities of sorcerers. However, if one is willing to study this closely, one will realize that it concerns the very nature of sorcery. Seen from this perspective, sorcery acquires a new dimension since "darkness" and "night" do not only constitute the prerogative of certain individuals in the society but extend, so to speak, to all of creation. Indeed, according to the Bambara, there exists in everything and every being at least one part which remains incomprehensible and impenetrable by the mind. Thus, to varying degrees, anything can be accused of sorcery. According to this same people, however, the woman more than any other creature is intimately related to "darkness" and "night" because she is the most mysterious and unfathomable. This is why she is closely linked to sorcery.

Woman's enigmatic and impenetrable character results first from her physical constitution, which is so different from that of the male. In her entirety, the woman "is" the earth, that is, the inert matter which encloses life within it and supports all that is necessary for man's existence. She "is" also water, the element of proliferation and abundance. Each of the woman's sexual organs, as well as its adjacent parts, reveals by the analogies it evokes the different parts of creation, each as mysterious as the next.

Her genitals represent the hollows and grottos which tear open the surface of the earth and permit access to the depths of its entrails. These grottos and caves provided man with his first habitat and also symbolize his final home after death. Female genitals, grottos, and tombs are similar concepts, all three related to the ideas of rest and transformation, which are considered "closed" concepts because of their inaccessibility to the mind.

The uterus and its adjacent organs express the receptive and germinative aspects of the soil. What is more mysterious than the development of a seed, the flowering of plants, and the production of fruit? And what is more incomprehensible than women's menstrual blood and ability to conceive?[4]

The breasts recall the nourishing power of the earth. Do we know the mechanism of life, springing out of the earth and passing through plants to man? The breast is a subject of astonishment as great as that of life, seemingly born from death. As the earth only vivifies insofar as it engulfs and absorbs, so does woman nourish only to the extent that she assimilates her food.

However, again among the Bambara, if the woman is astonishing because of the constitution and particularities of her physiological being, she is all the more amazing because of the psychological features of her soul. As a result of her intuition, and also because of her skill in bringing unexpected solutions to problems which are presented to her, men immediately classify her among those beings endowed with clairvoyance. Her mental apparatus is made up in such a way that, in contrast to man, she always follows the inclination of her desires. Similarly, her powers of seduction and guile make her a being who both attracts and inspires fear. Woman is both obstinate and incorrigible; this is why these character traits have been turned into a proverb, and it is said: "The woman is like the rib; she can never be straightened."

We can go even further in the analysis of Bambara thought on this subject. The impermeability which woman sets up against the intelligence of whoever wants to understand her is due to the very obscurity of the metaphysical concepts which are at the base of femininity as a principle of nature. These concepts are matter, fluidity, understandability, and void, which the Bambara express respectively as earth, water, shadows, and cavity. Like the earth, woman is inert and passive. Like water which follows the form of any container, woman does not have a single "form"; she defies this obstacle, is changeable, and does not let herself be mastered. Like the night and shadows, woman is difficult if not impossible to fathom. Finally, like a cavity or a hollow, woman does not allow herself to be grasped; she is the "void" which can only be appropriated by being filled.

Considering these conditions it is not surprising to realize the immense place occupied by woman in nyctosophy. Among the Bambara she is the supreme "sorcerer"; it is even said that the younger she is the greater are her powers in this field. Among the Lovedu, who distinguish between "nocturnal-sorcerers" and "diurnal-sorcerers," the former, who are "sorcerers" from birth, are almost all women.[5] Among the Songhai the ancestor of all "sorcerers" (*tyarkaw*), "who are spread throughout the entire world," is a woman.[6] The Ashanti evidence the same predilection for "women-sorcerers," who are encountered more often than "men-sorcerers."[7] From the point of view of "sorcery" the Azande possess a certain balance of the sexes, as both men and women can be "sorcerers." Yet, among them a man can be "bewitched" by an individual of either sex, while this can be done to a woman only by another woman.[8] This same people consider any unusual action concerning female sexuality (e.g., lesbianism and exposing the genitals within sight of a man by way of provocation) to bring misfortune and to be related to the evil brought about by sorcery.[9] Among the Thonga, the power of the *baloyi* (sorcerers) "is transmitted by the mother and not by the father."[10]

The nyctosophers possess another important characteristic: they are destroyers of members of their own family yet do not attack those who, like them, are "sorcerers." The deterioration of which they are the cause also takes on a distinctive form: they are not always content to destroy the victim's goods and to bring about certain defects in his being; they sometimes go so far as to annihilate him through "eating." Oral folk literature on this subject is so vast, and the rites of protection against the noxious maneuvers of the nyctosophers are so numerous and varied, that any attempt at analysis risks seeming presumptuous and schematic. Nevertheless, only the apprehension of phenomena by their principles permits one to move with ease through the labyrinth of a subject which is inextricable and strange at first sight.

To explain the problem of sorcery in its destructive and evil-doing aspect, recourse is sometimes taken in the psychological and sociological concept of conflict.[11] Certainly a conflict situation can lead one of the parties to do harm to the other, and, as antagonism only appears between those who know each other and maintain relations with each other, it is easily conceivable that sorcery is more readily practiced between relatives and neighbors. One wonders, however, if more profound motivations cannot be introduced to explain social attitudes that are so characteristic and even so universal.

The Bambara have a slightly different theory for explaining this typical behavior by nyctosophers towards their relatives. To them, the sorcerer is an incomplete creature; indeed he is the only being in creation which does not possess a *dya*, that is, a double. This characteristic is expressed by the myth of creation of the "mother" of sorcerers, Nyale, the ancestor of the nyctosophers. Nyale (one of whose names is Mouso Koroni Koundge), was born from the tree Balanza, the vegetable avatar of the creator god, and the particular symbol of life, death, and rebirth. Having dried out, the tree fell, leaving only a kind of plank called Pèmbélé. So as not to remain alone on the earth and to have a wife, the Pèmbélé kneaded the decaying wood issuing from him with his saliva. In giving it form he thus incorporated into it his soul-breath (*ni*). This feminine being was also endowed with an immaterial double (*dya*). But to limit the evil which could be done by this creature, which he distrusted, the Pèmbélé entrusted its *dya* to the master of the sky and waters, Faro, who became the guardian of all *dyas*.[12] Thus Nyale, the first sorcerer, was deprived of her double, and, like her, so was the nyctosopher. From this stems the nyctosopher's incessant quest to regain "his" *dya*. It is thus to fill the void of his imperfection that he pursues before all else the double of the humans issued from his own flesh and, secondarily, from that of other men.

Let us be clear that the cannibalism of the nyctosopher should not be understood as eating, pure and simple. The sorcerer is not thought really to eat the flesh of his victims. In his attempt to appropriate the double he takes possession only of that very element which he himself is lacking; the *dya* alone corresponds to his abilities to assimilate. Furthermore, such an operation only proves possible after a transformation of the double into an animal, generally a domestic and edible one.

Aside from these activities, the sorcerer operates in the extremely vast domain of human imperfections. It is thought that nyctosophers are capable of reaching the human being particularly during his fetal life and thereby inflicting upon him faults which make him unable to completely fulfill his role in society. These defects are not unrelated to the double of their eventual possessors, as they constitute actual deficiencies of the *dya*. Those afflicted with such psychic or physical malformation are struck in the very double of their personality and are considered imperfect beings. Still, it should be noted that while the sorcerer's self always contains a fault of a psychic or physical order, all human beings afflicted with such flaws do not necessarily become sorcerers. The defects are given material form by diverse objects placed secretly in the settlements, objects which the initiates of the *nama* secret society do their utmost to discover and destroy.[13]

One domain, however, escapes the harmfulness of the nyctosophers, that is, the one to which they themselves belong. A sorcerer can not harm another sorcerer in the same way that he harms the common run of mortals. If a conflict breaks out between two nyctosophers, the one who is defeated is held to deliver over to the other a victim chosen from among his family so that it may be "consumed" according to the ways already discussed. This characteristic of conflict between sorcerers is explained by the fact that since the nyctosopher's personality is deprived of its *dya* it can not be depossessed of it.

Still, since he is deprived of his double, the nyctosopher is incapable of exercizing the powers of his mind in the usual way. He does not behave normally, but often expresses himself in movements and gestures which in the eyes of his peers place him in a separate category. He makes himself conspicuous and, by that very fact, becomes a being who ends by being rejected from social life.

Building on observations transmitted from one generation to another by means of oral tradition, different societies have succeeded in elaborating veritable typologies of sorcery, which are extremely rich from the psychological and social point of view. All nyctosophers are classed as such according to their behavior, their character, and their "specialization." The Bambara among others recognize several dozen of these "types."

Without having penetrated the world of sorcery as we were able to do among the Bambara, Junod remarks that among the Thonga similar concepts govern the world of the *baloyi*.[14] Likewise, J. van Wing establishes that among the BaKongo the actions of the *bando ki* (sorcerers) within the clan contributed, through their destructive character, to the separation of families and the disintegration of communities.[15]

The spectacular character of nyctosophy is not limited, however, to the choice of relatives and neighbors as victims or to the perceivable results of the sorcerer's noxious action. It also appears in the ways in which this action is performed. Generally, when a nyctosopher throws himself into an undertaking, he can carry it through only at the price of a metamorphosis which he imposes on himself. Habitually deprived of a double, he chooses one for himself when he needs it and leaves it in his place, while he goes off to perform the task on which he is set.

These changes have always attracted the attention of specialists in the problem of sorcery. Still, they have not usually been studied with the depth and precision which they merit, given their character, which is fantastic in appearance. Indeed, the accounts on this subject by those involved in it abound with sequences where the authors seem to have given their imaginations free rein in transforming the sorcerer into a wide range of animals, plants, and diverse objects. At first glance, then, it would seem that the nyctosophers' metamorphoses do not obey any rule. But this is not at all the case.

The thorough analysis which we have conducted among the Bambara (and of which we have only provided a sketch here) allows us to state that the sorcerer's transformations obey certain principles and occur according to a particular classification of beings and things. Nyctosophers find correspondents for their metamorphoses only among objects and beings presenting certain characteristics which make them conspicuous and detach them from the group to which they normally belong. These characteristics are classed according to well-defined ideas such as the unusual appearance of certain plants and animals and the physical or psychic characteristics and behavior (when it recalls human attitudes) of certain beings. The evil character, scarcity, distinctive modes of life, and the strange faults of certain individuals in a given species also constitute categories relating to sorcery. The same can be said of the unusual size, ambiguity, and murderous character of certain tools. Briefly, any object or being which is distinguished for specific reasons from the rest of the group in which it is otherwise integrated is susceptible of becoming a material basis for sorcery. In other words, it is isolation and uniqueness which attracts the nyctosopher. This recognition corroborates one of the mythic themes of the Bambara according to which evil came into the world with the appearance of unique things.

To this it should be added that each type of sorcerer possesses one or more avatars which it especially prefers for its "incarnations." These preferred changes reveal the relationship which exists for the Bambara between certain asocial types of the human being and the corresponding types in the animal and vegetable kingdom. They also give, from the literary point of view, precious information on narrative themes and epic cycles. By way of examples we should note some which enjoy particular favor among the sorcerers: the hare, which is thought to be astonishing because of its shrewdness and supposed ability to sleep "with open eyes"; the toad, which is believed to become a mouse during the dry season and which thus enjoys a sort of ambiguity; the baobab, because of its powerful trunk and small number of leaves; and "fonio," due to the very small size of its grain. The needle, knife, and *dyele* axe are also suitable to nyctosophers because of their murderous nature. So, far from being oddities resulting from an overflowing imagination, the sorcerer's transfigurations are integrated according to a precise logic into a systematization of the real which the mind has created for its own satisfaction and for the achievement of social well-being.

The problem of the sorcerer's transformations presents yet another aspect, this time negative, which is related to the specific taboos observed in sorcery. There exists among the Bambara, as in other African ethnic groups, an entire set of things and beings towards which nyctosophers manifest a real repulsion and which in no case will they take as bases for their metamorphoses. From the study of these elements we find that the sorcerer's taboos are associated with the ideas of conservation, society, and light and that, because of this, they are opposed to the concepts underlying sorcery, that is, destruction, uniqueness, and darkness. It is thus natural that sorcerers can not make such things their avatars. Accordingly, the nyctosopher will never transform himself into mistletoe of any type because this plant is believed to contain the quintessence of the plant on which it grows as a parasite. The same is true for the dog, symbol of vigilance and fidelity, and for the rooster, herald of the day. Also classed as taboos for the sorcerer are, among other things, honey, which represents the complete food and the most perfect product of nature, and the beehive, symbol of the ideal society.

Those things tabooed because they are considered alter egos of sorcerers should be accorded special attention. Never, say the Bambara, will a sorcerer transform himself into, for example, a chameleon, since this animal is himself a "sorcerer" and is thus a facsimile of the sorcerer. The same is true of the gun, which can kill its bearer, and the castor oil plant, sign of ruin. In other words, while a certain "distance" is required between the nyctosopher and the object or being capable of serving as material basis for his metamorphosis, too great a "distance" or lack of "distance" are bound to make it fail.

In light of the preceding thoughts it is possible to include in a total view not only the problem of the sorcerer's changes but also the problem of sorcery itself. The nyctosopher is located in some way between two series of realities, his alter egos and his antagonists. On the one hand there exists a sort of confusion between the nature of the nyctosopher and his alter egos, and it is this lack of separation which excludes the possibility of metamorphosis. On the other hand, an absolute gap exists between the nyctosopher and the realities located at the "antipodes" of sorcery, and it is this gap which prohibits symbolic association and incarnations.

These rules constitute the complement of the norms concerned with metamorphoses, of which those described as preferential are only examples. Moreover, in this case it is no longer the idea of "distance" which governs the metamorphoses, but that of affectivity. The nyctosopher has a predilection for the beings and things which permit him to realize himself according to his nature. Among these he prefers the ones which are especially apt to contribute to the manifestation of his personality by virtue of their greater conformity to his nature.

The sorcerer's changes and the taboos observed by him represent only one of the aspects of sorcery, that which throws light on the relationship which exists between the sorcerer and the environment to which he belongs. His presence and his role in society constitute the other aspect. At this point the observations already made by many ethnologists should be recalled. Although in all African societies sorcerers can be unmasked—and in fact are by those who take them as such—no objective investigator has ever been able to enter into direct contact with any of them. No one has yet been able to acquire an object of sorcery still preserving its harmful power, neither has anyone been able to be present at the doubling of a nyctosopher. Even more, observation has shown that many so-called evil objects, which according to the belief of Africans have caused sickness or death, are nothing other than simulacra prepared in advance and disposed in propitious spots by those who are responsible for finding them and presenting them as elements of sorcery (e.g., the initiates of *nama*). In light of such facts some have concluded that these are acts of fraud performed in all good faith by certain individuals interested in exploiting the credulity of people in order to arrogate power. Others have automatically classified sorcery and the sorcerer among the products of the imagination of indigenous people who are incapable of discerning the objective causes of phenomena. Finally others have played the sociologist in their brooding over these problems and have defined sorcery as an element of social control or as a set of conflict-ridden situations and social tensions.

There is no doubt that sorcery and the sorcerer have an intimate and profound connection with society. Nevertheless, it seems that the reasons for their existence are actually different from those commonly recognized. Sorcery exists only in terms of an ideal society, communal in form, which by its very structure excludes the principle of the individual, of the isolated man. Parallel to this "model," which implies the community and the good that results from it, the mind possesses another "pattern" involving the unusual, the singular, and the unique. The former is opposed to the latter as the social is to the antisocial, and as good is to evil. The sorcerer and sorcery are associated with the singular and unique, and any manifestation of beings and things according to these modalities stems from undertakings of sorcery. The problem which then arises in any inquiry into this subject is neither, in our opinion, the investigation of the manner in which those concerned grasp the relation between cause and effect, nor the statistical delimitation of conflict-ridden situations in society, but the tracking down within the society of the border between that which is social and that which is singular. It is worth noting, for example, that the more strongly socialized the structures of a human group are, the more its attention will be drawn by the singular and unusual, thus sensitizing it to the problems of sorcery. It is therefore not astonishing that sorcery is rampant precisely within those units which are most significant from the point of view of social cohesion, the clan and the family, that is, within kinship. If supplementary proof of these claims is desired, it can be found in the fact that in order to escape sorcery different African societies have found no better solution than the disintegration and dispersion of traditional kinship, in other words, the rupture of ancestral social cohesion and the modification of models of thought concerning society.

Of course this aspect of the problem does not embody the totality of concepts concerning sorcery when considered on the level at which we presently envision it. It is impossible to omit the psychological elements which also define it.

The sorcerer and sorcery are incomprehensible outside of the particular conception of the human person in African societies. The analysis and study of nyctosophy is based above all on the mobility and fluidity of this entity. The Western conception of the person as unitary presents a great obstacle to the apprehension of phenomena dependent on different evaluations of that same human person. The African mind, however, moves with ease over its own terrain, even though we are disconcerted when it presents us with the doubled sorcerer: one part of his being is busy "eating" his victim while the other sleeps in his home. We are also disconcerted when informed that a human being can be entirely "eaten" when he still has many days to live. We can thus understand H. A. Junod's stupefaction when he writes on this subject:

> How it is possible for a man who has still some days or months to live to be regarded as already entirely eaten up, I do not pretend to explain. Such is however the Native idea. One of my informants tried to overcome the difficulty by saying that what the noyi [the sorcerer] takes with him to eat is the inside, the bowels; the outward frame alone remains, and the man will soon die! Most of the Natives, when the absurdity of the idea is pointed out to them, laugh and say nothing.[16]

Still, the duality of the human person does not arise only in the domain of sorcery. It appears, perhaps less clearly but just as necessarily, in that of magic. For if the sorcerer is presented as a deviation from the social ideal and as the invasion of the individual and the singular in the heart of social cohesion, the magician is defined as a constructor of society. His principal function is to do battle against sorcerers and sorcery and to destroy them. Yet the realization of this goal is itself subject to the use of means which stem from the concept of the double, of the dynamic duality of the magician's being.

The African magician is a personage who joins to his medical skill, which is based on the knowledge of diseases and remedies, an exceptional gift for detecting sorcerers and their actions. In ordinary life he behaves like everyone else and, aside from a few details of clothing, hairstyle, bracelets and necklaces (which do not, however, constitute a general rule), nothing would distinguish him from the common run of mortals. He does not make himself conspicuous by his behavior and does not live apart from others; he blends in, so to speak, with the masses, and is an integral part of the society in which he lives.

It is at the cost of a long period of exertion that the magician acquires his medical skill. As a candidate for the profession he is to practice, he begins by seeking a qualified master whose teaching he will follow for several years. Then he undergoes a veritable initiation at the end of which he will be allowed to "heal." It sometimes is the case that medical knowledge is transmitted from father to son, in such a way that the magician's family remains the sole holder of the secrets concerning diseases and their cures. This latter form of acquisition of medical skill is perhaps more widespread in African societies than the preceding one.

The battle against sorcerers depends upon a knowledge and technique which the magician acquires by initiation, that is, through a progressive unveiling of things conducted simultaneously with the opening of the mind and intellect. This latter step is often integrated into profoundly religious rites which touch upon the mystical life. However, what is important in practical terms in this period of formation, is the neophyte's initiation into the manipulation of symbols and into the logic concerning the relations between things. This is, of course, never taught in a theoretical fashion but according to the norms of concrete thought: by images and representations which are related to reality by analogy and similarity.

In many cases, during the period of apprenticeship, the magicians disappear from society by retiring to some secret place in order to perfect their "scientific," moral, and mystical personalities. This retreat also increases their prestige in the eyes of their future clients. For a Thonga magician the sea constitutes an ideal "hiding place" during this period of his existence since, being an object of terror for the common people, it furnishes the magician with the elements necessary in the preparation of medicines, elements which he himself takes from its waters. As Junod recounts:

> Sinandondo was a wonderful man, dwelling on the Western border of the Nkomati, at Shifukundju. He had disappeared for two or three years, and was regarded as dead, but he unexpectedly reappeared, saying that he had lived at the bottom of the sea during the whole time. There he had not eaten anything; he was like a fish. The chiefs of the country, under the water, had given him his great drug called ndzundzu, and he returned home bringing with him a bunch of the precious roots. His people welcomed him and made a feast on his return. He then became a great magician.[17]

The desert, which is inhospitable and no less frightening than the sea, also lends itself well to the technique of isolation of the magician desirous of increasing his power. The same author reports on this subject that:

> Nwashihandjime, the great Nkuna magician, a splendid creature, his eyes beaming with a certain supernatural light...is said to have disappeared from his village for months, and to have come back from the desert emaciated but full of new magical powers.[18]

In each of these two cases the provisional abandonment of society and temporal solitude are, for magicians, a means of "hurling" themselves into public life.[19] This is because everything, in their conduct as much as in the ritual objects which they possess, breathes sociality. Junod adds on the subject of these same magicians:

> Their activity is not secret, nocturnal, and more or less unconscious. They act openly, in the light, during the day, and do not hide their magical powers; on the contrary, they make a show of them.[20]

The magician is the personage who centralizes in and of himself and his home all the tendencies and interests of the group. He channels in a single direction that which is important or appropriate to each of his peers. By his knowledge of them he is a sort of central organ towards which converges all the information concerning them. He is the uncontested master of the public stage whose background is private. He "holds" everything, men and things, in his hand as does the chief. This is why it is not surprising that actual political chiefs sometimes also exercise the office of magician.

Among the external marks of the magician's high position one almost always finds a tail of which the tuft of hair is without doubt the most important and meaningful part. This tail is, as it were, the usual insignia of office. Inside it the magician hides certain of his "drugs." The use to which he puts the emblem is characteristic: he employs it to indicate the "sorcerer" whom he has just unmasked; he places it on his head and buries his nose in its mass of hairs before accusing the guilty person and whipping him. But the tail is also an insignia of the chief and the chieftaincy. Any chief conscious of his duties and authority will carry with him one or more "fly whisks" (as they are called in a vocabulary scarcely concerned with nuances), that is, tails, because they are symbols of society and social cohesion. Among the Thonga, the tails of bovines constitute in addition the sign of union between uterine kin and their affines, as it is this part of a cow killed at a village celebration which the latter send to the former.[21]

We can now understand the importance of this insignia in the hands of the magician. For him it constitutes the effective symbol of his influence, power, and mastery with regard to the group over which he watches. Armed with his insignia, the magician is a sort of sacred being comparable to the divinity who governs the world.

Among other African groups the religious and social personality of the magician is revealed particularly through the special preparations which he himself concocts and which for him are weapons against evil and sorcerers. For the Kissi, the magician's essential attribute consists of a small personal "altar," the *gbindo*, which the magician makes by himself. The information collected on this subject seems to show that this altar too has a profound social meaning. Indeed the *gbindo* is composed of a stone taken from each of the community's places of worship, "two stones collected from each of the paths at the exit of the village, two stones gathered at the central square . . . , small iron and copper bells . . . , [and] a bull's tail."[22] In another *gbindo* there is found "slag and stones collected at the lineage's place of worship."[23] Among the BaKongo the fabrication of antisorcery "weapons" involves the participation and "communion" of all the inhabitants of the village, who thereby place themselves under the protection of the sacred object and submit themselves to the vigilant control of the magician.[24]

Sometimes these more or less complex preparations do not seem sufficient to demonstrate the social role of the magician. They are then augmented by more spectacular activities: the magicians organize dances during which they publicly display their power. J. Rouch remarks concerning this subject that among the Songhai "the magician's dance is one of the most effective means of protection and of the temporary acquisition of an extraordinary power."[25] Indeed all exceptional events call for these dances. These include the purification of the village, the celebration of the young girls' initiation, the completion of circumcision, and the death of a magician. The atmosphere in which these demonstrations take place deserves to be described in full, since it shows so well the profound contact which is established at that time between the magician and his public. Rouch, who was an eyewitness to one, recounts:

> . . . Yedyo [the magician], resumes his dance. It becomes increasingly slow and majestic. Yedyo's son, with bulging eyes, comes to dance next to his father. But Yedyo suddenly kneels down, trembling, and from his mouth he literally vomits a small, very fine chain, which seemed to me to be made of copper and which balances, like a tiny snake, in front of his face. Then he sees things even better than usually. He sees evil in four directions, and "pricks" the surprised *tyarkaw* [sorcerers]. During these few seconds he is the dangerous master of all the bush and all the villages. Then, bending over double on his haunches, he painfully re-swallows the small shining chain. He does not utter a word, or make any sign, but all of his assistants are taken by a sort of intense emotion at the mere sight of that chain. They tremble, raise their arms to the sky, wander wildly and cry; right next to me the village chief, shaken by sobs, falls on the knees of Sourgya (the chief of the village-group Yatakala) and, with his head buried in his ample robe, cries at length.[26]

The techniques utilized by magicians in their hunt of sorcerers are worthy of interest. Schematically speaking, they consist in the discovery and then the destruction of harmful objects, illnesses and diseases, and the inflicters of evil. In each of these cases the appropriate procedures are put into effect by the magician.

Speed is often the keynote of the search for objects said to be harmful to the human community. These objects, it is said, are "fabricated" by sorcerers who then hide them in places favorable to their evil action, that is, where those whose harm is wished must pass, or in a house, or on the outskirts of the village, and so on. The magician makes an effort to detect them in the presence of his fellow citizens, and in the course of this activity he does not merely walk. On on the contrary he runs, moving about with extreme speed.

Among the Bambara the *suba siriw* ("harmful objects" or, literally, "sorcerer's attachments") are "officially" discovered by initiates chosen for this function. This occurs once a year, at the time of the appearance of the *nama* secret society.[27] One of them, a stick in hand, takes command of a small troop, and all dash about throughout the village. The leader is responsible for searching with his stick any spot which seems to him to conceal a *suba siri*. In a frantic race he penetrates everywhere including houses, storerooms, and wells. He climbs trees and scales walls, searches under the mats of sleeping people and sometimes under the clothes of the inhabitants he encounters, and no one is able to offer the least resistance to him. During the whole rite, one of the initiates in the troop never stops casting abuse at the sorcerers.

Abruptly, the leader points his stick toward the earth, in the crack of a wall or the hollow of a tree. Another initiate then bends over, digs, and after having discovered the harmful object sought, grabs it by his mouth. Then, in the middle of the uproar, the entire troop retraces its steps in order to bring the object to the chief of the brotherhood. Next, the great magician comes closer and, with his sacrificial knife, pricks the *suba siri*, which the bearer has just let fall to the ground. A sacrifice of a chicken is performed at this time on the object, which is then set aside. The scenario is repeated until the *suba siriw* are exhausted. By the end of the night one can count several dozen "attachments" which have been identified and "immolated." They are all carefully suspended from a post or a tree located in the village square while the women, who had been excluded from the preceding ceremonies, are urged to come see them. It is thought that this is their best guarantee against the evils capable of striking their offspring. Those concerned say that the *suba siriw* "shiver and shake" while the women look at them. At the close of the *nama* celebration, all these "harmful objects" are taken off and thrown into the fire.

Among the Bambara the "sorcerer's attachments" are varied objects made of earth, wood, iron, and the like. They represent, among other things, the shapes of animals and people or even utensils and everyday objects. Their essential characteristic is the deformed figuration of what they are supposed to represent. Their true significance is as symbols of the physical and moral faults and flaws of the human individual. In fact, they take the place of the different deformities capable of attacking the *dya* and the body of the human being during his conception and gestation in the maternal womb. This is why the women are invited to come see them, once the magician has succeeded in "stopping" their harmful influence by detecting them and "putting them to death."

The people and even the majority of the *nama* initiates are convinced that these objects are "fabricated" by the sorcerers in order to do harm to humans. Yet the truth is otherwise. During the weeks preceding the *nama* celebration, and in the greatest secrecy, the group of initiates appointed to detect the "harmful objects" prepares and hides all of the "attachments." It is then easy for them to find these objects at the time of the search. Still, it cannot be emphasized strongly enough that, despite its appearance, this constitutes neither a hoax nor a deceit. Rather it concerns a technique intended to anchor deeply in people's minds the certainty that the magician watches over the birth of human beings healthy in mind and body. With speed as its keynote, his action to achieve this end is fast and effective. Nothing can proclaim his desire to resist evil and his intention to conquer resistance better than the effort which he displays in finding and confounding this same evil.

Similar procedures for tracking down the sorcerer's "preparations" are found throughout Africa. Junod describes them among the Thonga,[28] and Paulme does the same for the Kissi.[29] Among the latter people, the hunt for dangerous "talismans" held by sorcerers takes on the character of the pursuit of death (incarnated by the sorcerer) by life, of which the magician avails himself.[30] Reduced to these essential elements, the position of the two social antagonists in this "race" is characterized by a symmetrical opposition between right and left and between the individual and the social. The sorcerer holds in his right hand the knife, which he uses to open the chests of sleepers to tear out their hearts (the significant organ of the human body according to the Kissi and what is at stake in the battle between sorcerers and magicians), while in his left hand he carries his personal "altar" (the *sambio*), which contains his own heart. The magician himself displays in his right hand the essential attribute of his profession, the *gbindo*, which represents the social, while he carries in his left hand a pot filled with medicines, the antidote to the *sambio*. The left and the right of the sorcerer are presided over by death and destruction, the former because the *sambio* is synonymous with dryness and burning, the latter because the knife brings about the arrest of life and annihilation. At the same time, for the magician the left and right hands represent life. The left is the bearer of humidity and freshness because of the receptacle containing "medicines"; the right, by supporting the *gbindo*, conveys society itself, that is, the "living."

To this opposition should be added another, that which exists between the sorcerer's left and the magician's right, both of which carry "altars." Indeed, this opposition is quite clear during the "pursuit" of the sorcerer by the magician. As will be seen later, it is erased from the moment the sorcerer hides his altar beneath that of the magician. The first opposition about which Paulme speaks expresses a battle which is finally resolved by the magician's victory over the sorcerer. The second points out a confusion in the elements of opposition and results in the identification between the sorcerer and the magician. Indeed, as among the Bambara, where the "hunter" of the sorcerer's attachments is also their "maker," the Kissi *wulumo* tends to identify himself in the minds of the people with the *kuino*, whose personality becomes in some way unreal. The only magician who matters is the one who polarizes in himself the two aspects of sacred knowledge: that which is tied to life and that which is concerned with death. Paulme recounts:

> Public opinion does not contest the beneficial role of the hunter of sorcerers: the *wulumo* combats a public danger, as "the sorcerer is the enemy of all." But the idea of such a battle does not seem less suspect: how, we were told several times and with a tone of conviction, how would the hunter of sorcerers recognize the sorcerers and how would he be able to combat them, if he himself were not initiated into their secrets—if he himself were not a *kuino*, an assassin who eats human flesh? . . . The *gbindo*, which guides him in his pursuit, is of the same nature as the sought-after *sambio*; it is merely stronger: "if not, the *wulumo* would fall." . . . Certain people let it be understood that the *wulumo* can go so far as to play a provocative role, to fabricate a *sambio* which he hides with the sole aim of causing problems of which he will be asked to discover the cause. . . . It is again explained that the best hiding place for a *sambio* is *under* the pottery containing its antidote.[31]

An aspect of the acts described above extends far beyond the boundaries of the Bambara and Kissi ethnic groups, as it is found, for example, among the Kanda, Nyakyusa, Thonga, Mossi, and Samogo. There always exists a certain ambiguity in the minds of the people regarding the exact role of the sorcerer and the magician. Yet, in spite of this ambiguity, men and women everywhere are accused of sorcery and pay with their lives for the actions which society attributes to them and which it judges to be crimes directed against it. Are these religious and social attitudes with regard to sorcery contradictory? Is this an instance of illogicality in African thought, a thought incapable of considering phenomena objectively?

It should be said, first of all, that magic and sorcery (like many other cultural phenomena) do not demand any explanations on the part of those concerned. In their eyes, these are not phenomena deducible from a previous system. With the exception of a few wise men, the whole of a community (sometimes including magicians and sorcerers themselves) accepts things as they are presented in their immediate succession.

It should be noted next that the antagonism which characterizes the two orders of phenomena does not manifest itself as oppositional except on the level of the discontinuous. Rather, on the level of the continuous, the connection between the two orders of phenomena is such that the opposition changes into participation: "the *sambio* is often found hidden in the hand of the *wulumo*"[32] ("the best hiding place for a *sambio* is under the receptacle containing its antidote").[33]

In reality, then, the ambiguity denoted by the data of sorcery and magic flows, as does the role of the magician, from the way in which the complex domain of these phenomena is apprehended: sometimes as a whole, sometimes by means of its elements. Furthermore, the mind of those concerned easily and spontaneously performs a sort of slide from the discontinuous to the continuous in order to express its conception of reality. However, this is only possible because the data in question stem from two complementary aspects of the real.

In sum, the existence of the individual and society is grasped on the social level in terms of opposition and undergoes the treatment befitting the elements of a linear series, while it is perceived on the deep level of existence in terms of conjunction and is subjected to the treatment befitting cyclical elements. In both cases we are concerned with death and life. These two ideas confront each other when society thinks of itself and watches over its own security; they are "in rhythm" when society thinks of them by envisaging the incessant renewal of existence. In the latter perspective, death is hidden under the appearance of life and, inversely, life is sheltered under the rags of death, much like the "altar" of the sorcerer which is sheltered under its antidote and the sorcerer himself who disappears under the features of the magician. In reality, if one goes to the bottom of things according to African thought, one can incontestably state that any magician is potentially a sorcerer just as life is but a latent period of death.

Ethics and
Spiritual Life

Each thing gives birth to its child;
speech gives birth to its mother
(that is, silence).

Silence does not exist so long as
you are not master of yourself.

Self-mastery is the fruit of self-
knowledge.

Bambara proverbs

8

African morals and ethics belong to a domain which Western researchers have scarcely explored. To be sure, they have not failed to note
various aspects of the moral conduct of the Africans: fidelity, hospitality,
sense of justice, love and respect for relatives and traditions, modesty
surrounding relations between the sexes, unselfishness and self-
sacrifice. These qualities of the African soul have also been observed in
the vast field of oral literature often used by the people themselves for
the education and moral formation of the young.

Nevertheless, these observations have most often been buried by the
investigators in the mass of conventional acts or else they have been
arranged according to the perspective of Western culture, thus losing
their African specificity. No one has ever truly concentrated on the ultimate scope of African ethics and morals. Yet it would have been relatively easy to perceive that the African valorizes above all the mastery of
the self, making it, in fact, the foundation of his conduct.

This "virtue" possesses an essential preliminary which is also the
basis of African thought and philosophy. It is through the knowledge of
the self that the human being arrives at the mastery of the self; self-
knowledge is, as it were, the motive force behind the mastery of the self,
that is, the foundation of ethics. For the Bambara, as well as for other
peoples of the valley of the middle Niger, to know oneself means to be
aware of one's humanity, of the favorable position which, as a man, one
occupies in the universe. Self-knowledge makes manifest the eminent
character of the human being with regard to the rest of creation.

To be sure, this perspective does not prompt man to feel the smallness
of his condition or his state, or the weakness of his nature and his ways.
Much to the contrary, he depends on it to assert himself as the incon-

testable master of his surroundings. Man commands plants and animals, exercizes his authority over the march of time, obliges the clouds
to let rain fall and enjoins the thunder to recede. By his knowledge of
himself the human being becomes a miracle worker, or thinks of himself
as such, since in knowing himself he knows others, tied to him by
invisible links. He can also determine the value of everything which
surrounds him. As the center of a universe of relations, man becomes its
sovereign. The accounts of the first explorers of Africa abound with
details concerning this feeling of power presumed by chiefs, rainmakers,
African doctors, or simply the common people. Father Proyart recounts,
concerning the inhabitants of Loango: "One could not insult a man more
than to call him a coward, just as one cannot pay him a more flattering
compliment than to tell him he seems intrepid and warlike."[1]

Yet, to brave the elements in order to submit them to one's power or
to attempt to dominate the world would be of no interest if man did not
achieve a profound hold on himself. In fact, in African ethics self-
knowledge inevitably leads to self-mastery. An African's esteem for
someone is a function of his ability to dominate his passions, emotions,
behavior, and actions.

Apprenticeship in this conduct begins during the first years of a
child's life. It immediately focuses on the domination of suffering,
physical as much as moral. The child constantly learns to check his
reaction towards painful situations which are imposed on him by the
group during his progressive introduction into society. It would be a
humiliating dishonor both for the little man and for his family if he were
not able to repress his tears and especially his shrieks during the trials to
which he is subjected. The word "stoicism" comes naturally to the
memory of those who have long been witnesses to this quality of the
African soul. Thus, in an account of a voyage to West Africa more than a
century ago, A. Raffenel remarked:

> The blacks have a profound disdain for pain. They take pride in
> affecting indifference when they receive serious injury or when
> they are afflicted with painful illnesses: to make a single cry would be
> a dishonor. With equal success the women practice the stoicism of
> their husbands. While in labor they must seem not to feel the
> least discomfort. As soon as they have delivered, they clean their
> child and make it comfortable by themselves. That day or the next they
> go about the ordinary concerns of the household.[2]

As Father Trilles was able to note among the Fang, the real reason for
this attitude among women resides in the repercussions which they
believe the mother's conduct can have on that of the child: "The less she
shouts, the stronger the child will be."[3] If the African mother takes such

great care in not showing the pain of childbirth through excessive moaning and groaning, it is because by acting otherwise she would run the risk of bringing into the world a child who is feeble and without character.

Circumcision and excision (where they are practiced), as well as the initiation of the child into religious life, constitute so many stages in an apprenticeship in suffering. Among the Dogon, those in charge of circumcision and excision

> exhort the children to be brave before the operation, any demonstration of fear or pain bringing with it the contempt of their companions and of adults. Cowardice in this circumstance is so very ignominious that it must be kept secret in the village. Young girls must also accept without resistance or complaint the placing of rings in the nose, lips, and ears.[4]

Similar documentation can be cited in great quantity, so much are African traditions identical from this point of view. Other landmarks on the way to the formation of the individual by suffering appear along with the initiatory instruction itself. In all initiation societies physical suffering and its domination are, as will be seen later, the supreme attributes of spiritual life. In all cases a single rule governs the human being's education; this is the stoic bearing of pain, which is felt to be the best training in self-mastery. Self-mastery thus becomes a real factor in the social integration of the individual who is accepted by the group only to the extent to which he acquires a great facility for inhibiting the reflexes of affective sensitivity. Thus the real *homo socialis* is a closed being; he does not show himself on the outside. The "virtue" to which he aspires, and which he must practice above all else, makes him a being who is indifferent, who does not betray any emotion, feeling, or disturbance. We will see in what follows the way in which this attitude is valorized religiously. Indeed, the distance between repressed pain and its elevation to the rank of happiness and joy is not great. African mysticism plunges its roots into ethical values of the highest order.

Among all the reflexes capable of undermining the mastery of the self, there is one towards which the African is particularly sensitized, and that is speech. The man who talks too much or who does not know how to keep a secret is for the African a being without value. In fact, the African places the true basis for the human being's dominion over his acts and his conduct in the power and control exercised over his speech.

We can thus measure the importance accorded in ethics not only to speech but also to its opposite, silence. To be sure, speech is involved in man's life and exuberance and is the source of achievements and advances, but it carries within it its own limits. It can not go beyond certain boundaries tacitly recognized by society without exposing its author to the severe judgment of others. The chatterer is without doubt the sole human being towards whom the African is not afraid of allowing himself the right to nourish feelings of hatred. Silence has nothing in common with other moral values aside from constituting at once their beginning and end. It is the supreme virtue, as it subsumes integrity, courage, the power of the soul, prudence, modesty, and temperance. Silence defines the man of character, and is the attribute of the wise man; it is a type of wisdom. He who knows how to be silent possesses true happiness, interior peace, and detachment.

In light of this, it is quite useful to try to understand in detail the way in which certain African peoples conceive of silence. Obviously, this analysis and the conclusions which are drawn from it can not apply in their entirety to the whole of Africa. Still, it is not unlikely that more thorough research in this area would reveal a striking similarity between the Bambara or Dogon conception of silence and that of the Bantu peoples of southeast and southwest Africa.

Among the Dogon, silence is highly valued when it does not result from the timidity or weakness of the individual. It is not only the opposite of unnecessary chattering, which is defined as "speech without a path and without seeds," but it constitutes the antidote for the misdeeds of speech. He who knows how to command his tongue avoids quarrels and misfortunes and shows himself to be the social being par excellence.

> He is patient . . . ; he knows how to hold back his words when it is necessary; he does not get angry and he avoids disputes by not responding to provocations. This rare quality requires much force of character; . . . the patient man is sometimes sad and must make an effort to forget the "bad words" to which he did not wish to respond. Such a man is highly valued in the village; he makes the people around him happy; "the patient man has peace," goes the proverb. . . . He is "refreshing" like water.[5]

Like many other African peoples, the Dogon hold that women do not share this quality with men. Chattering is a fault which is attributed to them by their nature, putting them in direct relation to sickness and death, since a surfeit of words engenders illness. Various ritual practices applied to women find their religious and social motivations in this. The wearing of earrings and rings in the lips and nose and the filing of incisors constitute for a girl so many "trials intended to insure the harmonious development of her linguistic apprenticeship and to aid in making her mistress of her speech."[6]

The Bambara profess identical ideas on this subject. The role of silence in their moral life is even more profound than it is among their immediate neighbors. Speaking of the man who easily becomes angered, or who in his speech allows himself to be carried away by the fire of passion, the Bambara say "he is unable over himself," meaning that he does not know how to dominate himself. Similarly, the man who, being ignorant of the ingenious combinations and constructions of the language, expresses his thought in too direct a fashion does not merit his peers' high regard, even if he otherwise gives proof of great learning. Such a man does not possess real dominion over his speech. He does not master it, nor does he know the real workings of communication, according to which a message is understood by another in an indirect manner. Here also woman is distinguished from man by her fashion of speaking too directly. Detours and sinuousity characterize her action but not her speaking. Furthermore, she is a chatterer, speaking with intemperance and not knowing how to impose limits on her words. And, because of this fact, she is likely to divulge her secrets and those of others. These factors indirectly furnish the explanation for one of the strangest rites in Bambara religion, which consists of the beating of the corpse of a woman whose husband never subjected her to any correction while she was alive. The flagellation is equivalent to an affirmation of the perfection of the deceased. In this way it is indicated that she was so accomplished in the mastery of her tongue during her life that her impassivity was equalled only by the insensitivity of the corpse. The Bambara also strive to remedy what they suppose to be a "congenital" defect in woman, her loquaciousness. All young girls on reaching marriageable age undergo the tatooing of their gums and lower lip, which lose their pink color and become violet. Thus it is hoped to confer a certain mystery to women's speech: their words will leave the organ of speech under the protection of obscurity evoked by the color indigo. "The balm which is made to penetrate the two areas will confer a discipline upon them,"[7] a discipline, it is thought, which will be capable of containing and subduing speech itself.

On a more general level, men and women are unconsciously submitted to a constant apprenticeship in the mastery of speech. How could it be otherwise in a society where the use of implication, euphemism, symbol, allegory, and secret is a part of the everyday technique of oral expression? There the concepts used by thought are never perfectly defined and clear entities. They possess blurred outlines, sometimes contracting in order to indicate a diminution of their applicability, sometimes expanding so that their content may flow out to the limits of the unusual and unexpected. Speech and discourse follow this same movement, so that speech is richer in hidden meanings than in its apparent expressiveness. "In this way a single term can have an abundance of meanings since so many concepts enter the same channel."[8] Speech, then, constitutes a sort of sonorous mask behind which thought hides, obliging the interlocutor to detect its true face.

Among very young children games and secret languages constitute the ideal pedagogical means for apprenticeship in the mystery and camouflage of thought. To be sure, these games are above all recreational activities. Nevertheless, it would be ridiculous, in Africa, to reduce them to that function alone. Basically, the games of young Africans are theater pieces played by actors unconscious of their role and ignorant of the meaning of the themes which are treated in them. Through these diversions children are plunged directly into an organized universe, whose essence their minds cannot grasp. The "libretto" of these clever constructions particularly escapes them. The children unconsciously pour their psyches into the mold of the game and, identifying themselves with their own activity, progressively follow its hermetic and obscure character. They themselves become hidden, dissimulating, and inner-focused. Like the games, they cannot be reached.

The secret languages which children enjoy using contribute to the same end. Their "pig Latin," while still allowing communication, conceals the meaning of the message from those who do not possess the code. In the art of secrecy, it appears as a neutral instrument whose manipulation entails a double effect. First, on the social plane, the users of "pig Latin" consciously familiarize themselves with the handling of "reserved" knowledge which, in another form, will be the sole knowledge that will concern them after initiation. Secondly, on the individual plane, "pig Latin" contributes to the modeling of the mind and intellect of those who practice it and permits them to acquire a greater mobility in grasping the relationships between things. For children, oral "gymnastics" are the best introduction to the gymnastics of thought.

The early childhood of a Bambara person thus begins in an atmosphere amenable to confidences, complicity, and mysterious allusions. In fact, it is a "climate" of silence. Is not confidence the enemy of divulgence?

Thus prepared, the little men begin the fundamental phase of their childhood, their first initiation, which introduces them into the complex mechanism of successive revelations where the secret can only be divulged at the price of the teller's life.

The initiation into *n'domo* can be considered a minor form of introduction into the mysteries. The personages who take part in the epiphanies of this initiation society are all uncircumcized children. Officiants and candidates are openly in a position of authority, and adults carefully avoid interfering in the affairs of *n'domo*. But the society's goal is grandiose since it is concerned with the children "playing" at the discovery of mankind. Indeed, the central figure in this sacred play is a masked child whose face is hidden behind a hollowed piece of wood representing human features. During his choreographic maneuvers the actor is obligated to maintain the most absolute silence. His attitude is significant: the absence of speech is analogous to interior life, monologue, and meditation. It also constitutes an appeal intended to send the small members of the society in search of man as he was when he left the hands of the creator, of that man who can be discovered behind any human face. The major point of the lesson put forth by the "play" is that "man is only revealed in the isolation and silence of the soul."

Parallel to this exterior aspect of the practice of silence, the *n'domo* is intended to act on the children's innermost character. As can be expected, this action makes use of the theme of physical pain. Ritually provoked, this pain is not envisaged in itself but only inasmuch as it signifies other things. It interposes itself as a symbol of the evil which speech can cause under certain circumstances. In this meaningful complex the child's attitude toward the signifier acquires the value of a test relative to the signified. In either case one must impassively endure suffering and demonstrate the mastery of self. A close analysis of the diverse elements figuring in this symbolic whole shows, as we will see, that in reality it is silence that is still at issue here, since the goal which the *n'domo* seeks to attain is to build the human being's strength of character on the mastery of his tongue.

The rite which concretizes these theoretical remarks is quite simple. It is summed up in the beatings which the members of *n'domo* inflict on each other during the brotherhood's annual celebration, when each strives to hit the feet and legs of his adversary. The instruments used in these violent acts are rods which must be cut from branches of the *grewia* (*villosa* and *bicolor*) because of this plant's particular symbolism. The *grewia* is related to the notion of communication. Indeed, someone who wishes to sell an object easily will first expose it to the smoke obtained by burning the wood of this bush. Similarly, the walking sticks of old men are made from *grewia*. It is through this semantic content that the plant is related to the tongue. Is not the fundamental function of this organ to allow and to encourage communication between humans? Thus to whip oneself with switches of *grewia* is symbolically equivalent to inflicting oral injuries on oneself. In addition, the stoic endurance of pain becomes the best test of dominion over oneself and one's speech.

One may perhaps think that aside from this complicated network of man's attitudes and behavior through which silence is discovered with some difficulty, Bambara culture does not possess more direct ideas concerning the fundamental element of moral life. But this is not the case. The oral literature of this Sudanese people is filled with sayings and maxims concerned with the eminent value of verbal sobriety. They also have many practices whose efficacy is a function of silence. In these two domains in particular the same richness and esteem for "the moment of silence" can as easily be established across the entire African continent as among the Bambara.

Without doubt the Bambara possess an unusual way of apprehending silence: silence is not an absence, still less a lack, but a present reality, and this recognition is fundamental. Silence is said to place itself before and after speech. It engenders speech which, however, is its "mother": normally, it is said, the mother brings the child into the world, but in the case of speech and silence it is rather the child (speech) who gives birth to its mother (silence). The inversion of filiation, which constitutes the power of this image, bears witness to the profound valorization of silence. Silence is the ultimate reality, it is the power capable of engendering itself while giving rise, in the act of its generation, to the other reality, speech. For this reason, the Bambara affirm that speech and discourse—language—only acquire their full value in relation to the silence which underlies them.

We understand from this the glorification of silence which we find in sayings concerning the world, the village, creation, cohesion between humans and the individual:

> If speech constructs the village, silence builds the world.
> Silence adorned the world, speech made it hum.
> Speech dispersed the world, silence reassembles it.
> Speech destroys the village, silence makes its foundation good.
> Silence hides man's manner of being from man, speech unveils it.
> One does not know what the silent man thinks, but one knows the thought of the chatterer.
> The secret belongs to he who keeps quiet.
> Silence delimited the paths, speech confused them.

Silence is also one of the conditions, if not the only one, of interior life:

> Silence pondered; speech did not want to think.
> Silence soothes the *dya*, speech frightens it.[9]

It is on a collection of thoughts such as this (the fruit, perhaps, of a long observation of men and things) that the experience of silence is set against its opposite, speech. The first belongs to the category of the true and the serious; the second belongs to lightness, diversion, and confusion. The first is also a medicine capable of curing all illnesses; the second opens the doors to misfortune:

> Silence gave birth to the serious, speech to diversion.
> Any serious thing is made in silence, but any futile thing in
>   tumult.
> Marriage [for example] is made in silence, free love in amuse-
>   ment and noise.
> If speech burned your mouth, silence will heal you.
> Silence is the antidote for all, speech opens the door to all
>   [evil].
> What silence could not improve, speech can not improve
>   either.

If we compare all these maxims with each other, a pattern seems to emerge which reveals the underlying ideas of the different situations determining the oppositions brought about by the mind between silence and speech. Silence evokes contraction, intimacy, concentration, closed space, the interior; speech evokes enlargement, the impersonal, dilution, open space, the exterior. Silence brings man back towards himself like a centripetal force; speech alienates him by acting like a centrifugal force. This realization allows us to appreciate the true value of numerous taboos entailing the interruption of speech, which are felt by those involved to be directly related to normal life. For all these "forbiddens" would expose the transgressor to the heaviest of consequences, dissipation. We understand from this that these "forbiddens" are considered as means of protection and not simply as unwonted prescriptions.

The satisfaction of certain biological needs naturally places man in communication with the exterior. The rule has it that one abstains from speaking on these occasions; otherwise one would risk increasing one's own fragility already begun by the opening of the bodily orifices. The same prohibition is in effect for bathing because nudity is also an interaction with the exterior.[10]

The silence required of the man who transports seeds to the field and the man who sows *fonio*[11] seems more difficult to locate in the schema just proposed. And yet here too man manifests his intention to avoid the dispersion and scattering of that which, by necessity or by nature, is already engaged in expansion and diffusion. The seeds only promise a good crop on the condition of being first spread on the field. But while the distribution, seed by seed, in the soil is necessary, too great a dissemination is harmful. *Fonio*, with its tiny round grain, naturally possesses a great power of dispersion. What would happen to it if the sower "amplified" this property? Surely it would be better in either case to try to establish a fertile union between the arrangements which suit the human being's moral life and those which are in conformance with the life of the seed.

There is also a rule that engaged couples among the Bambara observe a total silence between themselves during the entire prenuptial period. The reason for this prohibition is commonly explained by the symbolism of the partners in marriage. They are likened to the sun (the man) and the earth (the woman). As soon as they are betrothed, meeting and speaking to each other is equivalent to admitting that the sun can reach the soil with a goal other than fecundation. At a certain level the explanation is undoubtedly valid. Yet, if we look at the prohibition morally, in terms of the ethics of marriage, a complementary and more profound meaning immediately appears. For the Bambara, marriage evokes the concepts of unity and cohesion. Within marriage man and woman combine to form a harmonious whole based essentially on intimacy and the interior. This is why coquetry is thought to be the worst enemy of the family, for it orients the human being towards the outside.[12] We thus understand the prohibition which forbids the engaged couple from addressing words to each other prior to their union.[13] Before marriage the future spouses are located on the path of the realization of unity; they are thus more exposed to dissipation than actual mates. In this state speech could only increase the fragility of their situation.[14]

Death and the practices which accompany it are equally marked by silence on the part of the living. Thus, for example, one should not speak in the presence of a dead person until he has been washed. During the burial the bearers of the corpse must observe silence; a widower does not speak during the first three days of his widowhood; and a widow does not speak during the washing of her head which occurs before her husband is placed in the tomb. Anyone crossing a cemetery must abstain from speaking. These types of conduct are integrated in the conception of silence as just defined. More than anything else, death marks separation, withdrawal, and dispersion. It wounds the unity of the human being whose constituent parts fall into disintegration and confusion with the termination of life. Death provides man with the experience of dissolution. But the character of necessity that it takes on does not destroy life's hope.[15] It obliges every mortal to a constant and unconscious effort of concentrating his being on himself, as if life were somehow experienced as gathering and convergence. As is sung in a lamentation: "Come closer, come closer; stay close together so that the hyena [death] does not eat us; stay close together so that the lion [death] does not eat us. Stay close together."

Thus emerges, according to Bambara thought, the true nature of silence. It is tied to life; it is a source of life since it leads to the conservation of existence which it otherwise protects. Its adoption as a fundamental moral virtue allows us to detect the specific features of the Bambara ethic. According to this ethic, human conduct is oriented directly towards life, that is, it follows life's plenitude and burgeoning, its advance and retreat. Just like life, which is above all adaptation over time, man's moral comportment is marked by adjustment and adaptation. In this domain there is no invariability but, on the contrary, a very great plasticity on the part of man.

The value of human action is gauged in terms of its positive or negative charge with regard to life. Only the endeavors tending to affirm one's essence are good and worthy of interest, that is, those which bring the human being back toward himself so he may affirm his everlastingness. The basis of the Bambara soul is thus concentration and meditation, and nothing is more despised by this Sudanese people than the individual who does not know how to, or cannot, have an inner life.

The ideal man, the hero, occupies an important place in the culture of this people precisely because their ethic valorizes above all the notions of subjugation and domination. In this respect the ethic creates the hero; further, any man who conforms to this ethic is a hero. Can one speak of courage and fearlessness greater than that necessary to conquer oneself, to become master of one's self? The Bambara do not think so. The ethic of this people goes beyond the framework of human conduct; it is a sort of wisdom. It brings man closer to the divinity, for he who is able to assure his domination over himself possesses interior peace and equilibrium, true detachment. Unshakable even before death, such a man has no reason to envy God.

The *korè* society is intended precisely to urge man to this final stage of his moral life by means of symbolic death and resurrection. These are not, however, vain words, for the inhibition of fear in the face of death is acquired during initiation into *korè* by the most realistic application of physical suffering and asceticism. The neophytes undergo the most painful vexations, beatings, burns, pricks, and suffocations, all of which they must endure with cheerfulness and perfect impassiveness. The "death" of the senses thus becomes the indispensable preliminary to symbolic death and, under these circumstances, one can naturally wonder if this symbolic death is not something more than a signifier pure and simple. Indeed, the distance between real and symbolic death is reduced to a minimum by that beginning of bodily destruction of which pain is the signal. Besides, socially, the entrance of men into *korè* is felt as a real death and resurrection. And when certain neophytes actually succumb to the treatment inflicted upon them, their disappearance is simply ascribed to the failure of the officiants in the "technique" of resurrection. Further, these "cases" are not even commented upon in the village. Silence merges here with death itself and both give to ethical life its true dimensions, those which elevate man above his humanity.

It should be noted, however, that the doctrine of *korè* does not allow equal rights to all human beings for the ennoblement which it bestows.

First, women are excluded from it because of the particular nature of their being; they realize as it were the goal intended by *korè* for men, the granting of "life." Thus, as generators and bases of humanity, they carry within them their own "letters of nobility." It would then be superfluous and unnecessary for them to be subjected to the *korè* rites. Secondly, men themselves are divided into "lords" and "slaves" and only the former are admitted to initiation into the *korè*, as if Bambara morality definitively distinguished two rules of conduct, one reserved for nobles and the other for "captives." In truth, the ethical principles outlined above are valid only for "nobles," for they alone are considered to be Bambara. One is thus led to study more closely the conceptualizations concerning "nobles" and "slaves."

Among the Bambara, man receives his social and ethical "definition" in relation to the profession he practices or the materials he manipulates. Thus for this Sudanese people there exist systems of conceptualizations related to agriculture, the forge, wood- and leather-working and the art of speech. The man who devotes himself to working the earth is "noble," he constitutes the *horoya* or "aristocracy," for this occupation allows the human being to be his own master. The farmer provides for all his alimentary needs by himself; his "fate" is played out, so to speak, in the relation between his diligence and the soil. There is no intermediary between him and the earth from which he draws his subsistence. Nobility, according to the Bambara, is fundamentally characterized by one's independence from others.

The holders of other skills manifest themselves quite differently. Their essential activity consists in assuring the farmer of that which he needs to fully accomplish his task. The blacksmith extracts iron and makes tools that are indispensable for working the earth. Artisans in wood and leather furnish, respectively, utensils necessary for the preparation of food and for its consumption, and objects intended for protection against contact with the ground (sandals) or for permitting the transport of drinking water (water-skins). Finally, the "master" of speech, the praise-singer, enhances the glory of the farmer through compliments and praises which he addresses to him in the most varied circumstances.

The skill of these four types of "technicians" does not directly procure for their holders the means of subsistence. The blacksmith, "carpenter," leather-worker, and praise-singer depend for their livelihood on what the farmer exchanges for their services. Their lives are dependent on him and they are practically his "slaves." As subordinates, they are despised by the farmer, who does not even consent to associate with them in marriage. The "slaves" live as castes, and if the "master" fears them because of the power which their skill confers upon them, they usually meet only with disdain on the part of "free" men.

Such are the ideas and attitudes concerning the two social categories which at the same time oppose and complete each other in daily life. It is fitting to note that in terms of ethics each of them lets a special type of man appear.

The farmer, a free and socially independent personage, is as it were conscious of his dignity. He is reserved and sober in his words and actions; he is proud and modest; he knows how to keep from speaking his feelings; he is preoccupied by his "salvation," which he pursues methodically and relentlessly. In his capacity as "master" he is often disdainful of others and surrounds himself with a considerable number of secrets and taboos which, like a spider's web, weave a complex network of prescriptions and rules around him. The farmer sees himself as exclusive, and only the earth is worthy of his company. His morality is sober and severe since in the final analysis it rivets him in the solitude and isolation of "law."

The man of caste, by contrast, represents freedom of behavior and relaxation. He does not live by inhibitions and has no reserve in his gestures and words. His force resides in the very power of his speech which he manipulates with elegance and skill. The praise-singer, in particular, is the consummate artisan of speech. His activity gave birth to a literary "genre" known under the name of *pasa* which includes all "literary" productions intended to stimulate the individual, to provoke awareness of his physical and moral strength, and to maintain his "tonicity." This concept allows us to understand that the praise-singer's action presupposes the existence of a latent force which resides in any living element in the universe and which certain words or actions have the capability of drawing from dormancy and of exalting. "This force is the *nyama*, which is probably comparable to a vibrating movement, and is the common principle of all beings, identical in inorganic matter and living beings though with several differences in degree."[16]

Indeed, all men of caste are manipulators of *nyama*, hence their common name *nyamakalaw* ("handles of *nyama*"). This permits us to better understand the moral situation of this category of human beings who are placed practically above the morality applicable to the society as a whole as represented by the farmers. The strength and moral liberty of the people of caste reside in the ease with which they treat *nyama*—that obscure power which, when freed from its material base, is capable of breaking out and causing the death of whomever confronts it.

The ethic of these men of caste thus finds its foundation in an element independent of the human being (or, it could be said, in an element of nature), while that of the nobles is rooted in the very souls of those who practice it. The former defines man in terms of his power of intervention. It emphasizes the human being's character of interference and intrusion in the forces of nature; it also reveals the mediating role of those who receive it as their share. The latter defines man in relation to himself; it allows the appearance of an actor at grips with the problem of himself. The ethic of men of caste opens onto action and the world; through it, the human being acts on the other. The ethic of the nobles opens onto itself; through it man acts on himself.

These characteristics of the morality of men of caste should not be considered as abstractions. On the contrary they are deeply fixed in the cultural traditions that concern this category of humans. Among the Bambara, as among other peoples of West Africa, the *nyamakalaw* play the role of mediators between two individuals or between two groups in a situation of conflict. If they are capable of fulfilling this function it is precisely because the ethical schema which suits them makes them intermediaries, that is, beings capable of effecting associations or dissociations. Turned toward the exterior, the *nyamakala* is the man of the elements, which he sometimes arranges in ingenious constructions and sometimes scatters and spreads in all directions.

The distance between mediator and warrior is not great. Both are combatants and both purpose to master and discipline discordant and antagonistic situations. This is why the man of caste is not only a conciliator and arbiter but also a warrior intimately associated with the fray of the battlefield. Among the Bambara, and in all of West Africa, the praise-singer was always found among the front lines of combatants. He was the first, it is said, to receive the "shock-wave" of battle.

All this helps us to better understand the connection which exists between the *nyamakalaw* and blood on the level of myths and legends concerning the origin of castes. Among the Bambara the ancestor of praise-singers, Sourakata, was created from the sacrificial blood of Faro (the water genie), while the blacksmith was created from the blood of his castration.[17] Among the Dogon the ancestors of men of caste were likewise considered to have issued from the Nommo (the homologue of Faro), who was sacrificed in the sky by God. The praise-singer was born from the blood of the throat, the blacksmith from the blood of the umbilical cord and the genitals.[18] A recent inquiry bearing on the legend of the Malinké praise-singers shows a similar relationship between them and blood. The praise-singer of old is intimately involved in scenes of violence if not war.[19] Thus myths and legends combine social phenomena and together find their foundation in an ethical conception of the human being, a conception divided between the power over oneself and the power over the other.

Because of the numerical superiority of people without caste and especially by reason of the autonomy which working the earth confers upon the human being, the holders of the power over the self deem themselves superior to the upholders of the ethic of power over the other. The differentiation between the two human groups goes so far that a social dichotomy is perceivable on the level of clans and lineages: nobles and slaves are exclusive in relation to each other, without the castes being exclusive among themselves (members of different castes marrying among themselves). This sentiment of superiority of the "nobles" towards their antagonists, the "slaves," does not however reflect the true reality. It proceeds more from a need to affirm the self (proper to the one who measures himself against himself) than from the consciousness of moral supremacy.

"Nobles" and "slaves" are found in a position of complementarity characterized by the play of reciprocal gifts. Yet this reciprocity is restrictive and never results in structures of matrimonial alliances. At first sight this might seem incomprehensible, given that the exchange of women undoubtedly expresses the most profound and perfect form of gift. However, if one looks closely at it, one perceives that there is a fundamental incompatibility between this sort of exchange and the nature of the partners. Thus the prohibition of marriage between the caste groups and the nobles, instead of being an aberrant norm, becomes the very rule of logic of the system regulating the relationships between the two groups. Indeed, the exchange of women results in an association which guarantees at every instant the power of the givers of women over those who are their takers and, inversely, the power of the takers of women over those who give them. The uterine nephew is thereby the focal point in this clash of power between the two groups. In the case of a marriage between nobles and caste members, the latter would be clearly at an advantage since, by their nature, they "have power" over others while the nobles "have power" only over themselves. Such a marriage would occur more as a rupture of the forces present and as a disequilibrium profiting the caste members than as a symmetrical agreement.

In support of these claims it should be noted that it is generally the nobles who prohibit marriage between themselves and people of caste, as if the feeling of repugnance toward this type of partner unconsciously revealed the admission of their own inferiority in terms of the groups' respective powers.

We are thus confronted with the most unexpected implications of the moral conceptions of the African. Through the mastery of self and the mastery of the *other,* man in West Africa actually rejects his own alienation. The two moral attitudes sketched here lead the human being to wish to be himself, to seek himself in his own blood and to reject that which is foreign. On the level of overt social behavior, this leads to long and detailed analyses of the "situation" of the spouse prior to marriage. It also leads to the overvalorization of the autonomy and independence of one's own lineage, one's own clan, and one's own country. Finally, one must not dismiss the possibility that the isolation of Africa over the centuries was due in large part to such ethical conceptions as those exemplified by the Bambara and Dogon and several other West African peoples.

Mysticism and Spirituality

9

Undoubtedly prompted by the demon of literature, the ethnographers who tell us of African trances emphasize their brutality. But African mysticism has its nuances, half-tones, and melodic lines. Among the Yoruba and Fon there is an entire civilization of spirituality comparable to that of the wood carvings and bronzes of Benin.

R. Bastide
Le Candomblé de Bahia

Until recently African religious practices hid from foreigners one of their most subtle and engaging aspects, the one which, by its appearances and motivations, is related to what the "great" religions call mystical life. There have been numerous factors limiting the analysis of religious phenomena and preventing the "noninitiated" from attaining the "sacred." The African was likened to the gentile for whom Christian revelation was lacking and who, because of this, was devoted to the worship of idols. African religion seemed devoid of nobility, elevation, and grandeur. Blood sacrifice and the comportment of the believer in the performance of his duties toward the revered powers (a comportment seemingly dominated by fear)—are these not evidence of a lesser religion, one incapable of lifting the follower to the heights of spirituality? Can there be a divine basis for beliefs which often tolerated drinking bouts and licentious behavior and the immolation and consumption of human beings? And what can be said of the strange phenomena of possession and "sorcery," which seem to stem more from dealings with demonic powers than from relations with the divinity?

Patient and meticulous research has been necessary in order to realize that African spirituality does not cede anything to that of the great religions. In both cases the human being is in search of a sort of deliverance capable of transfiguring his terrestrial condition. Like the believer in the so-called superior religions, the African is not only content to implore the pardon or aid of the divinity or to express his gratitude to him. He aspires to have contact with his god, he wishes for the sight of the one he adores, he longs to become the Other through a transformation which he nevertheless wishes not to be radical. Indeed, if the African neglects nothing in resolutely undertaking the path to celestial metamorphoses, he still insists on retaining his status as a man and living his life on earth. His mysticism thus does not correspond to a definitive and total change but rather to an indefinitely repeated experience of the divine. We will see how in his search for the beyond the African seeks, in sum, his life "insurance," the supreme remedy for death. This profoundly differentiates it from Christian mysticism, which is a conditional guarantee for life in the beyond, a leap of the soul leading to the irrevocable union of the subject and God.

The preliminaries of African mysticism are located on the level of the perishable casing that is the human being. The duality between the "soul" and the body is sharply felt by the African, who attributes to the first of these elements the characteristics of permanence and continuity, while he grants to the second change and growth. But, according to him, there can be no mystical life if the importance given to the body does not diminish to the advantage of the soul. Hence the eminent value earned in his eyes by the practices whose goal is physical suffering, mortification, and privation. All initiation societies emphasize this aspect of spiritual life. Asceticism of the body, it is thought, sharpens the sensitivity of the mind, conferring upon it a greater liberty by orienting it toward interior life.

Still, it would be wrong to consider the African mystic as a sort of contemplator whose "ecstasies" place him in a separate state. The mystical life of the African does not isolate the individual, nor does it strip him of his social loyalties, his duties, or his work. Rather, it permits him to realize himself more fully in his daily activity and his usual occupations. In fact the state of beatitude, the moments when man communicates with the Invisible, seem to be just as "natural" and consistent with the duties of life as any other type of activity. Generally speaking, there is to our knowledge no limitation either on the subject's sensitivity or ability to move, and often the person in a state of ecstasy displays a distinctive manner of behaving, a characteristic gestural expression. It is by these very signs that one can recognize man's entrance into communication with the world which is usually foreign to him. If we were to study the reactions of the "ecstatic" more deeply, we would be tempted to acknowledge that a supplementary, latent sense exists in the human being, a sense of "vision" whose activation is tied to the presence of certain specific stimuli of a linguistic, musical or biological order. Still it is certain that these stimulants do not act as isolated units but in the form of complex, perceptible schemata. They are shown and perceived in a ritual "atmosphere" of celebration. Finally, they are an integral part of a certain "climate" and it seems logical to think that under these circumstances and according to these modalities they provoke reactions on the part of man. We must, however, avoid reducing African mystical phenomena to simple relations of this type, since nothing obviates the hypothesis that the stimuli of which we have spoken are also sensitive mediators belonging to a much more subtle chain of elements whose exact nature escapes us.

From this point of view it is fitting to note the social character of "ecstasy" as well as its occurrence in time. In Africa the phenomenon of mysticism is rarely limited to individual cases. Most often it concerns "visions" affecting a group of subjects who pursue the same religious goal. In this respect one can speak of a conditioning of "believers" to perceive the principles which ordinary experience prohibits them from attaining. "Ecstasy" thus finds a place in a specialized technique of which certain members of society, the masters, are highly aware, while those who are subjected to it are usually ignorant of its ways and goal. It also seems that ecstatic phenomena do not "happen" unexpectedly, like "gifts" made at any time by the invisible powers. They coincide with events which are well defined in time: the period of initiation, the period of rites for obtaining rain, divination seances, and so on. African "ecstasy" thus appears as the result of a very precise knowledge on the part of the society which, by using the appropriate intermediaries (the "ecstatic" and the person responsible for his "training"), opens to it the paths of communication with the world inaccessible to human senses. It realizes society's endeavor to bring within the limits of the possible that which man cannot attain, know, or understand through ordinary sensory experience. It is surely here that the human being's true power as a "magician" resides. For even if, according to our point of view, the knowledge thus acquired is qualified as subjective, it is nonetheless true that for those concerned the irruption into the beyond constitutes the most profound expression of enjoyment and happiness. For them the vision of what is hidden is like a *challenge* issued to suffering and death and is also a proof that these two realities do not exhaust by themselves the totality of the contents of human destiny.

We can confidently affirm that throughout all of Africa the techniques for acquiring the state of "ecstasy" contain a common denominator, the temporary alienation of the very being of the person concerned. Participation in mystical life through ecstasy is "leaving" in order to "return," "abandoning" one's kinsmen in order to "find" them afterwards, and especially letting go of oneself totally in order to "recover" oneself anew. Mystical ecstasy is a "death" followed by resurrection.

It is fitting to say now that, thus defined, the situation of the mystic is only a specific case of a much broader cultural phenomenon which includes, as we will see, the case of the person "possessed" by spirits other than God, the case of the warrior and that of the hunter. In sum, the mystic seems to be differentiated from his peers only by the referential element to which he relates the acts centered in him.

In recent years "possession" by the divinity has been particularly well-studied in several West African peoples. It is thus to this geographical area that our remarks will be limited.

Among the Ashanti mystical life takes on a character more individual than social. The "call" is, so to speak, spontaneous and generally occurs at the time of celebrations and customary religious ceremonies. The person affected by divine favor abruptly changes the rhythm of his dance by accelerating it and giving evident signs of a rupture in communication between him and others. He can also fall into convulsions and, with wild eyes, start to tremble all over his body. Both of these symptoms are generally interpreted by the officiating priest as the surest index of divine solicitation; it is thus that the divinity chooses its servant in order to make of him his "wife." If the "chosen one" responds appropriately to these signals concerning his vocation, he begins an apprenticeship with a priest, who takes charge of his spiritual education.

Entrance into the service of the divinity actually corresponds to temporary detachment from the previous environment. For the two or three years of his instruction, the novice avoids his family and the society in which he lived previously; he goes to live with his master. Whether he is married or not, sexual relations are strictly forbidden since, as the "wife" of the divinity, he is obligated to remain faithful to his new partner. This obligation ceases as soon as the apprenticeship is finished and normal life is resumed.

According to Rattray, during the first year of his training the neophyte is familiarized with the ritual ablutions intended to strengthen his ankles, to make him more attractive to the divinity or, further, to permit him to enter into contact with the divinity.[1] The sight and hearing of the candidate are the object of altogether special care. If new trances are late in appearing, the priest applies certain "medicines" to the eyes of his pupil. He puts others under his pillow in order to "force," as it were, the spirit to become visible and audible. Plants which grow on graves are used in the preparation of these ablutions which aid contact with the beyond. During several consecutive nights the novice even takes his bath in the cemetery, although for these lustrations neither soap nor sponge is ever used, and cold water is required. All these techniques visibly lead to the isolation of the postulant, and they serve to create an atmosphere of exterior void and arid calm around him rather than, as we might think, one of fear. Particular prohibitions reinforce this climate of solitude for, in addition to the obligation of abstaining from certain social activities (the extraction of palm wine, the setting of fish traps, and so on), the candidate is required to live close to the sanctuary in order to strive "to hear and to listen to the voice of his god."[2]

During the second year the isolation of the novice becomes even more pronounced. He is strictly forbidden to go out at night with other young people, to go to the chief's court without being summoned there, and to participate in quarrels or to fight or gossip. He is henceforth provided with means of "protection," or *suman*, types of talismans which the postulant always keeps on him. He grants them special attention, for the *suman* is endowed with particular prohibitions which even further limit their owner's margin of freedom. According to the information furnished by Rattray, the wearing of "phylacteries" determines the conduct of those chosen while they eat. Thus, for example, in order to respect the prohibitions of his *suman* called *gyeme*, the Ashanti novice does not have the right, during his meal, to name by their proper names those animals known to be particularly voracious, such as the lion, hyena, or panther. He can only avoid this prohibition by using euphemisms. This undoubtedly reveals one of the characteristic traits of the mystic's alimentary behavior, ritual gluttony, which (as we will see later among the Bambara) symbolizes man's greediness with regard to knowledge.

Finally, during the third year, the neophyte devotes himself to the acquisition of knowledge intended to develop his gifts as a "clairvoyant." In particular he learns how to divine by means of water. He also strives, as will be seen concerning the Bambara, to deepen his intellectual aptitude for grasping the relationships between things. Towards this end he is presented with a pot filled with water, in which various ingredients are placed. He is then asked to remove the substances from the container while his master reveals to him their meaning(s).[3] It is thus during this period that the novice learns to go beyond reality. He is instructed in how to surpass immediate sensory data in order to grasp and understand their significance. In sum, the final phase of the Ashanti mystic's education consists of apprenticeship in the most subtle "detachment" of the human being with regard to things.

Such training necessarily leads the candidate to the "sacerdotal" office. In addition, special rites of enthronement consecrate him to this new state: he becomes the "spouse" of the divinity and can in turn go on to the instruction of other adepts. For these the "priests" often recruit women who, after their mystical training, become auxiliaries (*woyo*) of the "priests." It is they, in fact, who are responsible for periodically entering into trance in order to bring the message of God to the believers who ask them for it. These initiates receive a new name and often learn a secret language. They become

the passive instruments of the gods and carry no authority whatever except when they are possessed. The priest himself is never pos-

sessed. He would be ineligible for the prie
receives the messages, and any instructions
those messages are issued by him. Each god h
appointment is an official one, and she live
worshippers as does the priest himself.[4]

The Ashanti mystical "system," to which tl
in the northern Mossi kingdom) as well as th
undoubtedly be connected, seems to correspond to the
contemplators:

1. The priests who, after having given the overt signs of their calling
and after an appropriate training, become "sensitized" to the beyond to
the point that they can be considered as permanent "ecstatics." Their
comprehension of "divine" things is such that they themselves can be
considered to be gods. Thus there is no need, once their novitiate is
finished, for them to enter into communication with the divinity
through the intermediary of the trance.

2. The women (*woyo*) who do not have access to the integral knowledge of things "from above," and so utilize the trance in order to communicate intermittently with the divinity.

For the "mystic-priests" the "incarnation" of the divinity continues
without interruption, while for the *"woyo* women" it is ephemeral and
transitory. But in either case the change in personality remains marked
by two characteristic events: the symbolic death and resurrection of the
ecstatic. This aspect of mystical rapture is even more evident among the
Fon.

Among the Fon, apprenticeship in mystical life possesses a collective
character. The initiation of boys and girls takes place in the "houses of
worship" or "houses of god," which are types of "convents." As among
the Ashanti, the recruitment of adepts is selective. It is determined
either by a "seizure" of possession, occurring at any time during the
year (but especially during the great annual festivals of the divinities), by
the consultation of an oracle which designates the future postulant, or,
finally, by the direct request of the priests to the family heads. In the first
case, the future novice is brought into the "house of god" during or
immediately after the "attack" itself; often he rushes into it on his own
while in trance. In the other cases the recruits are asked by the priest to
present themselves before him in the convent where they give their
official assent to their future mission as servants of god.

For the great cults, such as those of the gods of thunder and earth
(respectively, So-Shango and Sakpata-Shokpona), the ritual cycle in
which the postulants are engaged includes, at the beginning, the impressive public ceremony of their death and resurrection. The candidates
are asked to participate in that day's dance, occurring in front of the

y door, which is covered with a polychrome mat of red, white,
lack. As a preliminary a goat had been sacrificed and its blood
red on the principal sanctuary. When the dance reaches its climax:

the secretly designated candidate soon cries out, and works his way
through the excited crowd into the midst of the dancers, where he
begins to twirl wildly. He dances even more furiously until he falls
stark on the ground, as in an epileptic fit. The dancers, after circling
round the "corpse," wrap it in a shroud and, singing dirges, carry it
into the convent.

The laity believe that the neophyte has actually died. . . .

Once in the convent, the shroud is undone, and drink is given. The
novice is instructed in his future role and how to act. Each night for
seven nights he sleeps in his shroud. A goat is killed, and its blood
and skin reserved for later use. On the evening of the seventh day,
the wrapped body is borne into the temple, and the body smeared
with "medicine." Songs are sung round the "corpse," and the parents may be allowed to assist at this ceremony.

On the eighth day is held the ceremony of "resurrection." The
neophyte is held by outsiders to have been dead since the week
before, and now to be raised by the power of the god. Hence there is
great excitement and anticipation. The usual preliminaries of sacrifice
precede dancing in the public place.

The supposed corpse is then carried out of the convent by acolytes.
It is wrapped in reed mats, as for a funeral, and smells abominably,
because wrapped in with it is the putrefying skin of the goat or fowl
which was killed the week before. Women kneel by the corpse,
sprinkle it with water, and fan away the flies.

The priest then comes forward and, kneeling by the "corpse," he
calls upon the god for help to restore the dead one to life. Seven times
he calls upon the "deceased" by name, and it is not until the seventh
time, when the relatives begin to get anxious, that the body gives a
grunt. The others then press round and unfasten the grave clothes.
They lift up the neophyte, whose body is daubed red and white. With
their aid he staggers seven times round the drums, and is then led
into the convent to begin his training and become a new being, to the
thunderous applause of the excited crowd.[5]

Thereafter the novice is considered as a "prisoner of war" of the god
who "ravished" him. His family continues to see him each morning
when bringing him the provisions of food for which they are responsible. All contact with the child is strictly limited to this visit until the end
of his religious retreat, which lasts seven to nine months and corresponds, in fact, to the neophyte's moral, intellectual, and spiritual
training. For him it is a matter of acquiring a new personality consistent
with his new state. From a simple mortal he has become the "wife" of
the divinity and consequently he has the duty of anointing his body to

please his "husband," and of keeping watch on all his acts in order to remain faithful to him. Boys and girls take their meals separately, but each group utilizes a common dish and carries the food to the mouth with the left hand, as it is this one that belongs to god. The practice is perhaps even more significant if one realizes that, like all other African peoples, the Fon in ordinary life use their right hand for eating. It would tend to show the real position of the recluse, which is inverted in relation to that of the layman.

The change in the personality of the novice is equally apparent on other levels. During his retreat he receives a new name. After he has left the convent and goes about his usual tasks,

> if anyone calls him by his old name, he will fall down as if dead, or call out the person's name; for his own self died before his entry to the convent. A heavy fine will be imposed upon the offender, sacrifice must be offered to the deity, and all or part of the training of the novice may have to be undertaken afresh.[6]

The training given in the convent also operates in the area of language. The neophytes are generally made to learn a new language, one which does not seem to be either a secret way of speaking or a jargon, but simply the dialect of the region in which originated the cult of the god served by the candidate.

At the end of the period of his spiritual training, the novice receives from his master the final instructions concerning his conduct in life. He becomes familiar with the prohibitions of the god and the "commandments" he must observe, for example, respect for others, obedience to relatives and elders, and discretion. Finally, on the day of his departure from the convent, the new mystic is bought back by his family.

> Gathered in groups before the priest, he tells the families that these are prisoners that have been captured, which will they choose? Each family makes a pretence of looking out a good captive, but finally selects its own relative. A small present is given to the devotee, and he embraces his family and gives one cowrie in return. He then goes to his own home to live, but pretends to be a prisoner from a far country still, who has been exchanged for the true son of the family who is in exile.[7]

As can be seen, in spite of differing external characteristics, Fon mysticism is consistent with that part of the Ashanti model which deals with permanent "ecstatics." Although they are of different status, the Ashanti "priest" and the Fon "layman" enjoy a common intermediary state, one whose nature consists of a certain sacralization of man through the "descent" of the divinity in him.

The Bambara mystical "system" offers multiple points of similarity with the Ashanti and Fon models. The only striking difference is found in the recruitment of the mystics. Among this Sudanese people of the middle Niger valley, recruitment is selective only on the level of sex and social compartmentalization into free men and "slaves." For them neither women nor castes have access to the mystical experience controlled by the society. Conversely, all free men have the duty of becoming the "wives" of god by undergoing the appropriate initiatory rites.

In truth, Bambara mysticism does not occur in an individual's life as an unusual and unexpected phenomenon. It is anticipated since early childhood, so that at the moment when the man approaches it, it appears to him as the outcome of a considerable amount of effort and hardship. The mystical experience is here the crowning of the preceding initiatory activities, which might be justly considered as the "ferment" allowing man the profound interior change to which the final initiation, *korè*, leads.

In order to visualize the subtle mechanism to which the individual is submitted on the path to his "deification," a brief account of Bambara religious "doctrine" is indispensable. This "doctrine" does not constitute a theoretical corpus, even one oral in nature, which one would find "ready-made." It is rather a diffuse body of knowledge, more or less explicit, retained by old men of different social levels and occupying diverse religious offices. And above all it is a *praxis*, in the sense of an action which organizes and transforms the human being. The religious doctrine is put in concrete form by six initiation societies, or *dyow* (*n'domo, komo, nama, kono, tyi wara,* and *korè*), which must be braved by each individual desirous of conforming to the human ideal.

It would take too long to set forth in detail the various correspondences which the Bambara grant to the set of *dyow* and, in any case, that is not the aim of this work. Still, in order that the African's ascent toward mysticism be better discerned, we will briefly note a few details about the structuring of the initiatory process.

The *dyow* find their concrete model in the human being himself and so, say the Bambara, the *dyow* are associated with the six principal articulations of the body. The joints of the lower limbs are related to movement as a preoccupation of inquiry and research, while those of the upper limbs are associated with "doing." Parallel to this configuration, the Bambara establish a connection between the *dyow* and the sensory organs, since both reveal man's contact with exterior reality. Thus the initiatory societies are envisaged as elements of life oriented towards the exterior. Finally, the model of the human body furnishes another connection with the *dyow*, according to which they appear as a kind of living organism.

The *n'domo* and *korè* mark, respectively, the first step and the conclusion of initiatory life. They are so intimately tied to each other that one, the *korè*, is perceived on the model of the other. They represent the extreme, essential, and inseparable stages along the path to knowledge.

According to the Bambara, the structure of knowledge postulates that man be instructed first in that which he was before society took charge of him: an exemplary being, androgynous, beautiful, but living in and of his solitude. It is *n'domo* that is responsible for revealing this fundamental aspect of education. Associated with the ankle, the sense of direction, the foot and the leg, it is perfect for fulfilling this task for, in this context, it signifies balance, determination, and foundation. This being so, it is natural that *n'domo* is limited to uncircumcised children, that is, man before his socialization, when he carries within him both masculinity and femininity. The *n'domo* is thus unique among the societies, as it is a sort of model which "potentially" contains all the other *dyow*. Circumcision, which marks the departure from *n'domo*, emphasizes still further the deep chasm separating this initiation society from the five other *dyow*. At the same time, however, it orients all instruction dispensed to the individual afterwards. By stripping man of his original femininity (through the removal of the foreskin), circumcision both suppresses monologue and channels reflection towards the other. The latter is, depending on the circumstances, either knowledge itself, the soul, woman, or consciousness; this Other can also be agriculture, immortality and God.

From the "mouth" of *komo* the initiate learns all that is appropriate to know about the nature of knowledge and its relationship to humans. Associated with the knee, the sense of touch, and the vocal organs, the *komo* is qualified to instruct the initiate on the nature of speech and the "form" and "volume" of knowledge.

The same initiate learns from *nama* the nature of the union between the soul and the body, between man and woman, between good and evil. The correspondence of this *dyo* with the hip joint, the sense of smell, the thighs, and the genital organs enables it to "treat" these problems since all these parts of the body are considered as "makers" of society.

The *kono* teaches about that which deals with the nature of the human being and with the duality of mind and body. *Kono* is the *dyo* of man's judgment and consciousness. Its relation to the elbow, taste, the nose, and the ears is significant. The articulation of the arm recalls man's contact with God, the discernment of flavors marks the just evaluation of the soul and matter, and the organs of smell and hearing reveal intellectual sensitivity and flair.

Tyi wara encompasses everything that concerns man's relationship with the sun and the earth, the stars and seasons, animals and plants, iron and the techniques of producing agricultural tools, and clothing and ornaments. It is a synthesis of man from the perspective of the activity of his hands. This enables us to grasp the aptness of the connections drawn between this *dyo* and the shoulder, hearing, the hands, and the stomach. Owing to the fecundating power of received speech, the ear is directly connected to human achievements brought about by the other organs of this correlative set.

Finally, at the summit of the edifice of knowledge is *korè*, whose teaching deals with the spiritualization and divinization of man. By its vast initiatory program extending over two consecutive years and by the content and character of its revelations, this *dyo* marks the end and completion of knowledge. The wrist, eyes, and brain, to which this society is associated, clearly illustrate the determinant role which they play in the conduct of the person.

All that has just been said can be summarized in the following few sentences. The knowledge of self (*n'domo*) engenders the investigation of the subject of knowledge itself (*komo*) and leads man to confront what is social (*nama*). From this is born judgment and moral consciousness (*kono*), owing to which knowledge approaches the cosmos (*tyi wara*) in order to terminate in the divinity (*korè*).

One can thus see the manner in which mystical life, which blossoms in *korè*, is prepared for and based in long training over the course of the five other initiation societies. By eliminating the intermediary links between the first and last *dyo*, it could be said that the essential relation in this group is the one uniting the knowledge of self (*n'domo*) with the knowledge of God (*korè*).[8]

Knowledge of God, deification of man, overflowing of plenitude, ennoblement of man—*korè* is all these things. This, at least, is how it is seen by its followers. The eminent value of *korè* results from the fact that it makes the human being equal to God, that it deifies those whom it "kills." This is to say that it makes people "immortal" as would a kind of sacrament consisting of the granting of the eternity of God to mortals.

The effect of *korè* would nevertheless remain unintelligible if it were isolated from the "doctrine" of reincarnation, which is the very foundation of religious life among the Bambara. Greatly simplifying things, we can say that at death the spiritual principles of every human being return to God.[9] However, because of the nonconformity and disproportionality which exist between the divinity and man as he is when he leaves the "hands" of the creator, God preserves a part of these spiritual principles at each union. Thus "natural" man dies and is reincarnated a certain number of times, until the divinity has entirely "absorbed" him and does not agree to give him up again. It is to mitigate this disadvantage that *korè* proposes the divinization of the human being while he is living in order to endow him with another "nature" which connects him to the divinity and is even made to identify with him. Thus, while periodically attracting man to him (at the time of his death), God is no longer able to hold him back definitively, and so reincarnations will continue without end. Man will have conquered the prerogative of God.

The situation of the mortal deprived of the help of *korè* is recalled annually during the six years which precede the septennial ceremonies of this initiation society. Once a year the children of the village go to the market to steal the peddlars' merchandise for fun. The booty of this ritual pilfering is put away in a hidden place known only to them. The peddlars know that this is the prelude to the festivities of *korè*. When they become aware of it, they go to the head of this institution and, for a few cowries, buy back their goods. The rite presents in allegorical form man's situation on the "natural" religious plane; it is the image of reincarnation on the way to extinction. Like the merchants' goods, man is "stolen" by death and must, so to speak, search for himself in order to buy himself back. Supposing, however, that he is "stolen" very often, he will end up in ruin from these transactions. Without "ransom" it will no longer be possible for him to recover his own "merchandise" and he will cease to exist among the living.

To thwart this progressive "disembodiment" of the human being, *korè* proposes its own technique, which consists essentially of the sublimation of pain and death. The undertaking is subject to a basic preliminary: the adept's symbolic death, which corresponds at the same time to a sort of life in the tomb, the fetal stage, and the return to animality. By "being reborn" after his period of training, the mystic will be the revived person par excellence, the man become God, the permanent "ecstatic."

From the first day of their retreat in the brotherhood's sacred wood, the initiates in *korè* are submitted to tests meant to symbolize their death. The social isolation to which they are held during their initiation likewise contributes to maintaining, in them and in the social life of the village, this atmosphere of abandonment, separation, and solitude which characterizes the world of the dead. Among these trials the most commonly employed are the following: the placing of two knives, one iron, the other wood, on the tongue; "burial" under a skin impregnated with irritating substances; walking on burning cinders; passage under an arch; and a short stay in a straw hut. The test of the knives symbolizes, strictly speaking, the "life" and "death" of the postulants. The iron knife is believed to "kill" them, the wooden one to instill in them the germ of life. In truth it is only at the end of their retreat that the neophytes are considered to be "revived," but the wooden tool already introduces in them the seed of life, because wood and the tree are generally the image of renewal. The novices' "death" is felt in a very realistic fashion. Their bodies must be deprived of the care which a living person usually gives his body. In addition, the postulants sleep on a bed of leaves on the ground, and they drink without using their arms. The torture of the skin involves their entombment as well as their return to the maternal womb, since the skin signifies not only the shroud but also the placenta. The trial by ashes corresponds both to a purification and to a renunciation of personal taste and preference. The passage under the arch which the initiates can only execute while crawling on all fours recalls their obligation to seek the knowledge of God by experiencing their own weakness, for the arch represents the celestial vault. Finally, the stay in the straw hut is likened to the "smoking" of the neophytes: they represent the "food" of God while the straw hut evokes the kitchen. In sum, in a synthesis of acts and images, the five trials recall the condition of the man who "dies" in relation to society and himself in order to become a new being closer to God than to men.

Two weeks after the initiates' symbolic death the rite of their "resurrection" takes place. This rite, contrary to what we may recall among the Fon, does not contain the idea of a return to life of the decomposing "corpse." Rather, it is patterned after the model of birth from the maternal womb. Consequently the principal stages which mark this initial phase of life are characterized by the following ceremonies: the placing of the child on the ground, his being washed with ordinary water, the tasting of that water by the newborn, insufflation, ablutions with millet beer, impressing movements on the limbs, and dressing. This is why, when the initiates "return" to life, *korè* performs a procedure involving aspersions and anointings, bathings and insufflations, beating and the dressing of the postulants. The meaning of all these operations is, however, transposed onto the spiritual plane. The aspersions and bathings are intended to remove that which obscures the mind; the anointings to put the mind in "effervescence" and to give it the taste and pleasure of dealing with the Invisible. The insufflations, performed on the ears, eyes, nose, and mouth, tend to waken the corresponding senses in order to sensitize them to contact with spiritual realities. The beatings, complemented by the motions impressed on the newborn's limbs, correspond to the cooperative behavior which the initiate must adopt toward the teaching dispensed to him. Finally, the dressing with a new cloth marks the appearance and display of the new man in all his spiritual beauty. At the end of the rite of "resurrection" a meal is served to all the initiates. It consists of a thick porridge of millet accompanied by a sauce of baobab leaves which is necessarily devoid of all condiments. It is thought that the blandness of the food shows the excellence of the new being's "taste," which is capable of experiencing the flavor of any substance.

The very day of their "return" to life, and thus of their entrance into communion with the divinity, the initiates are divided among the eight classes of *korè*, each of which signifies their accession to the "residences" of mystical life. This event marks the beginning of the next phase of initiation into *korè*, which takes place one year after the first and, like it, lasts two weeks.

The subject of the second phase, whose basic principle is divine "illumination," takes as its theme the period of the individual's life between birth and the completion of circumcision. The prominent features of this model consist of the granting of the newborn's soul (*ni*), the dropping off of the umbilical cord, the cutting of hair and the giving of a first name, followed by the ceremonies which mark the sixth day after circumcision (*daworo*) and, finally, the completion of this same rite. This is to say that this part of the initiation is marked in turn by five particularly significant corresponding events. By their "resurrection," the initiates become "deified" humans, although they still do not have the totality of their new soul. Like the newborn children who only acquire their *ni* six days after birth,[10] the adepts of *korè* receive the fullness of theirs on the sixth day of this second initiatory phase. This signifies that beginning with this event they are oriented towards a certain independence connoting the very status of the individual. This autonomy in relation to God is totally enjoyed beginning on the seventh day, which corresponds to the dropping off of the newborn's umbilical cord. The next day, which in the calendar of rites following birth is marked by the cutting of hair and the assigning of a name, is characterized in *korè* by various anointings and aspersions of the adepts' heads. But, in the same way that the rites concerning the child actually underlie the manifestation of the ancestor incarnate in him, so the corresponding rites of *korè* show the recognition of divine incarnation in the postulant. Beginning on the eighth day of this initiatory phase the initiates become gods. Better still, they are sons of a reincarnated God, lacking only the title of the divinity if the reincarnation of the divinity can be said to follow the rules of that performed by the ancestor in the world of humans.[11]

The period which, on the profane level, stretches between the eighth day after birth and the end of the fifth day after circumcision is not markedly valorized by *korè*. This is not the case for the sixth day after circumcision, which finds significant correspondences with and is assigned to the ninth day of initiation. On this day the initiates are furnished with a sort of sistrum made up of two circles of calabash with a space between them, from whose edge stems of a particular grassy plant hang like fringes.[12] The emblem resembles the sistra of the newly circumcised which, devoid of fringes the first five days following circumcision, are "dressed" starting on the sixth day. The process symbolizes the state of ignorance of the human being (the "naked" sistrum) and the state of man having attained knowledge (the "dressed" sistrum). During the day the adepts manipulate them with a twisting movement. By this motion the hanging ends of the stems are separated from their core, so that the object gives the impression of swelling with each movement and deflating when it returns to a state of rest. The rite is intended to exalt the arrival of the man-god at the supreme phase of knowledge. It celebrates that period in the life of the "revived" person when, like the other kind of "newly circumcised" person, he dons festival clothes in order to enter into communion with supreme wisdom.

Finally, by transposing it to the plane of initiation itself, *korè* valorizes the closing rite of circumcision. This is characterized by the burning at the village crossroads of all materials with which the circumcized had contact during their seclusion. From the perspective of *korè*, this rite is repeated under several forms: the sistra spoken of earlier are abandoned in the sacred wood of the brotherhood, and the debris of costumes and objects used during the initiatory period are burned. Like the closing rite of circumcision, this signifies the definitive renunciation of one state and the accession to another, considered perfect in relation to the preceding one. Both cases are concerned, in fact, with the rejection of the congenital "ignorance" which accompanies every human being coming into the world.[13] But while at the end of circumcision man only partially rids himself of his "incapacity" to grasp things, at the close of initiation into *korè* he completely frees himself of it. His soul attains supreme perfection.

Parallel to these characteristic phases of his training, the Bambara mystic undergoes an apprenticeship in depth, one more refined and subtle, which has to do with gaining awareness of his ascension towards God. This aspect of the adepts' spiritual life is visible at the level of his belonging to one of the eight classes of *korè.*

These classes appear as a succession of stages, marked at the bottom by the category of *sulaw* and at the top by that of *karaw*. They are the phases which man is believed to pass through after his symbolic death, which he undergoes at the beginning of the initiation in his approach towards God. Without doubt, each initiate, by the office he holds within *korè*, belongs to only one class, which thus characterizes his definitive place in the brotherhood. However, *korè* integrates him into its own dialectic, which leads the neophyte to realize within him the essence of each of the eight categories.

The starting point of the adept's theomorphosis is constituted by his animality, as represented by the class of *sulaw* (literally, colobus monkeys): anyone admitted into the brotherhood must first become aware of his participation in animal nature. Indeed, *korè* reminds him of this quite brutally during the first period of initiation. The bodily trials and maltreatment to which he is subjected orient his mind in the same direction. The "presence" of his body is made acutely real by suffering.

Furnished with this idea, the man of *korè* reaches the stage represented by the *bisatigiw* (literally, "masters of the whip"), whose essential characteristic is the spiritual quietude which results from the mastery of the tongue and power over oneself.

The fundamental consequence of the acquisition of self-mastery is the adepts' accession to the great knowledge belonging to the members of the class of *surukuw* (literally, "hyenas"). Contrary to what is represented by the gluttonous animal whose name they use as an epithet, the *surukuw* evoke the stability and balance appropriate to any being which is neither curious, greedy, nor unappeased.

From this stage the adept arrives at the phase of illumination and purification of the mind belonging to the *tatuguw* (literally, "firebearers"). The fire in question is constituted by the divinity itself, who sets fire to the initiate but does not consume him, or only consumes the "old man" in him. This fire is also the purifying element which rids man of his preconceptions and makes him capable of serving as guide to his fellow men.

The four stages which we have just sketched form a complex which, though profoundly mystical, is located on an "inferior" level of spirituality. Through effort and asceticism they place the wise man in the best frame of mind to "see God" and to lay out his path before he attains joy. The four following stages are the mark of the union and co-penetration between man and the Invisible.

The class of *korè dugaw* (literally, "vultures of *korè*") constitute the "abode" of spiritual joy and pleasure, features which are perceptible in the "obscene" and "lascivious" behavior of these initiates. The adept who has reached this stage experiences union with God as a marriage; man here becomes the "wife" of the divinity. Still, the "consummation" of this mystic marriage is only achieved at the following stage.

This stage is represented by the *kurumaw* (literally, "bruised ones")[14] whose spectacular behavior consists of tearing the body with the aid of thorns. The action is symbolically felt as the deflowering of a woman and the sacrifice of oneself, which mystically signifies God's taking possession of his wife, the adept. In realizing his theomorphosis, the adept undergoes, like a new bride, the deflowering of his soul, without which his "sacrifice" would be sterile.

The next to last marker on the path of the mystic headed toward his deification is symbolized by the *dyaraw* (literally, "lions") who are the expression of the nobility, justice, and serenity of God. This "abode" is that of the royal power of the divine "wife." After his "wedding" and his "fecundation," the adept takes his place next to his "husband"; like him he becomes "royal" and acquires the prerogatives of command. From the mystical point of view, the "lion-man" borders on identity with God, but he only achieves it at the following stage, the final one.

In the "abode" of the *karaw,* the initiate arrives at "identity" with the divinity. He is "the same as the Other" or, better, "the same and the Other"; he achieves "unity." This perfect likeness is represented by the emblem of the *karaw* class composed of one or several small planks representing God in the form of a hand but interpreted at the same time as a face.[15] By this is expressed the "initiate-God association" corresponding to the notion of "hand-face" or "do-say" or "act-speech," all aspects of the same being.

This is incontestably the culmination of the mysticism of *korè*. It is, however, a mysticism which to our knowledge does not offer ecstatic experiences through trances but which is the result of the adept's long labor in conforming to an invisible model inculcated in him through the rites. By analogy to the first four stages, those we have just described in turn form a whole which corresponds to the superior level of spiritual life, that of joy, pleasure, and gaiety. They mark the stages of intimate union with God, the soul's entrance into the domain of "fecundity" and "procreation," which corresponds to the maturity of the spiritual man.

The two parts of the mystical path should not be considered as corresponding to an actual dichotomy in Bambara mysticism. They are only two complementary aspects of a single whole, the first marked by the ideas of effort and struggle, the second by the concepts of abandonment and relaxation. When understood in this way, the mystic path of *korè* takes on its full meaning. It is an ascension towards "marriage" and intimate union with God, a ladder allowing one to rise to the divine being. The more one rises the more profound is the union with the coveted being. In fact, on the path of spiritual ascension, everything occurs as if, by approaching the divinity, man had changed his "sexual" identity in order to come closer to femininity. To put it whimsically, one might also say that according to Bambara mysticism the "kingdom of God" is the "kingdom of women."

If we now try to follow the mystic in the very practice of his life as an "ecstatic," his attitude towards his new condition appears to be characterized by two fundamental features which, moreover, run like a leitmotif all through his spiritual training. The *korè* adept displays a type of behavior which can accurately be defined as a return to childhood. He also adopts a stance towards pain and death that tends to deny their reality.

The adepts of the *korè dugaw* class in particular preach this "displacement" towards childhood. In their dress they openly sport costumes which provoke hilarity.[16]

> Next to men in baggy shorts are men in rags or in tight pants made of thirty-six pieces having thirty-six colors, one leg of which goes down to the ankle while the other does not even reach the knee. Some brandish wooden sabres, others jump and kick while astride a bamboo pole, a reed or millet stalk.[17]

The entire behavior of these initiates tends towards the comic and all that comes to their minds is expressed in a burlesque way. By his playful and facetious character, the *korè duga* appears as an adult whose mentality indicates a regression to the stage of childhood. This is corroborated too by the attitudes exhibiting foolishness and ignorance. The *korè duga* declares himself to be a "fool," "imbecile," and "idiot." He shows off his failure to recognize hygienic norms by eating in a thoughtless fashion or by concocting his "dishes" out of strange foods mixed together. He places himself outside the fundamental rules of well-being, as if he no longer possessed the idea of social life.

The *korè* adept's return to childhood corresponds, in truth, to the affirmation of his interior satisfaction. Feeling himself to be of the same nature as his creator, he channels the overflow of his joy into childish amusements and jests. His behavior, revealing simplicity if not ineptitude, is intended to express the feeling of blindness of the mind in its confrontation with the spiritual "discoveries" witnessed by the *korè duga*. In regard to these higher things, he is like a "blind hippopotamus" placed in the middle of a thicket with no exit. Ignorance here changes to the confession of the mind's inability to penetrate obscurity and mystery.

It should be said that a more careful examination of the diversions and drolleries of the *korè dugaw* reveals the intimate relationship which exists between this manner of showing oneself in public and the ideas attached to pain and death which also belong to this class of initiates. From one end of the two periods of initiation to the other, suffering is given free rein. The postulants feel it in the form of mortification and asceticism inflicted by their elders, but these practices teach man control over himself. Owing to them, he becomes master of his tongue, his tastes and desires, his movements and the social relations which he can establish. Through suffering, man becomes "his own owner" and this title confers on him the quietude and detachment which characterize the true wise man. Here, then, pain flows directly into pleasure and joy.

Death, which for most men is the greatest pain, is emptied by *korè* of any painful or distressing meaning. For the mystic it is union and marriage. This is so much so that in the past, at the death of a *korè duga*, his colleagues would announce everywhere that there had been a "wedding" among them. They would leave the neighborhood, and the dead man would be buried by the people of another neighborhood. Furthermore, *korè* forbids the use of the word "death" (*su*) in normal speech. Sidibé Mamby tells us: "Thus, by homonymy and sympathetic harmony, the *korè duga* also cannot say the name of the five-centime coin, a *sou*." This explains the meaning of one of the *korè* songs, which recommends that humans take more time in their reflections on the present and the conditions of their birth rather than on their death. Thus pain and death are both ultimately visualized as phenomena generating, for those who know how to "see," a sense of well-being and happiness. This happiness is procured by victory over oneself, the consequence of agonistic contact with suffering. It is also conferred by the unusual "marriage" that is death.

The sublimation of suffering and death as well as the interior fullness which it engenders prevent the *korè duga* from keeping his profound satisfaction to himself.

> Having arrived at this stage of perfection..., he has the duty of shouting his joy, of breaking the ties of inhibitions in order to reveal himself externally. He must show that he enjoys the most total freedom. He must dance...his gaiety.... His liberty can even go so far that he has the ability to execute this dance poorly, intentionally, so as to show that he is above his own game.... And it is thus that the "buffoons" give themselves up to the funniest jokes and amusements imaginable. By their dress, gestures, and words, they show their contempt for any conformity; they mimic in a burlesque way the most serious and sacred things; they publicly parody what is private and intimate. Lastly, they divert certain things from their finality to better show the simplicity and freedom of childhood. For the comedy which they create and the laughter to which it gives birth are the expression of the life which is not concerned with rules or obstacles, the life which ridicules halts and limits.[18]

In sum one can confidently state that the behavior of the Bambara mystic results from a certain experience of the divine. A question immediately comes to mind: what knowledge of God does the human being acquire through this confrontation? It is in the accounts of the *karaw* of *korè*, kinds of tirades meant specifically to provide the adepts with explanations on the subject of the nature of the divine being, that the answer to this fundamental question can in large part be found. Indeed, God often appears there under various names and epithets which allow a glimpse of his essence. He is *Yori*, sovereign authority and beginning of everything that exists; "crossroads," that is, pivot on which everything rests and around which everything gravitates; "meeting-space," thus omnipotence and domination; and "celestial vault," which indicates immensity and distance. God is also "furnace," which recalls the "burning" and "incendiary" character of the divinity; "transformation," that is, transfiguration of the man who approaches him; and "savanna," a term which reflects his richness and opulence. He is also called "tension of the mind" and "waiting of the heart" to signify respectively the immediate energy which he represents and his patience. But the "attribute" which best fits the divine being is surely the one which defines him as a "spindle," "fecundating" itself and getting bigger as the spinning progresses. The *korè* language means by this that the more one speaks of God, the more he becomes "thick" and unintelligible. Does this mean that man should never evoke God? Far from it. The *korè* has as its very mission to discover the path for arriving at God and to reveal this itself; it tries to communicate to man the overflow resulting from divine plenitude. Since, basically, if God is the profound and impenetrable being to which man is devoted in his mystical life, it is no less true that he is also a desire comparable to a "voice" buried in the soul. He is the "voice of the voice," as *korè* designates him, which the human being can and must make emerge for his ennoblement and continuity without end.

Initiation into *korè* is not only a recommendation but a social obligation necessary to maintain the harmony of humanity and the world. However, it should not be thought that the mysticism of *korè* isolates the brotherhood's adepts from the common run of mortals and makes them lose the sense of concrete realities. On the contrary, it is the crowning of the life of a Bambara man. Also, even while knowing himself to be revived and transformed into God, the Bambara man carries out his usual occupations by projecting his mystical marriage on the marriage which he contracted with his wife, on the one which he perceives between the sun and the soil, and also on the one which is periodically established between the hoe and the earth. In sum, this mystical experience does not at all destroy the daily life of the "ecstatic." Rather, it gives it a new dimension without which the perspective of humanity would be reduced to distressingly diminutive proportions.

The "possession" by God just sketched must not be separated, culturally speaking, from other phenomena, some of which, at first glance, do not possess any mystical character. Indeed, it is fitting to consider the position of the ecstatic as that of an intermediary between the visible and Invisible. He is at once man and God, and this quality locates him "midway" between earth and sky. This is why he is the supreme "living being," the being in possession of secrets hidden from common mortals. Often he is a diviner and prophet, capable of revealing the future; often, also, he learns during the period of his spiritual training a "secret" language. It happens that in other circumstances of life also related to possession and often to trance the human being assumes this role as intermediary between the visible and the Invisible.

The case closest to the mystical phenomenon resulting from the intervention of the divinity is that which stems from possession by "spirits." Let us take for example the *bori* of the Hausa, the *zar* in Ethiopia, the *ndöp* in Senegal, the *holey bari* among the Songhai, the "trembling" among the Dogon, the "folly of the gods" among the Thonga, and so on. This form of possession is extremely widespread in Africa. It even goes beyond the limits of the African continent and is easy to follow to southern Italy,[19] Haiti,[20] and Brazil.[21]

It is not possible here to study this phenomenon in all the ethnic groups in which it appears. Besides, this would be more for the sake of erudition than for the understanding of the phenomena. What we would rather do is to try to detect its structure or the model which it obeys so as to show the link which unites the different examples. We have found among the Bantu of southeast Africa an area of investigation which seems to lend itself admirably to this endeavor.

Among the Thonga the spirits believed to take possession of the human being are especially those of individuals belonging to foreign groups. H. A. Junod states:

> We must carefully note, at the outset, these two ideas: the tormenting spirits are the *manes of strangers* and not of the people of the country, and they frequently attack Thongas who happen to be travelling in such countries, and follow them in their further migrations.[22]

The first signs of possession come in the form of an attack, during which the patient is unconscious, or by the apparition of such symptoms as a persistent pain in the chest, uncontrollable hiccoughing, unusual yawning, an abnormal loss of weight, an unexpected and lasting limp, and so on. Still, divination alone is capable of indicating with certitude whether it is a case of interference by spirits or a phenomenon with a "natural" cause. If the oracle pronounces in favor of the first possibility it is necessary in treating the invalid to turn to the intervention of the "exorcist" (*gobela*), who himself must have once been possessed. This follows the rule that only such people are competent in this therapeutic domain. In the past the treatment of this type of affliction entailed only the balancing of a palm leaf in front of the patient. Junod recounts that:

Now the treatment is much more complicated...it comprises four principal rites: the drum performance, the ablution in the *gobo* calabash, the drinking of the blood, and the *hondlola* ceremony.[23]

From the descriptions recorded by Junod it appears that each of these rites possesses a canvas on which are added details particular to the healer's undertaking of this treatment.

"The drum performance" must begin at night, at the appearance of a new moon (this should be remembered, since, as will be seen in the following, possession by spirits among the Thonga is related to the moon). Its purpose is to plunge the patient into a confused and disorganized acoustic environment whose outcome is expressed by a melody constituting a personal song entoned by the patient himself at the end of the rite. The possessed person's state is felt as an upsetting of his normal way of being. The patient is in the most complete disarray which often leads him to behave aggressively towards the audience or to throw himself into the fire without burning himself. The discordant music is also intended to obtain a twofold result: first, to make the patient reveal the name of the possessing spirit and, second, to provoke the appearance of the opposite material sign, also acoustic in nature, which marks in the patient's psyche the passage from disorganization to reorganization. Indeed, as soon as the spirit "declares" its name, it can be interrogated by the officiant, who desires to know the circumstances under which it took possession of its "mount," while the personal song from then on becomes a means of provoking or healing future seizures. Such songs "are generally in Zulu [a foreign language for the Thonga] and it is asserted that, even if the patient does not know this language, he will be able to use it in his conversation, by a kind of miracle of tongues!"[24]

The "rite of the *gobo* basin" immediately follows the preceding one and is organized around the theme of the distant voyage, during the course of which the invalid "saw everything" and even learned the art of divination. During this ceremony, the *gobela* plunges the patient's head in a basin filled with water so that his eyes are immersed.[25] He then orders him to open his eyes while his head is maintained in that position. This is the "medicine" which "makes him see."

These two phases of the ritual of "exorcism" are, from the evidence, dominated by the separation which exists between the person possessed and the society to which he usually belongs. The invalid lives with foreign "spirits" and finds himself under their dominion; he belongs to another "world." He even lives in another time which can be classed as "rapid" and "hot," if one considers the aggressiveness often shown by the possessed person and the fact that he can throw himself in the fire without suffering its effects. The rites of noise and the basin of water aim at clarifying a confused situation and leading the "foreigner" and the "savage" to "domestic" life. This result is only definitively obtained after the completion of the second part of the ritual.

The "drinking of a victim's blood" takes place the day following that of the ablution in the *gobo* calabash.[26] The invalid is offered a fowl or, better, a goat, whose blood he will drink.

> The exorcist who has been in charge of the cure orders the bystanders to repeat the song which had induced the first crisis. The possessed again shows excitement, and exhibits the same symptoms of raving madness.... Then the animal is pierced beneath the foreleg...and the patient throws himself on the wound, greedily sucking the flowing blood, and, in frenzy, filling his stomach with it. When he has drunk his fill, he has to be dragged away from the animal by main force.[27]

Then he is given "certain medicines" to drink, of which one is "apparently" an emetic. He is also tickled on the uvula, which provokes the vomiting of the blood that was drunk. The invalid is then smeared with ochre and dressed with bands of the skin of the sacrificed animal tied together by small cords made from *mounga* roots,[28] "which have a pleasant odor; this has the property of 'rejoicing the nose' of the spirits."[29] The cooked goat meat is consumed by the invalid and those exorcized on preceding days, while the bones (except for the astragals, which are attached to the patient's sternum) are burned in a cool place. The invalid thereby enters into the period of "convalescence" which lasts an entire year. During all this time he must wear the garment made from bands of skin of the sacrificed animal and is required to observe the strictest sexual continence. The period of convalescence is also an initiatory period since, from the "invalid" which he was until this point, the possessed person is transformed into a disciple of his healer. He accompanies the healer everywhere in his movements, helps him in cures, and is initiated into the art of exorcism.

The *hondlola* or "purification" rite takes place at the end of the period of convalescence. It consists essentially of the neophyte's consumption of the foam of a "medicine" prepared by the master, as well as of the rubbing which the latter performs on the entire body of his pupil in order to collect the body dirt. This is carefully gathered and part is put into the "amulet-bags." The remainder is pressed into a ball which is deposited in the back of the disciple's hut, on the spot where, that same day, a forked branch is planted constituting the altar of the new exorcist.

From then on the formerly possessed person is completely changed in status. He belongs to the society of those who are capable of "manipulating" the world of the spirits. From being their slave as he had been, he becomes their master. However, to maintain himself in this state, he will have to observe numerous prescriptions. Some of them are intended to protect him against evil influences, others to "calm his gods and disperse them when they wish to do him violence." Still others are meant to assure him continual renewal in his preoccupation with belonging to a world opposed to the one he previously left, an indispensable condition for assuring dominion over the spirits. The latter prescription consists of drinking at each new moon a liquid which he vomits immediately afterwards, thereby maintaining the relationship previously established between him and the moon.

Two ideas emerge from this second phase of the ritual of "exorcism." By drinking goat blood, the "possessed person" is introduced into the category of "domesticated" beings; he achieves his "return" into the "human" world, a "return already initiated by the preceding phase of the rite."[30] The *hondlola* ceremony makes him a new being, one capable of "commanding" the spirits.

In sum, the image of the possessed person which appears after this brief description is that of a being intermediary between the visible and the Invisible. Having "departed" for the world of the "spirits" and thus become a "stranger" to his own people, the possessed person needs "domestication" so he can again be counted among humans.

This image becomes more prominent when compared to those of the warrior and the hunter. By nature the warrior is a killer of men. Aggressiveness attains its highest value in him, since by definition he is led to deprive his fellow man of life. Among the Thonga there exists a special "medicine" which is administered to warriors so that they are capable of killing. This "medicine" is intended to remove all human conscience from them so that they become similar to bloodthirsty animals.[31] But by killing human beings the killer runs great risks:

> To have killed an enemy on the battlefield entails an immense glory for the slayers; but that glory is fraught with great danger. They have killed. . . . So they are exposed to the mysterious and deadly influence of the *nuru* and must consequently undergo a medical treatment. . . . [The *nuru*] is the spirit of the slain which tries to take its revenge on the slayer. It haunts him and may drive him into insanity. . . . He will go out of his mind, be attacked by giddiness . . . and the thirst for blood may lead him to fall upon members of his own family and to stab them with his assagay.[32]

To forestall this danger, the warriors who have killed must remain apart for a certain time.

> They put on old clothes, eat with special spoons because their hands are "hot" and from special plates . . . and broken pots. They are for-

bidden to drink water. Their food must be cold. The chief kills oxen for them . . .; but if the meat were hot it would make them swell internally "because they are hot themselves, they are defiled. . . ." If they ate hot food, the defilement would enter into them. "They are black. . . . This black must be removed". . . . During all this time sexual relations are absolutely forbidden to them.[33]

To "purify" the killers of men ("to remove the black" from them), the doctor uses all sorts of seeds which he roasts in a broken pot with medicines and the undigested contents of a goat stomach. The patients rub themselves with the mixture on the joints of the limbs. Finally, coals of the medicines are collected and put in small skin-bags (*tintébé*) which the killer of men will wear around his neck.[34]

Further, the portrait of the warrior indicates the gap which separates the killer of men from those who have not performed the supreme act of "bravura." The warrior is also a "stranger" to his own people and, like the possessed person, is in need of "domestication" before he returns to normal life.

The hunter is marked by an aggressive attitude just as distinctive as that of the warrior. He is thirsty for blood, but with him the thirst is for animal blood. When he prepares himself for the hunt, rites are performed which tend to "separate" him from the familial and village community and to "bring him closer" to the animals which he will kill. Sometimes a chicken is sacrificed before the hunter leaves, although no adult has the right to eat its meat since the success of the expedition would be compromised. Only young children may eat it: "they are quiet" (that is, they do not have sexual relations).[35] It is also forbidden for the hunter to bring salt along on his hunting expeditions, and before leaving he must be inoculated in the wrist with *tintébé* "medicines" which, as we know, are used for warriors. The "dehumanization" of the hunter sometimes goes so far that anyone intending to hunt hippopotamus—an animal reputed to be particularly dangerous—must have sexual relations with his own daughter before leaving, although otherwise incest is severely reprobated by society.[36] Conversely, during the hunt itself sexual relations are strictly forbidden as much for the hunters as for their wives remaining in the village. The reason for this prohibition is found, according to Junod, in the fact that

> there is in the sexual act something wild, fierce, passionate which . . . has an influence on the hostile forces; these will be excited and more difficult to overcome: enemies in battle, the animals of the bush during hunting and fishing parties, disease, danger of contamination at death. . . . Life is, so to speak, accelerated by the sexual act.[37]

In fact, during his expedition in the bush the hunter must behave like a being who adopts the life of the wild. One of Junod's informants states,

> "The hunter must forget everything about home. Were he to have relations with women, his charms would get heated, whilst they must remain cool (*titmeta*). He must himself become a man of the bush (*wa nhoba*), similar to the animals which are found there."[38]

The more important the animals that are killed, the greater the hunter's danger of remaining definitively "won over" by the bush. It follows in this case that certain rites are indispensable in order to avoid the "madness" which can take possession of him, making him incapable of resuming life in the village. For example, he who has killed an eland must take a louse from the animal's forelock as well as a root from the spot where its head rests and, as soon as he returns to the village, call a doctor who will free him from the animal's *nuru*.

> Should you omit this treatment you may lose your senses, be unable to find the way home or, when you are back, you may forget everything about your hunting trip. People will say to you: " . . . you are cracked"; you act as if you had killed an eland and had not been *lurulula*, delivered from its nuru![39]

Furthermore, any return from the hunt is ended by the sacrifice of a chicken, performed by the head of the village at the principal entrance of the settlement before the hunter passes through it.

Thus, the case of the hunter follows practically the same model as that of the possessed person and the warrior. Like the latter two, the hunter needs to be returned to "domestic" life after his hunting trip. An analysis of the elements common to all of them would allow the "kinship" which unites these three personages to be seen more clearly.

Aggressiveness seems to be a constant which underlies the behavior of each. Prior to "exorcism," the possessed person is so menacing that those surrounding him jump on him to hold and contain him. His character of destructive antagonism reveals itself in opposition not only to his fellow men, but also to himself, since at the time of the seizures he throws himself into the fire. The warrior manifests his combativeness with regard to other humans; he is filled with the war medicine and his "hatred" pushes him to kill them. He is the supreme "killer" because he glories in the death he causes. Only the hunter is his equal, with the sole difference being that the hunter concentrates on wild animals.

The destructive "instinct" places the possessed person, the warrior, and the hunter in intense duration; they live in rapid time, which the Thonga translate by the concept of heat. They are "hot." The "heat" which characterizes the state of the warrior who has already caused death is so intense that it is believed to have "burned" him. The warrior who has killed men is "black"; he has passed beyond the limits of life in society. His own destruction is avoided by preventing him from eating hot meat. Placed in "accelerated" time, each of them must also abstain from sexual relations which, according to the Thonga, already constitute the human being's "hot" and "rapid" life.

It is by returning anew to "normality" that they all reintegrate the slow time and "coolness" that characterize everyday life. Protected from the disorderly ascendancy of the spirits, the possessed person becomes "cool." The bones of the goat sacrificed in his honor during the rite of calming by blood are burned "in the shade of a large tree, where it is cool. So the possessing spirit will also be cool . . . and not too wild."[40] The whole life of the exorcized person is marked, after his return to the normal state, by the coolness of calm and peaceful existence. This is appropriate to him even after his death, for he is buried with a bouquet that has been made from an aquatic plant and placed on his head.

> *"This is to cool him,* because his poor head has been so tired, it has suffered so much from anguish, pain, excitement!" The grass, being taken from the water, also appears *to cool the spirits.* . . . Moreover, a little hut is built on the grave itself . . . to protect the exorcized against heat and fatigue.[41]

For the warrior and the hunter it is the *tintébé* "medicines" that assure stability in "coolness" and protect them against unexpected and anarchistic rages. Moreover, these same "medicines" are ingested by the warriors at the *bukanye* festivals.[42] They are believed to remove the murderer's madness and prevent the participants in these drinking bouts "from killing any of their compatriots during the ensuing weeks of the *bukanye."*[43]

The analysis of some of the elements common to the possessed person, the warrior, and the hunter gives an account of the cultural model on which they depend. Each of these three personages possesses a mobile personality capable of living by turns two different lives, two opposing times. Each of them is founded in normal everyday life, that which is built within the framework of the visible, the attachment to a community and the village. Each of them also occasionally undergoes a change to another life, one which is marked by the invisible, the enemy, and the bush. The passage from one to the other of these existences is not, however, identical in all three cases. Despite himself, the possessed person is, so to speak, "taken" by invisible powers; the warrior and the hunter undergo appropriate rites in order to acquire, respectively, hatred of the other and de-domestication. Thus detached from normality, they all participate in what can be called ":madness," that state of which the least that can be said is that it denotes aggressiveness: the madness of the gods, of war, and of the hunt. In each of these cases, the "madman" displays a combative ardor and becomes incapable of normal life in the community. Hence the rites of "return," all based on "taming" and "domestication." The example of the possessed person who is made to drink greedily and until exhaustion the blood of the animal considered the most "domestic" of animals is illuminating.[44]

In sum, the possessed person, warrior, and hunter are each defined by two opposing terms: the possessed person oscillates between the visible and the invisible, the warrior between friend and enemy, and the hunter between village and bush. This signifies that not only do these three personages participate reciprocally in their respective significant values but also that the oppositional terms perform in each group a kind of "confusion." The possessed person borrows the distinctive features of the warrior and hunter, just as the latter two "are" possessed persons. Similarly, the visible merges with the "friend" and the "village," while the invisible becomes the "enemy" and the "bush." It is fair to say that at their most extreme the images of the possessed person, warrior, and hunter could merge into a single icon, that of any human being placed in an agonistic situation between security and insecurity, between life and death.

Having reached this level, we understand why all the rites in which the profound existence of the human being is engaged are rites of "departure" and "return." We also understand why the ceremonies concerning the "ecstatic" forcefully underline the "resurrection" of the initiate and his "return" (with his god) to humanity.

But the analysis to which we have been devoted also accounts for the similarity which numerous authors in different areas have established among the various phenomena of possession. In each case, the possessed person lets significant features appropriate to the hunter and warrior penetrate his behavior.[45] Inversely, the behavior of the latter two displays the "madness" of the possessed person. This goes even further, since in our own civilization the hunter and the warrior belong to that category of human being which is considered closer to the gods than to common men. If they do not astonish each other, they are made to astonish us, if only by the "gift" of speech of which they are the incontestable masters.

Thus we can see the two limits of the mystical phenomenon: that which connects it to the sky, where it is believed to receive the investiture of the mind, and that which unites it to the earth, purveyor of its appearances and manifestations as traced on the human scale. All along the way mysticism is identified by markers which death distinguishes by means of its imprint. The "wife" of God, the supreme possessed person,

offers himself to "death" to attract the divinity to him. The person possessed by spirits "travels" towards death but returns from it to better
"command" it. The warrior and the hunter cause death by striving to
avoid its distressing repercussions. In fact, everything occurs as if man
wanted to be master of that necessary confrontation between himself
and the Invisible which awaits him at the end of the path. It seems to
displease him to let himself be treated by God, his master, as an inert
and passive object; he works hard at making him adopt the arrangement
which follows his desire to live.

It would undoubtedly be rash to generalize the manifestations and
forms of mysticism described here to the whole of the African continent.
The experience of which we have just spoken may not be valid for all its
peoples, even though it is necessary to note in this regard the insuffi-
ciency of adequate documentation. In any case, even if among certain
peoples this characteristic of religion is lacking on the "institutional"
plane, it is no less true that the African, considered as an individual, is
profoundly mystical. We mean by this that he aspires, more than appearances would indicate, to a sort of intimacy and union with the
Invisible. This aspiration is expressed in practice by a great freedom and
a surprising familiarity which man adopts in his relations with God. We
certainly can not speak in this regard of relations based on love, since for
the African this sentiment is not the mainspring of the union, but rather
of a sort of marriage based on trust and abandonment.

Considered in this light, African mysticism has an appearance similar
to what ethnologists call a "joking relationship." Man and God are in
the position of partners tied together by the most subtle and noble
relationship, one which rejects carnal dealings at the same time as it
extols fusion through gesture and speech, that is, through the mind.

Thus, as in the "joking relationship," the meeting between man and
the Invisible turns into a sort of "game" in which sanction and fear do
not have a place, where death itself loses its disturbing character in order
to be no more than the reverse of the lost opportunity which is
immortality.

Conclusion

10

It is permissible at the end of this essay to sketch in broad strokes the portrait of African spirituality, a portrait whose features, as spread out over the many preceding pages, are sometimes too rich in detail to leave an overall image.

The African is above all a stubborn earth-dweller. His profound attachment to the soil finds its equal only in the immensity of the continent which he inhabits and to which he is riveted to the point of not being able to freely separate himself from it. This interest in the earth is significant, for the African's vision of himself, his life, and the world is affected by it. The African may bring to human culture a contribution which, if exploited rigorously, would undoubtedly have permitted a deepening of Hellenic philosophy and science prior to Plato and Aristotle. His "taste" for "matter" establishes the African wise man as a miracle-worker of the elements, a role which he fulfills even to our day among numerous peoples and according to a millenary knowledge of nature. This wise man wants to be master of the earth. "Miserable" in appearance and with insignificant means, according to our perspective, this man commands water and wind, acts of fire, and manipulates earth as if it were a part of himself.

In the presence of such an alchemy of the elements, one might think that the African was only "terrestrial," that he took no interest in the world above, that his thought did not extend beyond the tree tops or the horizon of the savanna. Yet this is not the case. The sky interests him just as much as, if not more than, the earth, if only because this place holds for him more secrets than the universe which he frequents daily. This place, in fact, is not foreign to him; ever since the death of the first man the sky has been humanized. It has its gaze turned toward the earth, like the "children" of the gods whose "mothers" (in the past, when celestial beings lived with men) carried them on their backs, feet up and heads down.[1] The sky is the "great village," it is the place of rest for humans who have "left" this world and who ask only to return to earth. It is far without really being so. A constant commerce is carried on between the high and the low; the sky and the earth communicate at every instant through channels that are invisible but felt as profoundly real.

To be precise, we may say that it is at the intersection of the terrestrial and celestial coordinates that African man is located. He sees himself as the synthesis of the universe, a sort of model which, from the moment that it *is*, matters little to call small or large. From this follows his sense of power.

This power is over the world, with which he "plays" in his myths and rites, like a child for whom the toy is sometimes an independent reality, sometimes an objectification of his interior universe, and often both at once. The African wants to possess the world, just as certain royal buffoons in West Africa who, by walking on their hands, mean to carry above their heads, in their palms, the great earth which normally supports them. The sky and God do not escape this will for power. The African means to control them; he obligates them to come down to him; he commands them. He tells them to come and they come, transforming man into an extraordi- nary mount, making him their "horse" and their "wife," making him a foreigner to his own people, pushing him to become like themselves. He tells them to depart and they depart, leaving behind them something of themselves. One sees in this *agônia* that man is neither a toy nor a straw between the hands of the forces which would escape him. He is the arbiter of his own game with these forces; he is above them. This is the essence of his spirituality. It is contrary to our ways of thought and goes against the superficial observation of the African's religiosity, yet it seems to us to be true.

The African could not nourish such ideas without a feeling of power over his own person. In reality the mastery of the self is the keystone of all the religious architecture of the African. It is present in his gestures and his behavior; it is realized in his language; it is actualized in his mentality and his entire way of being. It is a mode of being, but power over himself and the feeling which he has of it lead the wise man to solitary insensitivity and happiness. They lead to the isolation of the human being, an isolation whose only remedy is in the integration of the individual into a deperson- alizing social system. This same "power over the self" leads directly to the self-esteem and dignity which constitute the background of African spirituality and account for many attitudes that have been softened by time and colonial domination but that were characteristic of the era of the first explorers. This legitimate pride is the "faith" very much alive in the value of mankind and the consciousness of the superiority of the human being in relation to the rest of creation. It is this "something" which explains, at least in part, not only the African's penchant for blood sacrifice but especially for the sacrifice of the self, whose most subtle form appears in mystical life at the time when the adept who has become the "wife" of God makes a gift of himself.

For such is the paradox of African spirituality: man both affirms and denies himself. He affirms himself through the feeling of his own power, and denies himself by giving himself away. Yet the paradox is only apparent: the gift of self is the means which allows him to better realize himself. The mystic "dies" in order to relive. Death becomes a position of retreat which allows one the better to conquer life.

Notes

Introduction

1. This does not preclude the existence of a similar spot, located elsewhere than on the East African coast, which could be the place of origin of the Thonga and their creation myths.

2. See respectively: E. G. Parrinder, *African Traditional Religion* (London: Hutchinson's University Library, 1954 [2d ed., 1962]), and E. Dammann, *Die Religionen Afrikas* (Stuttgart: W. Kohlhammer Verlag, 1963). The latter work has been translated into French as *Les Religions de l'Afrique* (Paris: Payot, 1964). Note that Parrinder has also published a study on this subject which is restricted to West Africa, *West African Religion* (London: Epworth Press, 1942 [2d ed., 1961]).

3. Parrinder, *African Traditional Religion*, p. 25.

4. Ibid.

5. Dammann, *Religions de l'Afrique*, p. 15.

6. Ibid., p. 16.

Chapter 1

1. In particular, among the Pygmies of Gabon, the Fon, and the Dogon.

2. Among the Thonga and the Zulu, for example.

3. Among the Herero.

4. Among the Kurumba, the Tswana, the Tallensi, and others.

5. Among the Kurumba and the Tallensi.

6. A motif which is found among the Kabre, the Burundi, the Akamba, etc.

7. There are numerous examples of this; see in particular the account of the Pygmies, R. P. Trilles, *Les Pygmées de la Forêt Equatoriale* (Paris: Bloud et Gray, 1932), pp. 287ff.

8. For example, among the Tallensi; see M. Fortes, *The Dynamics of Clanship among the Tallensi* (London: Oxford University Press, 1945), pp. 22–23.

9. Paul Radin, "Introduction," in *African Folktales and Sculpture*, ed. Paul Radin, Bollingen Series, no. 32 (New York: Pantheon Books, 1953), p. 4.

10. See R. C. Stevenson, "The Doctrine of God in the Nuba Mountains," in *African Ideas of God*, ed. E. W. Smith (London: Edinburgh House Press, 1950), p. 216; C. M. Doke, *The Lambas of Northern Rhodesia* (London: Harrap, 1931), pp. 222–23; and H. Labouret, *Les tribus du rameau lobi*, Travaux et Mémoires de l'Institut d'Ethnologie, vol. 15 (Paris and the Hague: Mouton, 1931), p. 137.

11. It is certain that the meaning of a vast body of human behavior in so-called archaic societies has remained impenetrable to the Western world because of the philosophy which colors our thought. If Parmenides or Heraclitus had had the same influence on our mind as Aristotle, the distance between the "primitives" and us would undoubtedly be less great.

12. Because of the generality of this phenomenon we think we may dispense with ethnic and bibliographic references.

13. J. Roumeguère-Eberhardt, "La notion de vie, base de la structure sociale Venda," *Journal de la Société des Africanistes*, 27, fasc. 2 (1957): 184–85.

14. H. A. Junod, *The Life of a South African Tribe*, 2d ed. (London: Macmillan, 1927), 1:57, 2:356.

15. See Roumeguère-Eberhardt, "Notion de vie," p. 187.

16. See T. Cullen Young, "The Idea of God in Northern Nyasaland," in Smith, ed., *African Ideas of God*, p. 48.

17. See, e.g., D. Zahan, *La Dialectique du verbe chez les Bambara* (Paris and the Hague: Mouton, 1963), pp. 85–95.

18. See D. Zahan, *Sociétés d'Initiation Bambara, le N'Domo, le Korè* (Paris and the Hague: Mouton, 1960), pp. 126–28; A. C. Hollis, *The Masai, Their Language and Folk-lore* (Oxford: Clarendon Press, 1905), pp. 294–98; idem, *The Nandi, Their Language and Folk-lore* (Oxford: Clarendon Press, 1909), pp. 53–58; and Edwin M. Loeb, *In Feudal Africa* (Paris and the Hague: Mouton, 1962), pp. 236–49.

19. These symmetries are very widespread in Africa. The motivations for them vary, however, according to the different cultures and, often, according to diverse circumstances within the same culture. Thus among all the Bantu of southeast Africa, the left is feminine and the right is masculine, while among the Zulu there are women of the right hand and women of the left hand. See, e.g., J. Roumeguère-Eberhardt, *Pensée et société africaines* (Paris and the Hague: Mouton, 1963), pp. 80–81, 86.

20. On this subject, see D. Zahan, "Note sur la gémelléité et les jumeaux en Afrique Noire," *Bulletin de la Faculté des Lettres de Strasbourg*, March 1964, pp. 351–53.

21. This is valid even for societies which do not have age-sets.

22. For example, among the Bantu of southeast Africa; see Junod, *Life of a South African Tribe*, 2:57, 60–61.

23. M. Lamy, *Les Jumeaux* (Paris: Corréa, 1949), p. 14.

24. E. E. Evans-Pritchard, *Essays in Social Anthropology* (London: Faber and Faber, 1962), p. 162.

25. Ibid., p. 163.

26. This theme is widespread in Africa.

27. For example, in Nuba myths (see Stevenson, "Doctrine of God," in Smith, ed., *African Ideas of God*, p. 216), among the Dogon (see M. Griaule, *Masques dogons*, Travaux et Mémoires de l'Institut d'Ethnologie, vol. 33 [Paris and the Hague: Mouton, 1938], p. 48).

28. We find the theme in this form, for example, among the Banyarwanda and Barundi; see R. Bourgeois, *Banyarwanda et Barundi*, Académie Royale des Sciences Coloniales, Mémoire no. 8 (Brussels, 1956) 3:19–25.

29. See E. Dammann, *Les Religions de l'Afrique* (Paris: Payot, 1964), p. 86; and Trilles, *Pygmées de la Forêt Equatoriale*, pp. 66–68, 78.

30. It is not without interest to note that the two themes mentioned here are found throughout the world.

31. It is not possible here to go into all the details which "surround" these themes.

Chapter 2

1. See E. E. Evans-Pritchard, "Zande Theology," in *Essays in Social Anthropology* (London: Faber and Faber, 1962), pp. 178ff.

2. H. A. Junod, *The Life of a South African Tribe*, 2d ed. (London: Macmillan, 1927), 2:375n.

3. Ibid., 2:323.

4. G. Dieterlen, "Mythe et organisation sociale au Soudan français," *Journal de la Société des Africanistes*, 25, fasc. 1–2 (1955):39–76; and 29, fasc. 1 (1959):119–38.

5. J. Daget, "La pêche dans le delta central du Niger," *Journal de la Société des Africanistes*, 19, fasc. 1 (1949):68–70.

6. J. Roumeguère-Eberhardt, *Pensée et société africaines* (Paris and the Hague: Mouton, 1963), pp. 13–24.

7. Edwin M. Loeb, *In Feudal Africa* (Paris: Mouton, 1962), p. 244.

8. R. Bourgeois, *Banyarwanda et Barundi*, Académie Royale des Sciences Coloniales, Mémoire no. 8 (Brussels: 1956), 3:20ff.

9. G. Bachelard, *L'eau et les rêves* (Paris: Librairie José Corti, 1942), p. 206.

10. Junod, *Life of a South African Tribe*, 2:325–26.

11. Bachelard, *L'eau et les rêves*, p. 207.

12. See G. Balandier and P. Mercier, *Les Pêcheurs Lébou* (St.-Louis, Senegal: Centre IFAN-Senegal, 1952), pp. 5ff.

13. See Dieterlen, "Mythe et organisation sociale," 29, fasc. 1 (1959):136–38.

14. See R. Mauny, *Tableau géographique de l'ouest-africain du Moyen Age* (Dakar: IFAN, 1961), p. 272.

15. J. P. Lebeuf, *L'Habitation des Fali* (Paris: Hachette, 1961), pp. 369ff.

16. In fact, what is involved here is the fabrication of cast iron, although for Africans, sensitive to manifestations of life and movement, rigid and unmalleable cast iron remains static while iron becomes in some way a living symbol.

17. Dim Delobsom, *L'Empire du Mogho-Naba* (Paris: Editions Domat-Montchrestien, 1933), p. 283.

18. See A. Lestrade, *La médicine indigène en Ruanda*, Académie Royale des Sciences Coloniales, Mémoire no. 8 (Brussels, 1955), pp. 214–16.

19. M. J. Tubiana, *Survivances préislamiques en pays zaghawa*, Travaux et Mémoires de l'Institut d'Ethnologie, vol. 67 (Paris and the Hague: Mouton, 1963), pp. 25ff.

20. Ibid., pp. 45–46, 149–50.

21. See D. Zahan, *Sociétés d'Initiation Bambara: le N'domo, le Korè* (Paris and the Hague: Mouton, 1963), pp. 323–24.

22. Without knowing the precise role of these places of worship associated with *komo*, G. Szumowski has described such a grotto in the region of Bamako; see his "Notes sur la grotte préhistorique de Bamako," *Notes africaines*, 58 (April 1953):35–40. The fact that this grotto served as a place of initiation into *komo* is shown by the presence of object no. 2 in Szumowski's plate III. This object belongs to the *sacra* of *komo*. On the existence of these types of places in West Africa, see H. Hubert, "Grottes et Cavernes de l'Afrique Occidentale," *Bulletin du Comité d'Etudes Historiques et Scientifiques de l'Afrique Occidentale Française*, 1 (January-March, 1920):43–51.

23. Tubiana, *Survivances préislamiques*, pp. 43–44, 83–84.

24. Ibid., pp. 46–47. See also an example of a grotto with this symbolism in Junod, *Life of a South African Tribe*, 2:597.

25. Zahan, *Sociétés d'Initiation Bambara*, p.232.

26. A significant example of this can be found in L. G. Binger, *Du Niger au Golfe de Guinée* (Paris: Hachette, 1892), 1:255.

27. R. P. Trilles, *Les Pygmées de la Forêt Equatoriale* (Paris: Bloud and Gay, 1932), p. 379.

28. Dieterlen, "Mythe et organisation sociale," 25:39–76.

29. Cited in G. Bachelard, *L'air et les songes* (Paris: Librairie José Corti, 1943), pp. 236–37.

30. Cited in ibid., pp. 242–43.

31. Junod, *Life of a South African Tribe*, 2:332–33.

32. Trilles, *Pygmées de la Forêt Equatoriale*, pp. 85–86, 136.

33. Bourgeois, *Banyarwanda et Barundi*, 3:68, 78; M. d'Hertefelt, "Le Rwanda," in *Les anciens royaumes de la zone interlacustre méridionale, Rwanda, Burundi, Buha*, Monographies Ethnographiques, no. 6 (Tervuren: Musée Royal de l'Afrique Centrale, 1962), p. 83.

34. Such is the case among the Nyanga; see D. Biebuyck, *De hond big de Nyanga*, Rituel en Sociologie, Mémoires de l'Académie des Sciences Coloniales, n.s., vol. 8, fasc. 3 (Brussels, 1956).

35. Water, for example, does not only possess a global meaning pertaining to fecundity but each type of water (rain, spring, river, pond, lake, sea, water found in the hollow of a tree, dew, etc.) also has a particular meaning.

36. Sacrifices of wild animals are relatively rare; one encounters them particularly in the equatorial forest.

37. It seems to be absent, however, among the Pedi.

Chapter 3

1. See H. Baumann, *Schöpfung und Urzeit der Menschen im Mythos der Afrikanischen Völker* (Berlin: Dietrich Reimer, 1936), p. 268; and H. Abrahamsson, *The Origin of Death*, Studia Ethnographica Upsaliensia, vol. 3 (Uppsala: Almquist and Wiksells, 1951), p. 4. For the synthesis presented here we refer with few exceptions to the myths cited by the latter author.

2. H. A. Junod, *The Life of a South African Tribe*, 2d ed. (London: Macmillan, 1927), 2:350–51.

3. See Edmond Perregaux, "Chez les Achanti," *Bulletin de la Société Neuchâteloise de Géographie*, 17 (1906):198, as cited by Abrahamsson, *Origin of Death*, p. 5.

4. See A. W. Cardinall, *Tales Told in Togoland* (London: Oxford University Press, 1931), pp. 27ff., as cited by Abrahamsson, *Origin of Death*, p. 6.

5. See J. Sieber, "Aus dem sozialen Leben der Nord-Tikar," *Zeitschrift für Ethnologie*, 67 (1936):273ff., as cited by Abrahamsson, *Origin of Death*, p. 9.

6. In African societies the "altar" of people struck by lightning is usually not permitted in the same place as the "altars" of normal dead people. In Buganda and Burundi a woman who has survived being struck by lightning legally belongs to the sovereign, who is considered to be of celestial origin.

7. The "cult" of thunder stones is explained in the same way.

8. Except in cases where the slow animal also enjoys great longevity, such as the tortoise. In this case slowness–death is overshadowed by slowness–long life.

9. H. A. Junod, *Life of a South African Tribe*, 2:437n.

10. Ibid., 2:339.

11. L. Frobenius, *Atlantis*, vol. 12 (Jena: E. Diederichs, 1924), p. 227, as cited by Abrahamsson, *Origin of Death*, p. 68.

12. Georg Haessig, *Unter den Urwaldstämmen in Kamerun* (Stuttgart and Basel: Evangelischer Missionsverlag, 1933), p. 98, as cited by Abrahamsson, *Origin of Death*, p. 36.

13. L. Frobenius, *Atlantis*, vol. 12 (Jena: E. Diederichs, 1928), p. 140, as cited by Abrahamsson, *Origin of Death*, p. 52.

14. J. van Wing, "Etudes Bakongo: Religion et Magie," Mémoires de l'Institut Royal Colonial Belge, vol. 9, no. 1, p. 25, as cited by Abrahamsson, *Origin of Death*, p. 98.

15. We have only enumerated those aspects discussed above. The myths of the origin of death take into consideration other aspects, such as activity, health, the distinction between men and animals and between men and plants, and time.

16. C. Tastevin, *Etudes Missionnaires*, 2:85, as cited by Abrahamsson, *Origin of Death*, p. 100.

17. S. F. Nadel, *The Nuba* (London: Oxford University Press, 1947), p. 268, as cited by Abrahamsson, *Origin of Death*, p. 101.

18. Frobenius, *Atlantis*, vol. 12, p. 174, as cited by Abrahamsson, *Origin of Death*, pp. 100–101.

19. One of the many examples of this theme can be found in R. P. Eugene Hurel, *La Poésie chez les Primitifs, ou Contes, Fables, Récits et Proverbes du Rwanda (Lac Kivu)*, Bibliothèque-Congo (Brussels: Goemaere, 1922), pp. 41–48.

20. I. Schapera, *The Khoisan Peoples of South Africa* (London: Routledge and Kegan Paul, 1930), p. 162.

21. P. Kolb, *Reise zum Vorgebirge der Guten Hoffnung,* ed. Paul Germann (Liepzig: F. A. Brockhaus, 1926), as cited by Schapera, *Khoisan Peoples,* p. 359.

22. T. E. Bowdich, *A Mission from Cape Coast Castle to Ashantee* (London: J. Murray, 1819), as cited by R. S. Rattray, *Religion and Art in Ashanti* (London: Oxford University Press, 1927), p. 106.

23. Winwood-Reade, *The Story of the Ashanti Campaign,* as cited by Rattray, *Religion and Art in Ashanti,* pp. 106–7.

24. A. le Hérissé, *L'Ancien Royaume du Dahomey* (Paris: Larose, 1911), p. 180, n.1.

25. Rattray, *Religion and Art in Ashanti,* p. 107.

26. Casalis, *Les Bassoutos* (Paris: Société des Missions Evangéliques, 1933), p. 304. A Christian influence in this threnody is not ruled out.

27. See H. Callaway, *The Religious System of the Amazulu* (London: Folk-Lore Society, 1884).

28. Junod, *Life of a South African Tribe,* 2:430.

29. It would seem that the opposition between these illnesses and the "glorious" state of the ancestors is among many peoples based on the impossibility of burying the dead according to the normal practices.

30. See J. Roumeguère-Eberhardt, *Pensée et société africaines* (Paris and the Hague: Mouton, 1963), p. 31.

Chapter 4

1. Audrey I. Richards, *Chisungu, A Girl's Initiation Ceremony Among the Bemba of Northern Rhodesia* (London: Faber and Faber, 1956). Also on this subject, but more from the point of view of art, see H. Cory, *African Figurines* (London: Faber and Faber, 1956).

2. J. Roumeguère-Eberhardt, *Pensée et société africaines* (Paris and the Hague: Mouton, 1963).

3. According to Audrey I. Richards (*Chisungu,* pp. 170–86), the puberty rites which she describes among the Bemba, as well as similar rites, cover a very wide area in central Africa (Northern Rhodesia, Zaire, and Angola). For her part, J. Roumeguère-Eberhardt reports an equally great distribution in southeast Africa of puberty rites similar to those she describes for the Venda. We should also note the striking similarities between the initiation rites of young girls among the Venda and among the Bantu of southwest Africa, as reported by Edwin M. Loeb (*In Feudal Africa* [Paris and the Hague: Mouton, 1963], pp. 236ff.).

4. Roumeguère-Eberhardt, *Pensée et société africaines,* pp. 87ff.

5. Ibid., pp. 89–90.

6. Loeb, *In Feudal Africa,* pp. 240ff.

7. Ibid., p. 243.

8. A. Hampaté Ba and G. Dieterlen, *Koumen, Texte initiatique des pasteurs Peul,* Cahiers de l'Homme, n.s., no. 1 (Paris and the Hague: Mouton, 1961), pp. 20–21.

9. Ibid., p. 21.

10. Ibid., pp. 29–30.

11. On this subject see André Raponda-Walker and Roger Sillans, *Rites et Croyances des peuples du Gabon* (Paris: Présence Africaine, 1962).

12. On this subject see E. de Jonghe, *Les sociétés secrètes au Bas-Congo* (Brussels: Polleunis, 1907), and J. van Wing, *Etudes Bakongo: Religion et Magie* (Brussels: Desclée de Brouwer, 1938).

13. For example, see R. P. Arnoux, "Le culte de la société secrète des *imandwa* au

Ruanda," *Anthropos,* 12–13 (1912–13); and R. P. Zuure, *Croyances et pratiques religieuses des Barundi,* Bibliothèque Congo, no. 22 (Brussels: Essorial, 1929).

14. On this subject see B. Gutmann, *Die Stammeslehren der Dschagga,* vols. 1–3 (Munich: Beck, 1932–38).

15. On these two peoples see A. C. Hollis, *The Masai, Their Language and Folk-lore* (Oxford: Clarendon Press, 1905), and idem, *The Nandi, Their Language and Folk-lore* (Oxford: Clarendon Press, 1909).

16. B. Holas, "Fondements spirituels de la vie sociale Sénoufo," *Journal de la Société des Africanistes,* 26, fasc. 1–2 (1956):9–32; Gilbert Bochet, "Le Poro des Diéli," *Bulletin de l'IFAN,* ser. B, vol. 21, nos. 1–2 (1959):61–101.

17. Bochet, "Poro des Diéli," p. 72.

18. Holas, "Fondements spirituels," p. 251.

19. Bochet, "Poro des Diéli," p. 75.

20. Ibid., pp. 97–98.

21. See D. Zahan, *Sociétés d'Initiation Bambara: le N'domo, le Korè* (Paris and the Hague: Mouton, 1960).

22. These are called the "buffoons" of *korè.*

23. *Grewia bicolor.*

Chapter 5

1. G. Wagner, "The Abaluyia of Kavirondo," in *African Worlds,* ed. Meyer Fortes (London: Oxford University Press, 1954), p. 33.

2. See Clement M. Doke, *The Lambas of Northern Rhodesia* (London: G. C. Harrap, 1931), pp. 30–31, 180–81.

3. See G. Niangoran Bouah, *La division du temps et le calendrier rituel des peuples lagunaires de Côte d'Ivoire,* Travaux et Mémoires de l'Institut d'Ethnologie, vol. 68 (Paris and the Hague: Mouton, 1964), pp. 47–48.

4. See Fr. Wilhelm Hofmayr, *Die Schilluk, Geschichte, Religion und Leben eines Niloten-Stammes* (Mödling: St. Gabriel, 1925), pp. 238ff.

5. Godfrey Lienhardt, "The Shilluk of the Upper Nile," in *African Worlds,* ed. Meyer Fortes, p. 145.

6. See Wagner, "Abaluyia of Kavirondo," p. 33.

7. See Niangoran Bouah, *Division du temps,* pp. 47–48.

8. Jean-Paul Lebeuf, *L'Habitation des Fali* (Paris: Hachette, 1961), p. 584.

9. Ibid., p. 212.

10. Ibid., p. 518.

11. On this subject see D. Zahan, "L'Habitation Mossi," *Bulletin de l'IFAN,* 17, no. 1 (January 1950):223–29.

12. On this subject see M. Griaule, "L'Image du monde au Soudan," *Journal de la Société des Africanistes,* 19, fasc. 2 (1949):81–87; and G. Calame-Griaule, "Notes sur l'habitation du plateau central Nigérien," *Bulletin de l'IFAN,* ser. B, 17, nos. 3–4 (1955):477–99.

13. The hearth, which also symbolizes respiration, is often formed by two stones placed against the wall in the back of the kitchen. The spherical container rests on the stones and leans against the wall.

14. Griaule, "L'image du monde," pp. 86–87.

15. See E. M. Thomas, *The Harmless People* (New York: Knopf, 1959), p. 41.

16. On this subject see E. Jensen Krige, *The Social System of the Zulus,* 3d ed. (London: Shuter and Shooter, 1957), p. 42–44.

17. J. Roumeguère-Eberhardt, *Pensée et société africaines* (Paris and the Hague: Mouton, 1963), pp. 82–83.

18. Ibid., p. 86.

19. See Edwin M. Loeb, *In Feudal Africa* (Paris and the Hague: Mouton, 1963), pp. 334, 337.

20. Ibid., p. 10ff.

21. On this subject, see D. Randall MacIver, *Medieval Rhodesia* (London: Macmillan, 1906); and G. Caton-Thompson, *The Zimbabwe Culture: Ruins and Reactions* (Oxford: Clarendon Press, 1931).

22. Paul Schebesta, *Les Pygmées du Congo Belge,* Mémoires de l'Institut Royal Colonial Belge, vol. 26, fasc. 2 (Brussels, 1952), p. 307.

23. Niangoran Bouah, "Division du temps," p. 36.

24. This is the case among the Lamba, for example, for whom the relations between the moon and the sun (which represent respectively the maternal nephew and the maternal uncle) can only be understood if it is granted that this "celestial" relationship constitutes the mirror-image of the son-father relationship (see Doke, *The Lambas,* p. 224). In both cases we are concerned with a characteristic antagonism related to the hostility of the younger generation toward the older generation.

25. By "minimum social signifier" we mean the group of kinsmen containing only the father and mother, their child, and the child's mother's brother.

26. See above, pp. 72–73.

27. Niangoran Bouah, "Division du temps," p. 139.

28. H. Kuper, *An African Aristocracy* (London: Oxford University Press, 1961), pp. 200–201.

29. Ibid., p. 201.

30. J. Roumeguère-Eberhardt, *Pensée et société africaines,* p. 57.

31. H. A. Junod, *The Life of a South African Tribe,* 2d ed. (London: Macmillan, 1927), 1:392.

32. Ibid., 1:388–92.

33. H. A. Junod, *Les chants et les contes des Ba-Ronga* (Lausanne: Bridel, 1897), pp. 40–43.

34. D. Zahan, "Aperçu su la Pensée Théogonique des Dogon," *Cahiers Internationaux de Sociologie,* 6 (1949):127 n.38.

Chapter 6

1. See H. A. Junod, *The Life of a South African Tribe,* 2d ed. (London: Macmillan, 1927), 2:564–68.

2. Divination by astragals is very widespread among the Bantu.

3. The connection between the "bird" and the spirit of the diviner which we are making here is corroborated by the initiation of diviners among the Nkouna, where the meat-receptacle of the divinatory bones is consumed by the master and his pupil without touching it with their hands, "seizing it with their teeth alone, 'the same as vultures do, which scent meat from far away.'" And where, in addition, "the heart of one of these birds has been cooked with other drugs, 'so that the new diviner will be able to dream of things which are far away and go straight to them.'" The new diviner "will be able to go and guess anything at once without fear or hesitation" (Junod, *Life of a South African Tribe,* 2:566).

4. Ibid.,2:565.

5. See E. E. Evans-Pritchard, *Essays in Social Anthropology* (London: Faber and Faber, 1962), p. 184.

6. J. A. Tiarko Fourche and H. Morlighem, *Les communications des indigènes du Kasaï avec les âmes des morts* (Brussels: Falk fils, 1939).

7. When the soul of a dead person is separated from its body, it follows the large branch of the Milky Way until the crossroads at the fork, where it undergoes judgment.

8. Tiarko Fourche and Morlighem, *Les communications,* pp. 29–30.

9. Ibid., p. 32.

10. We prefer not to make the classic distinction between "diviner" and "prophet."

11. The diviner sprinkles peanuts on these outlines. By coming to eat them, the jackal leaves its tracks on the divinatory matrices, and the diviner interprets these tracks the next day.

12. See D. Zahan, *Sociétés d'Initiation Bambara, le N'domo, le Korè* (Paris and the Hague: Mouton, 1960), p. 35.

13. See Tiarko Fourche and Morlighem, *Les communications*, pp. 14–26.

14. Ibid., p. 74.

Chapter 7

1. On this subject see D. Paulme, *Les Gens du Riz* (Paris: Plon, 1954), pp. 205–22.

2. See R. S. Rattray, *Religion and Art in Ashanti* (London: Oxford University Press, 1927), pp. 28, 29, 39, 167.

3. See J. Rouch, *La Religion et la magie songhay* (Paris: Presses Universitaires de France, 1960), pp. 255–302.

4. Among the Bambara the phenomenon of menstruation is associated with the flowering of plants.

5. E. Jensen Krige and J. D. Krige, *The Realm of a Rain-Queen* (London: Oxford University Press, 1947), pp. 250–70.

6. Rouch, *Religion et la magie*, pp. 283, 284.

7. Rattray, *Religion and Art*, p. 28.

8. E. E. Evans-Pritchard, *Witchcraft, Oracles and Magic among the Azande* (Oxford: The Clarendon Press, 1963), p. 31.

9. Ibid., p. 56.

10. H. A. Junod, *The Life of a South African Tribe*, 2d. ed. (London: Macmillan, 1927), 2:505.

11. See Jensen Krige and Krige, *Realm of a Rain-Queen*, pp. 263ff.

12. See S. de Ganay, "Aspects de mythologie et de symbolique bambara," *Journal de Psychologie Normale et Pathologique*, no. 2 (April–June 1949), p. 183.

13. The *nama* society specializes particularly in the battle against sorcery.

14. Junod, *Life of a South African Tribe*, 2:505–16.

15. J. van Wing, S.J., *Etudes bakongo, Sociologie-Religion et Magie*, Mémoires de l'I.R.C.B. (Louvain: Desclée de Brouwer, 1938), pp. 359–81.

16. Junod, *Life of a South African Tribe*, 2:511.

17. Ibid., 2:501.

18. Ibid., 2:520.

19. This is independent of the idea of "transformation," which is tied to the disappearance and reappearance of the subject. On this topic see the analogous technique of the chiefs, ibid., 1:383.

20. Ibid., 2:516.

21. Ibid., 1:329.

22. Paulme, *Gens du Riz*, p. 207.

23. Ibid.

24. See van Wing, *Etudes bakongo*, pp. 382–425.

25. Rouch, *Religion et la magie*, p. 290.

26. Ibid., p. 291.

27. See D. Zahan, *Le nama* (to appear).

28. Junod, *Life of a South African Tribe*, 2:529, 530.

29. Paulme, *Gens du Riz*, pp. 208, 209.

30. This part of our account is a systematization of documents provided by Paulme, *Gens du Riz*, pp. 205–22.

31. Ibid., pp. 209, 210.

32. Ibid., p. 209.
33. Ibid., p. 210.

Chapter 8

1. Abbé Proyart, *Histoire de Loango, Kakongo et autres Royaumes d'Afrique* (Paris: C. P. Berton, 1776), p. 168.
2. A. Raffenel, *Voyage dans l'Afrique Occidentale* (Paris: Arthus Bertrand, 1846), pp. 304–5.
3. R. P. Trilles, *Les Pygmées de la Forêt Equatoriale* (Paris: Bloud and Gay, 1932), p. 371.
4. G. Calame-Griaule, *Ethnologie et langage: La Parole chez les Dogon* (Paris: Gallimard, 1965), p. 370.
5. Ibid., pp. 374–75.
6. Ibid., p. 266.
7. D. Zahan, *La Dialectique du verbe chez les Bambara* (Paris and the Hague: Mouton, 1963), p. 46.
8. Ibid., p. 63.
9. In order to understand the scope of this saying, it should be remembered that the *dya* is one of the person's spiritual principles, his double, which makes up the totality of the conscious faculties of the human being. The *dya* enjoys a great mobility and is sensitive to any abrupt action operating on man. It can leave its owner without damage. See above, p. 8.
10. For the Bambara, nudity essentially consists of the exhibition of the genitals.
11. This kind of grassy plant is the *digitaria exilis.*
12. It is for this reason that the best wish that one can make on the occasion of a marriage consists in saying "Let it be a dirty marriage," that is, a marriage where affectations of coquetry are not present.
13. This prohibition is lifted by the sacrifice of a chicken, which is performed the day following the deflowering of the woman.
14. It should be noted that nothing destroys the stability of a Bambara marriage as much as household arguments.
15. The Bambara often express this character of death by the concept of contagion.
16. Zahan, *Dialectique du verbe,* p. 133.
17. G. Dieterlen, "Mythe et organisation sociale au Soudan français," *Journal de la Société des Africanistes,* vol. 25, fasc. 1–2, pp. 45–46.
18. M. Griaule and G. Dieterlen, *Le renard pâle,* Travaux et Mémoires de l'Institut d'Ethnologie, vol. 72 (Paris and the Hague: Mouton, 1965), pp. 375–79.
19. Hugo Zemp, "La légende des griots malinké," *Cahiers d'Etudes Africaines,* vol. 6, no. 24 (1960), pp. 611–42.

Chapter 9

1. R. S. Rattray, *Religion and Art in Ashanti* (London: Oxford University Press, 1927), pp. 38–47.
2. This does not exclude visits which the novice can make to his family on certain festival days; see ibid., p. 42.
3. This technique of instruction, as described by Rattray, in ibid., pp. 45–46, can be compared with the *kala ni* of the Bambara *korè;* see D. Zahan, *Sociétés d'Initiation Bambara: le N'domo, le Korè* (Paris and the Hague: Mouton, 1960), pp. 238–55.
4. See E. G. Parrinder, *West African Religion* (London: Epworth Press, 1942), p. 91.
5. See ibid., p. 94–95.
6. Ibid., p. 101.

7. Ibid., p. 105.

8. This statement is not at all theoretical, for while it is not necessary to be initiated in the four societies (*komo, nama, kono,* and *tyiwara*) in order to accede to *korè*, it is indispensable to have been initiated into *n'domo*. See Zahan, *Sociétés d'Initiation.*

9. We have elsewhere set forth the foundations of this "doctrine." See D. Zahan, "Aspects de la réincarnation et de la vie mystique chez les Bambara," in D. Zahan, ed., *Réincarnation et vie mystique en Afrique noire* (Paris: Presses Universitaires de France, 1965), pp. 175ff.

10. The granting by God of the soul (*ni*) begins with the human being's uterine life. This principle, however, is only fully acquired on the sixth day after birth.

11. It is highly probable that the *korè* initiates receive a new name on this eighth day of the second initiatory period.

12. *Andropogon gayanus.*

13. The Bambara express this concept by the term *wāzo,* which principally designates the innate capacity of the human intelligence relative to self-knowledge and general knowledge, of which God is a fundamental object. *Wāzo* also designates all that is opposed to the full realization of man from the social and religious point of view.

14. This word alludes to the scars resulting from wounds which the initiates inflict on themselves with the aid of thorns.

15. The word *kara* designates the wattles which are used to erect provisional fences. When in repose, these objects are rolled in the form of big cylinders. At the time of their use they unroll spontaneously when the strap tying them is undone. It is in this rapid movement of loosening that their analogy with the *karaw* of *korè* resides. Rolled up, they conceal wisdom and hide it from the view of humans, while unrolled they expose it so that it shines. Indeed, the *kara* emblems have as their function to "unroll" an instruction, thereby exposing a thought concerning divine wisdom.

16. We intentionally call attention only to the comic aspect of the *korè dugaw*'s dress. It goes without saying that all these details of dress possess extensive meanings which can not be analyzed here.

17. Abbé Jos. Henry, *L'Ame d'un peuple africain: les Bambara,* Bibliothèque Anthropos (Munster and Paris: Picard, 1910), p. 123.

18. Zahan, *Sociétés d'Initiation,* p. 357.

19. This is the "tarantulism" or "tarantism" on which a very suggestive study was recently undertaken. See Ernesto de Martino, *La Terra del Rimorso* (Milan: Il Saggiatore, 1961). This has been translated into French; see *La Terre du Remords* (Paris: Gallimard, 1966).

20. See Alfred Métraux, *Le Vaudou Haïtien* (Paris: Gallimard, 1958).

21. See Roger Bastide, *Le Candomblé de Bahia* (Paris and the Hague: Mouton, 1958).

22. H. A. Junod, *The Life of a South African Tribe,* 2d ed. (London: Macmillan, 1927), 2:480.

23. Ibid., 2:482.

24. Ibid., 2:488.

25. Undoubtedly, the basin contains various ingredients as well.

26. Junod observes that the racket can be prolonged for three or four days, if not a week, and that at the end of the rite of the basin of water the invalid may sometimes fall deeply asleep (ibid., 2:487, 489).

27. Ibid., 2:491.

28. An unidentified tree.

29. Ibid., 2:492. According to Junod, these roots are always used in the ritual of possession.

30. Our interpretation of the acts differs on numerous points from that given by Junod (ibid., 2:495–96). Concerning the drinking of blood, for example, he states (p. 495): "By the

drinking of blood, he has become a superior being, a man who does not fear that which makes others tremble."

31. Even the warriors' costume is conceived so as to bring about a "reconciliation" between them and the animal; see ibid., 1:450–55. For the description of the ritual concerning the war medicine, see ibid., 1:464–68.

32. Ibid., 1:478.

33. Ibid., 1:479.

34. Moreover, the warriors carry these medicines with them on the field of battle, for "the insanity which threatens those who shed blood might begin early" (ibid., 1:480).

35. Ibid., 2:60.

36. Ibid., 2:68.

37. Ibid., 1:189.

38. Ibid., 2:62.

39. Ibid., 2:64.

40. Ibid., 2:493.

41. Ibid., 2:502–3.

42. This is the Thonga "national" holiday, which corresponds to the beginning of the men's year.

43. Junod, *Life of a South African Tribe*, 1:400.

44. "The native mind has a much profounder conception of the unity of the animal and human worlds than we have. Spoon [one of Junod's informants] once said to me mysteriously: 'The astralagus of the goat truly represents the people of the village, because these animals live in the village; they know us, they know what is in us'" (ibid., 2:570).

45. By way of exemplification one can cite here Michel Leiris, *La possession et ses aspects théâteaux chez les Ethiopiens du Gondar*, L'Homme, Cahiers d'Ethnologie et de Linguistique, n.s., no. 1 (Paris: Plon, 1958).

Chapter 10

1. A Thonga tradition; see H. A. Junod, *The Life of a South African Tribe*, 2d ed. (London: Macmillan, 1927), 2:382.

Works Cited

Abrahamsson, H. *The Origin of Death*. Studies in African Mythology, Studia Ethnographica Upsaliensia, vol. 3. Uppsala: Almquist and Wiksells, 1951.

Arnoux, R. P. "Le culte de la société secrète des *imandwa* au Ruanda." *Anthropos*, 12–13 (1912–13).

Bachelard, G. *L'eau et les rêves*. Paris: José Corti, 1942.

——. *L'air et les songes*. Paris: José Corti, 1943.

Balandier, G. and P. Mercier. *Les Pêcheurs Lébou*. St.-Louis, Senegal: Centre IFAN-Senegal, 1952.

Bastide, Roger. *Le Candomblé de Bahia*. Paris and the Hague: Mouton, 1958.

Baumann, H. *Schöpfung und Urzeit der Menschen im Mythos der Afrikanischen Völker*. Berlin: Dietrich Reimer, 1936.

Biebuyck, D. *De hond bïg de Nyanga*. Rituel en Sociologie, Mémoires de l'Académie des Sciences Coloniales, vol. 8, fasc. 3. Brussels, 1956.

Binger, L. G. *Du Niger au golfe de Guinée*. Paris: Hachette, 1892.

Bochet, G. "Le Poro des Diéli." *Bulletin de l'IFAN*, ser. B, vol. 21, nos. 1–2, 1959.

Bourgeois, R. *Banyarwanda et Barundi*. Académie Royale des Sciences Coloniales, Mémoire no. 8, vol. 3. Brussels, 1956.

Calame-Griaule, G. "Notes sur l'habitation du plateau central Nigérien." *Bulletin de l'IFAN*, ser. B, 17, nos. 3–4, 1955.

——. *Ethnologie et langage: La Parole chez les Dogon*. Paris: Gallimard, 1965.

Callaway, H. *The Religious System of the Amazulu*. London: Folk-Lore Society, 1884.

Casalis, E. *Les Bassoutos*. Paris: Société des Missions Evangéliques, 1933.

Caton-Thompson, G. *The Zimbabwe Culture: Ruins and Reactions*. Oxford: Clarendon Press, 1931.

Cory, H. *African Figurines*. London: Faber and Faber, 1956.

Daget, J. "La pêche dans le delta central du Niger." *Journal de la Société des Africanistes*, vol. 19, fasc. 1, 1949.

Dammann, E. *Die Religionen Afrikas*. Stuttgart: W. Kohlhammer Verlag, 1963. (French translation: *Les Religions de l'Afrique*. Paris: Payot, 1964.)

De Jonghe, E. *Les sociétés secrètes au Bas-Congo*. Brussels: Polleunis, 1907.

Dieterlen G. "Mythe et organisation sociale au Soudan Français." *Journal de la Société des Africanistes,* vol. 25, fasc. 1–2, 1955; vol. 29, fasc. 1, 1959.

Dim Delobsom, A. A. *L'Empire du Mogho-Naba.* Paris: Domat-Montchrestien, 1933.

Doke, Clement M. *The Lambas of Northern Rhodesia.* London: George G. Harrap, 1931.

Evans-Pritchard, E. E. "Zande Theology." In *Essays in Social Anthropology.* London: Faber and Faber, 1962.

———. *Witchcraft, Oracles and Magic among the Azande.* Oxford: The Clarendon Press, 1963.

Fortes, Meyer. *The Dynamics of Clanship among the Tallensi.* London: Oxford University Press, 1945.

Ganay, S. de. "Aspects de mythologie et de symbolique bambara."*Journal de Psychologie Normale et Pathologique,* no. 2, April–June 1949.

Griaule, M. *Masques dogons.* Travaux et Mémoires de l'Institut d'Ethnologie, vol. 33. Paris and the Hague: Mouton, 1938.

———. *Dieu d'eau.* Paris: Editions de Chêne, 1948.

———. "L'Image du monde au Soudan." *Journal de la Société des Africanistes,* 19, fasc. 2, 1949.

Griaule, M. and G. Dieterlen. *Le renard pâle.* Travaux et Mémoires de l'Institut d'Ethnologie, vol. 72. Paris and the Hague: Mouton, 1965.

Gutmenn, B. *Die Stammeslehren der Dschagga,* vols. 1–3. Munich: Beck, 1932–38.

Hampaté Ba, A. and G. Dieterlen. *Koumen; Texte initiatique des pasteurs Peul.* Cahiers de l'Homme, n.s., no. 1. Paris and the Hague: Mouton, 1961.

Henry, Abbé Jos. *L'Ame d'un peuple africain: les Bambara.* Bibliothèque Anthropos, Munster and Paris: Picard, 1910.

Hertefelt, M. d', "Le Rwanda." in *Les anciens royaumes de la zone interlacustre méridionale, Rwanda, Burundi, Buha.* Monographies Ethnographiques, no. 6. Tervuren: Musée Royal de l'Afrique Centrale, 1962.

Hofmayr, Fr. Wilhelm. *Die Schilluk, Geschichte, Religion und Leben eines Niloten-Stammes.* Mödling: St. Gabriel, 1925.

Holas, B. "Fondaments spirituels de la vie sociale Sénoufu." *Journal de la Société des Africanistes,* vol. 26, fasc. 1–2, 1956.

Hollis, A. C. *The Masai, Their Language and Folk-lore.* Oxford: Clarendon Press, 1905.

———. *The Nandi, Their Language and Folk-lore.* Oxford: Clarendon Press, 1909.

Hubert, H. "Grottes et Cavernes de l'Afrique Occidentale." *Bulletin du Comité d'Etudes Historiques et Scientifiques de l'Afrique Occidentale Française,* 1, January–March 1920.

Hurel, Fr. *La Poésie chez les Primitifs, ou Contes, Fables, Récits et Proverbes du Rwanda (Lac Kivu)*. Bibliothèque Congo. Brussels: Goemaere, 1922.

Junod, H. A. *Les Chants et les contes des Ba-Ronga*. Lausanne: Bridel, 1897.

―――. *The Life of a South African Tribe*, 2 vols. 2d ed. London: Macmillan, 1927. (French edition: *Moeurs et Coutumes des Bantous*. Paris: Payot, 1936.)

Krige, E. Jensen. *The Social System of the Zulus*. London: Shuter and Shooter, 1957.

Krige, E. Jensen and Krige, J. D. *The Realm of a Rain-Queen*. London: Oxford University Press, 1947.

Kuper, H. *An African Aristocracy*. London: Oxford University Press for I.A.I., 1961.

Labouret, H. *Les tribus du rameau Lobi*. Travaux et Mémoires de l'Institut d'Ethnologie, vol. 15. Paris and the Hague: Mouton, 1931.

Lamy, M. *Les Jumeaux*. Paris: Corréa, 1949.

Lebeuf, Jean-Paul. *L'Habitation des Fali*. Paris: Hachette, 1961.

Le Herissé, A. *L'Ancien Royaume du Dahomey*. Paris: Larose, 1911.

Leiris, Michel. *La possession et ses aspects théâtraux chez les Ethiopiens du Gondar*. L'Homme, Cahiers d'Ethnologie et de Linguistique, n.s., no. 1. Paris: Plon, 1958.

Lestrade, A. *La Médecine indigène en Ruanda*. Académie Royale des Sciences Coloniales, Mémoire no. 8. Brussels, 1955.

Lienhardt, G. "The Shilluk of the Upper Nile." In *African Worlds*, ed. Meyer Fortes. London: Oxford University Press, 1954.

Loeb, Edwin M. *In Feudal Africa*. Paris and the Hague: Mouton, 1962.

MacIver, D. Randall. *Medieval Rhodesia*. London: Macmillan, 1906.

Martino, Ernesto de. *La Terra del Rimorso*. Milan: Il Saggiatore, 1961. (French translation: *La Terre du Remords*. Paris: Gallimard, 1966.)

Mauny, R. *Tableau géographique de l'ouest africain du Moyen-Age*. Dakar: IFAN, 1961.

Métraux, Alfred. *Le Vaudou Haïtien*. Paris: Gallimard, 1958.

Niangoran Bouah, G. *La division du temps et le calendrier rituel des peuples lagunaires de Côte d'Ivoire*. Travaux et Mémoires de l'Institut d'Ethnologie, vol. 68. Paris and the Hague: Mouton, 1964.

Parrinder, E. G. *West African Religion*. London: The Epworth Press, 1942.

―――. *African Traditional Religion*. London: Hutchinson's University Library, 1954.

Paulme, D. *Les Gens du Riz*. Paris: Plon, 1954.

Proyart, Abbé. *Histoire de Loango, Kakongo et autres Royaumes d'Afrique*. Paris: C. P. Berton, 1776.

Radin, P. *African Folktales and Sculpture*. Bollingen Series, no. 32. New York: Pantheon Books, 1953.

Raffenel, A. *Voyage dans l'Afrique Occidentale.* Paris: Arthus Bertrand, 1846.

Raponda-Walker, André and Sillans, Roger. *Rites et croyances des peuples du Gabon.* Paris: Présence Africaine, 1962.

Rattray, R. S. *Religion and Art in Ashanti.* London: Oxford University Press, 1927.

Richards, Audrey I. *Chisungu, A Girl's Initiation Ceremony among the Bemba of Northern Rhodesia.* London: Faber and Faber, 1956.

Rouch, J. *La Religion et la magie songhay.* Paris: Presses Universitaires de France, 1960.

Roumeguère-Eberhardt, J. "La notion de vie; base de la structure sociale Venda." *Journal de la Société des Africanistes,* vol. 27, fasc. 2, 1957.

———. *Pensée et société africaines.* Cahiers de l'Homme. Paris and the Hague: Mouton, 1963.

Schapera, I. *The Khoisan Peoples of South Africa.* London: Routledge and Kegan Paul, 1960.

Schebesta, Paul. *Les Pygmées du Congo Belge.* Mémoires de l'Institut Royal Colonial Belge, vol. 26, fasc. 2. Brussels, 1952.

Smith, Edwin W., ed. *African Ideas of God.* London: Edinburgh House Press, 1950.

Szumowski, G. "Notes sur la grotte préhistorique de Bamako." *Notes Africaines,* no. 58, April 1953.

Thomas, E. M. *The Harmless People.* New York: Knopf, 1959.

Tiarko Fourche, J. A. and H. Morlighem. *Les communications des indigènes du Kasaï avec les âmes des morts.* Brussels: Falk fils, 1939.

Trilles, R. P. *Les Pygmées de la Forêt Equatoriale.* Paris: Bloud and Gay, 1932.

Tubiana, M. J. *Survivances préislamiques en pays zaghawa.* Travaux et Mémoires de l'Institut d'Ethnologie, vol. 67. Paris and the Hague: Mouton, 1964.

Wagner, G. "The Abaluyia of Kavirondo." In *African Worlds,* ed. Meyer Fortes. London: Oxford University Press, 1954.

Wing, Joseph van, S.J. *Etudes Bakongo: Religion et Magie.* Brussels: Desclée de Brouwer, 1938.

Zahan, D. "Aperçu sur la Pensée Théogonique des Dogon." *Cahiers Internationaux de Sociologie,* vol. 6, 1949.

———. "L'Habitation Mossi." *Bulletin de l'IFAN,* 12, no. 1, January 1950.

———. *Sociétés d'Initiation Bambara: le N'domo, le Korè.* Paris and the Hague: Mouton, 1960.

———. *La Dialectique du verbe chez les Bambara.* Paris and the Hague: Mouton, 1963.

———. "Note sur la gémelléité et les jumeaux en Afrique Noire." *Bulletin de la Faculté des Lettres de Strasbourg,* March 1964.

———. *Le Nama* (to appear).

———, et al. *Réincarnation et vie mystique en Afrique noire.* Paris: Presses Universitaires de France, 1965.

Zemp, H. "La légende des griots malinké." *Cahiers d'Etudes Africaines,* vol. 6, no. 24, 1966.

Zuure, R. P. *Croyances et pratiques religieuses des Barundi.* Bibliotheque Congo, no. 22. Brussels: Essorial, 1929.

Index